House of MYSTERY

UNDER NEW MANAGEMENT

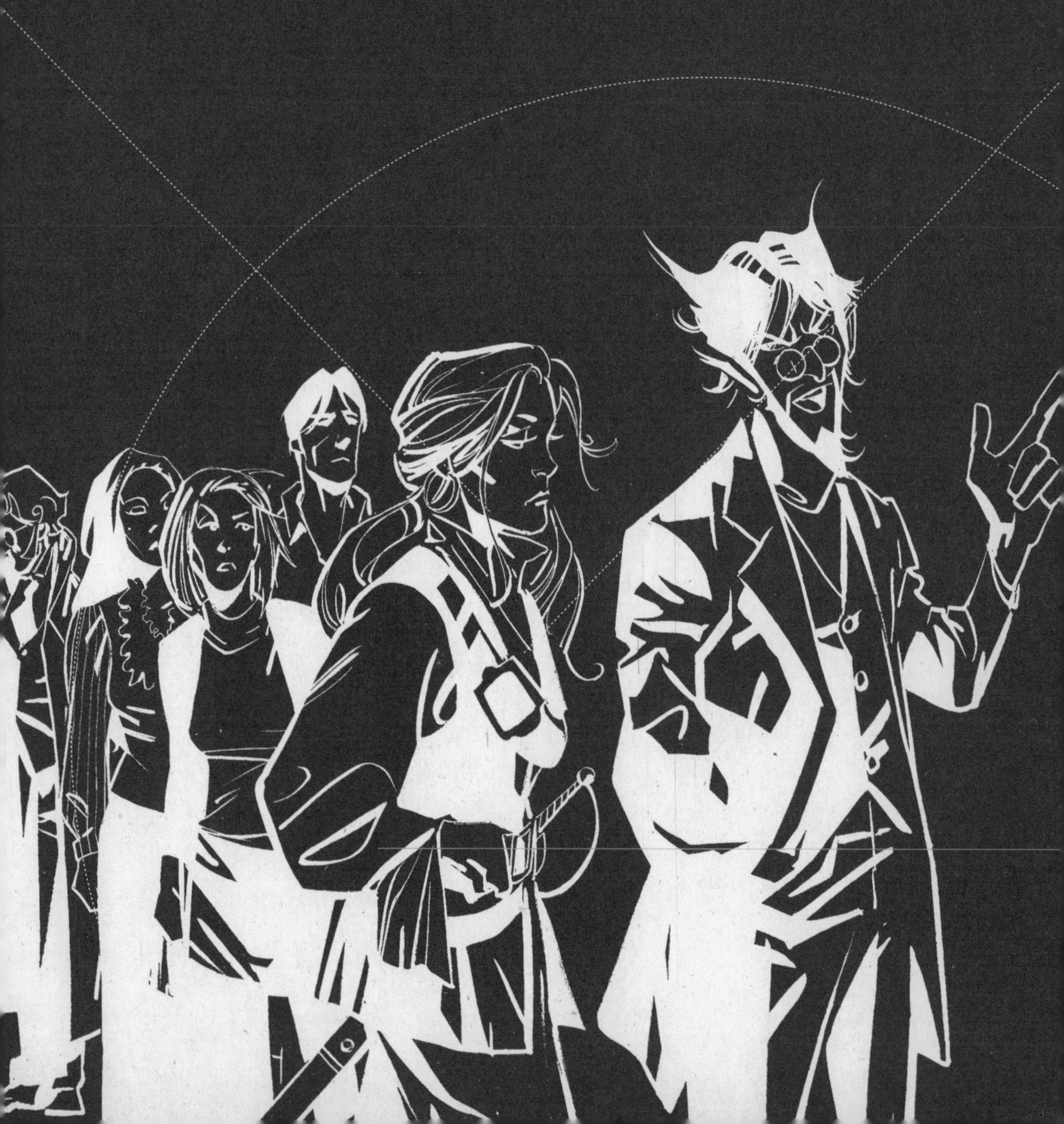

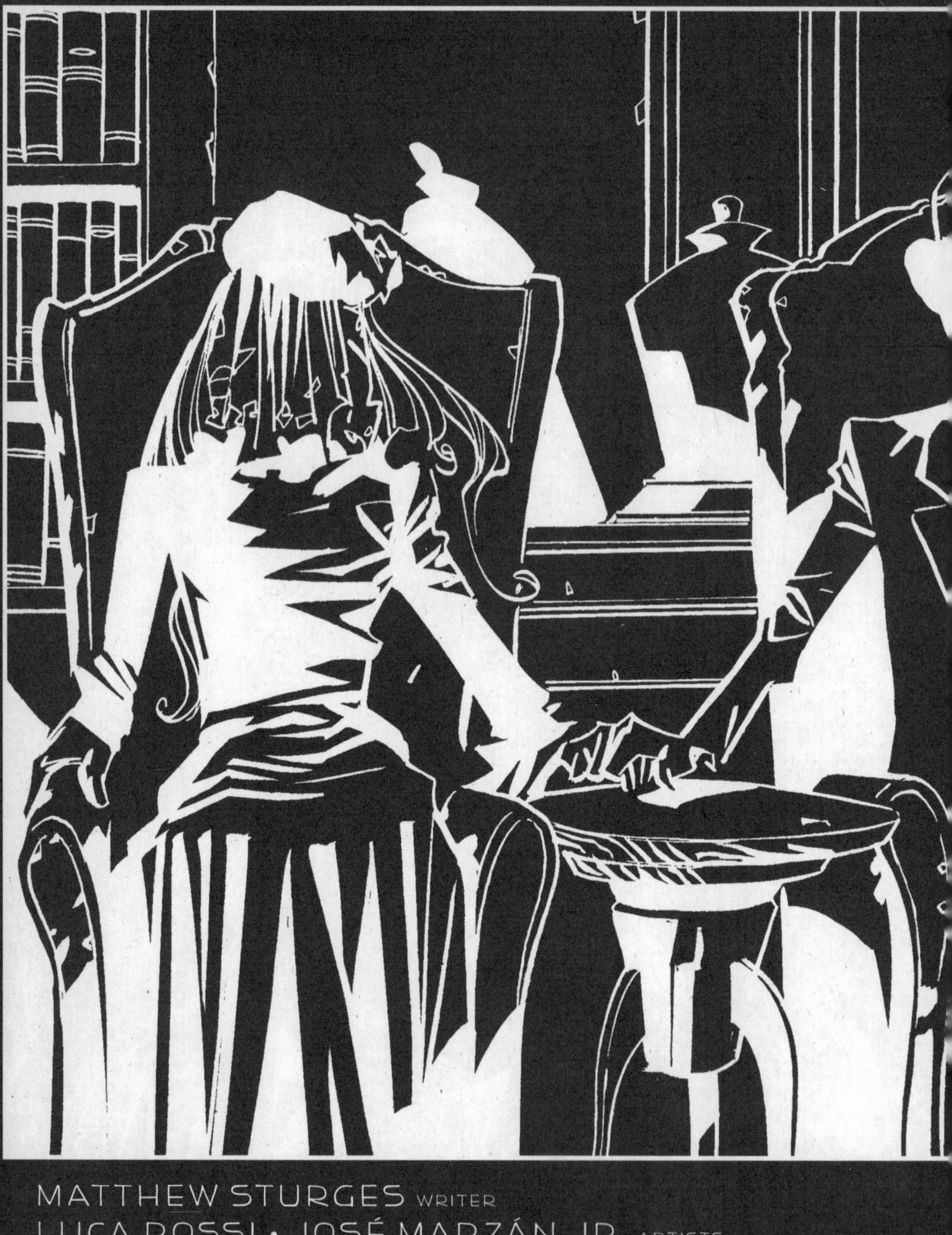

MATTHEW STURGES WRITER
LUCA ROSSI • JOSÉ MARZÁN JR. ARTISTS
LEE LOUGHRIDGE COLORIST
TODD KLEIN LETTERER
ESAO ANDREWS COVER ART AND ORIGINAL SERIES COVERS
BILL WILLINGHAM • DAVID JUSTUS
PAUL LEVITZ • ALISA KWITNEY SHORT STORY WRITERS
SERGIO ARAGONÉS • FAREL DALRYMPLE
SAM KIETH • JOHN BOLTON
LUCA ROSSI • JOSÉ MARZÁN JR. SHORT STORY ARTISTS

House of MYSTERY

UNDER NEW MANAGEMENT

KAREN BERGER	SVP – EXECUTIVE EDITOR
ANGELA RUFINO	EDITOR – ORIGINAL SERIES
BOB HARRAS	GROUP EDITOR – COLLECTED EDITIONS
SCOTT NYBAKKEN	EDITOR
ROBBIN BROSTERMAN	DESIGN DIRECTOR – BOOKS

DC COMICS

DIANE NELSON	PRESIDENT
DAN DIDIO AND JIM LEE	CO-PUBLISHERS
GEOFF JOHNS	CHIEF CREATIVE OFFICER
PATRICK CALDON	EVP-FINANCE AND ADMINISTRATION
JOHN ROOD	EVP-SALES, MARKETING AND BUSINESS DEVELOPMENT
STEVE ROTTERDAM	SVP-SALES AND MARKETING
JOHN CUNNINGHAM	VP-MARKETING
TERRI CUNNINGHAM	VP-MANAGING EDITOR
ALISON GILL	VP-MANUFACTURING
DAVID HYDE	VP-PUBLICITY
SUE POHJA	VP-BOOK TRADE SALES
ALYSSE SOLL	VP-ADVERTISING AND CUSTOM PUBLISHING
BOB WAYNE	VP-SALES
MARK CHIARELLO	ART DIRECTOR

HOUSE OF MYSTERY: UNDER NEW MANAGEMENT

PUBLISHED BY DC COMICS. COVER AND COMPILATION COPYRIGHT © 2011
DC COMICS. ALL RIGHTS RESERVED.

ORIGINALLY PUBLISHED IN SINGLE MAGAZINE FORM AS HOUSE OF
MYSTERY 21-25. COPYRIGHT © 2010 DC COMICS. ALL RIGHTS RESERVED.
ALL CHARACTERS, THEIR DISTINCTIVE LIKENESSES AND RELATED ELEMENTS
FEATURED IN THIS PUBLICATION ARE TRADEMARKS OF DC COMICS. THE
STORIES, CHARACTERS AND INCIDENTS FEATURED IN THIS PUBLICATION
ARE ENTIRELY FICTIONAL. DC COMICS DOES NOT READ OR ACCEPT
UNSOLICITED SUBMISSIONS OF IDEAS, STORIES OR ARTWORK.

DC COMICS
1700 BROADWAY, NEW YORK, NY 10019
A WARNER BROS. ENTERTAINMENT COMPANY.
PRINTED IN THE USA. FIRST PRINTING.
ISBN: 978-1-4012-2981-8

TABLE OF CONTENTS

MANAGEMENT

House of MYSTERY
UNDER NEW MANAGEMENT

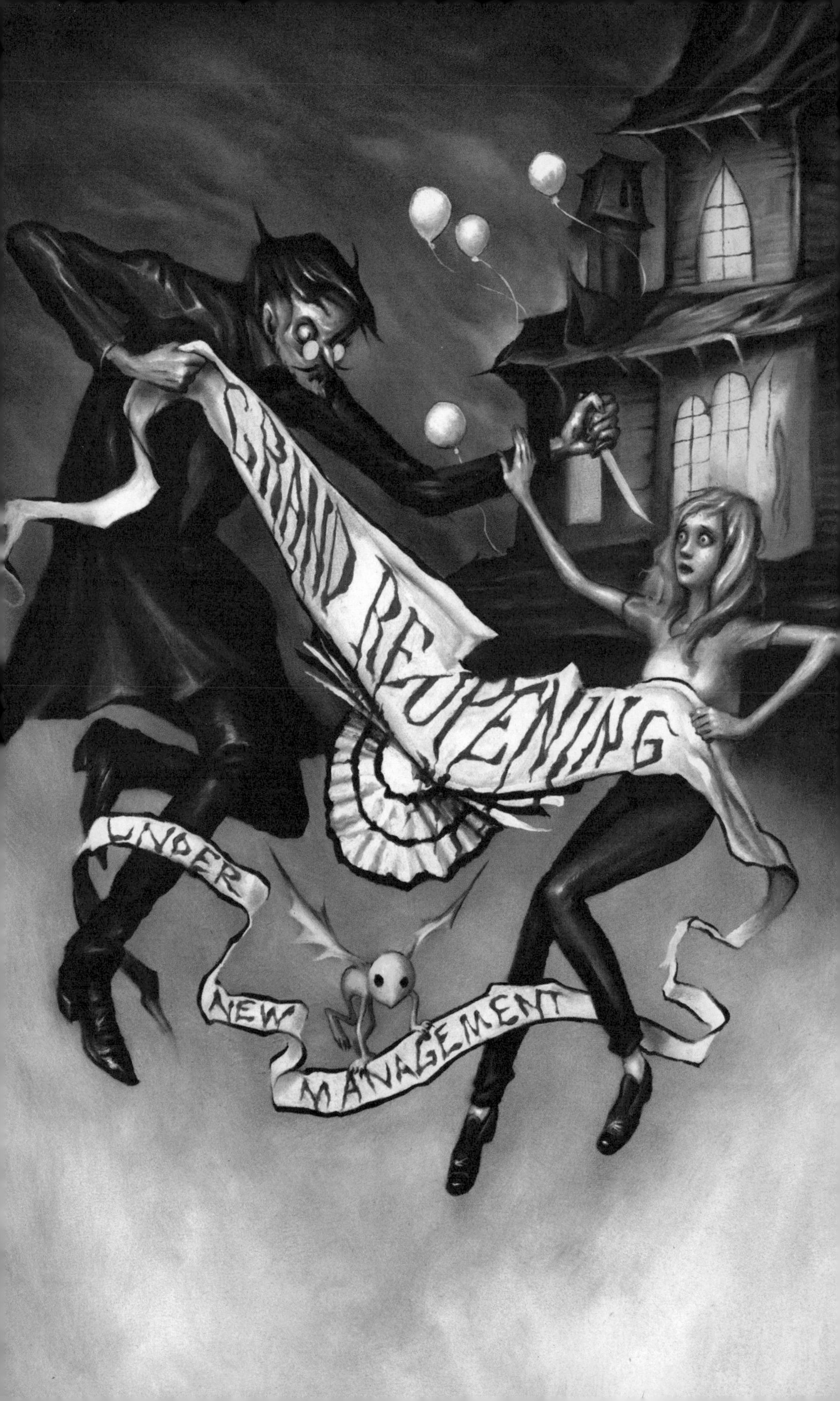
GRAND RE-OPENING
UNDER NEW MANAGEMENT

"DON'T LOOK AT IT!
WHATEVER YOU DO, DON'T LOOK AT IT!"

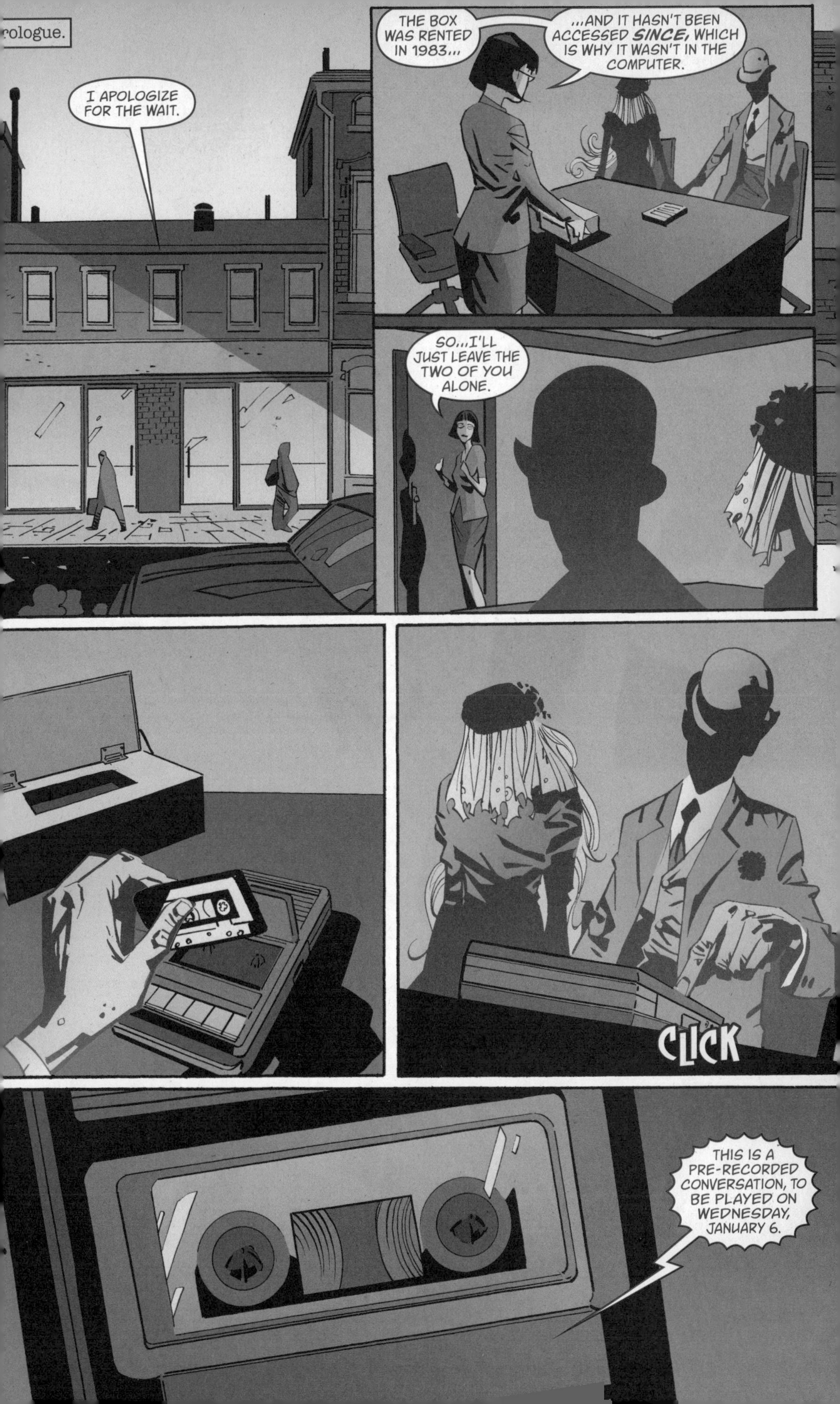

rologue.
I APOLOGIZE FOR THE WAIT.
THE BOX WAS RENTED IN 1983...
...AND IT HASN'T BEEN ACCESSED SINCE, WHICH IS WHY IT WASN'T IN THE COMPUTER.
SO...I'LL JUST LEAVE THE TWO OF YOU ALONE.
CLICK
THIS IS A PRE-RECORDED CONVERSATION, TO BE PLAYED ON WEDNESDAY, JANUARY 6.

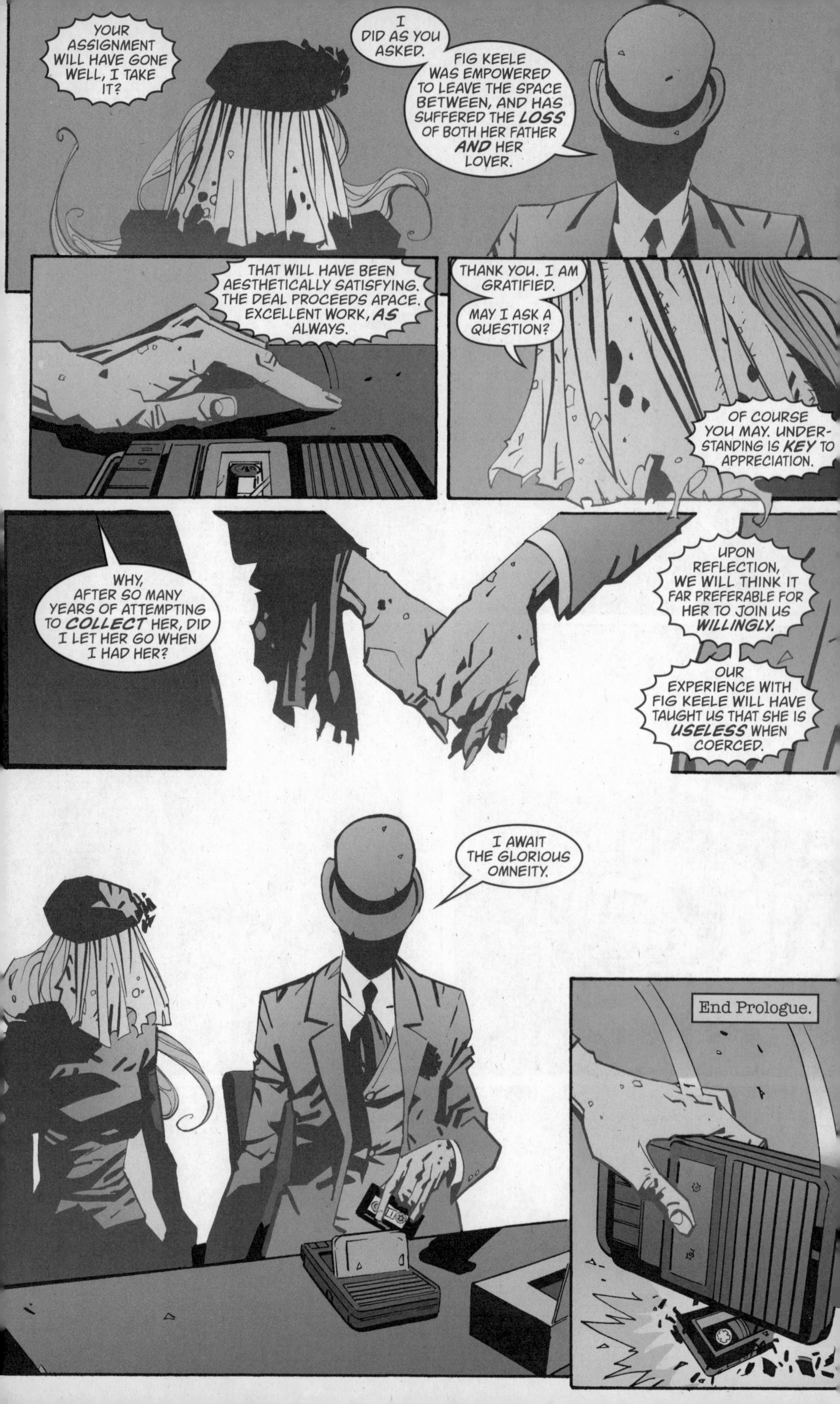
YOUR ASSIGNMENT WILL HAVE GONE WELL, I TAKE IT?
I DID AS YOU ASKED.
FIG KEELE WAS EMPOWERED TO LEAVE THE SPACE BETWEEN, AND HAS SUFFERED THE LOSS OF BOTH HER FATHER AND HER LOVER.
THAT WILL HAVE BEEN AESTHETICALLY SATISFYING. THE DEAL PROCEEDS APACE. EXCELLENT WORK, AS ALWAYS.
THANK YOU. I AM GRATIFIED.
MAY I ASK A QUESTION?
OF COURSE YOU MAY. UNDERSTANDING IS KEY TO APPRECIATION.
WHY, AFTER SO MANY YEARS OF ATTEMPTING TO COLLECT HER, DID I LET HER GO WHEN I HAD HER?
UPON REFLECTION, WE WILL THINK IT FAR PREFERABLE FOR HER TO JOIN US WILLINGLY.
OUR EXPERIENCE WITH FIG KEELE WILL HAVE TAUGHT US THAT SHE IS USELESS WHEN COERCED.
I AWAIT THE GLORIOUS OMNEITY.
End Prologue.

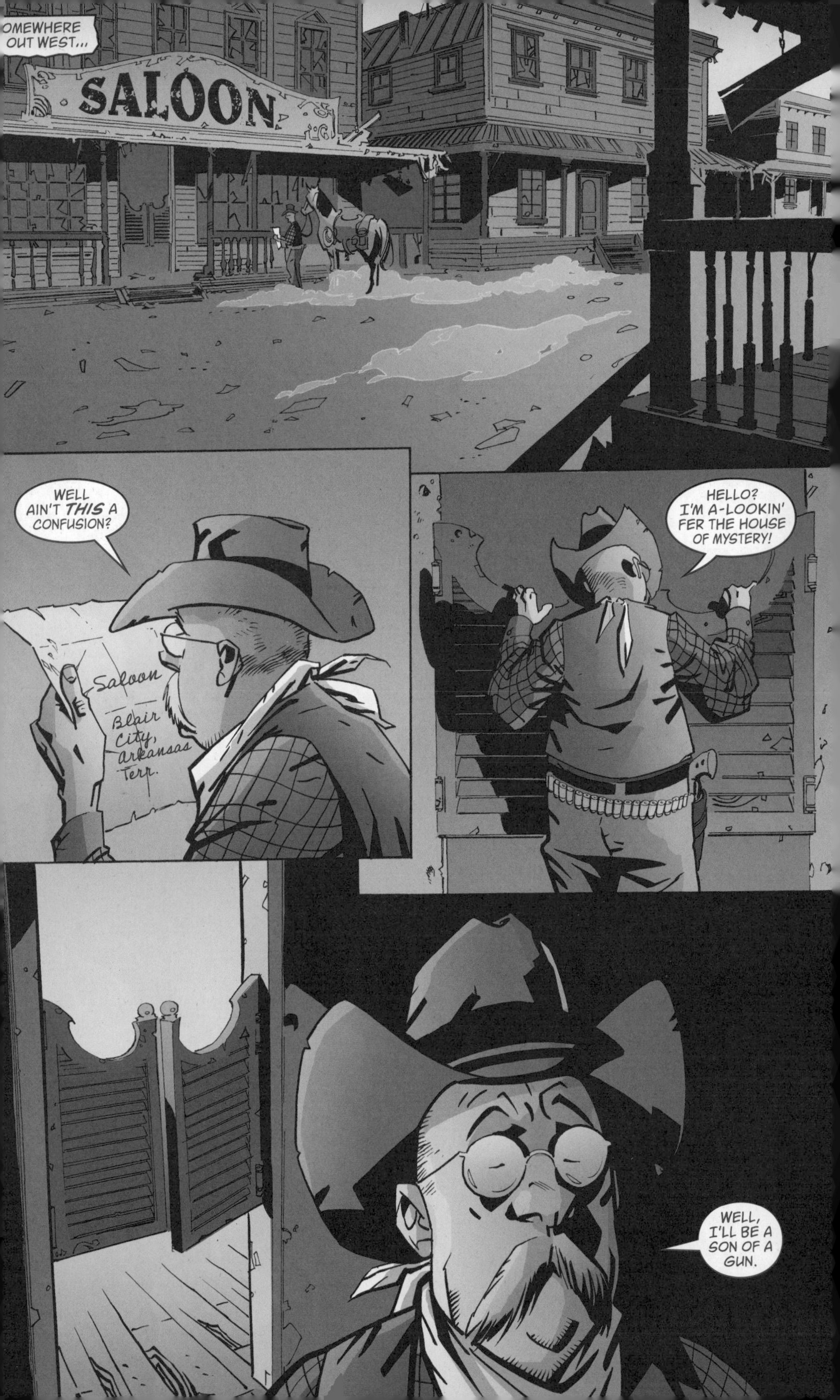
OMEWHERE OUT WEST...
SALOON
WELL AIN'T THIS A CONFUSION?
Saloon
Blair City, Arkansas Terr.
HELLO? I'M A-LOOKIN' FER THE HOUSE OF MYSTERY!
WELL, I'LL BE A SON OF A GUN.

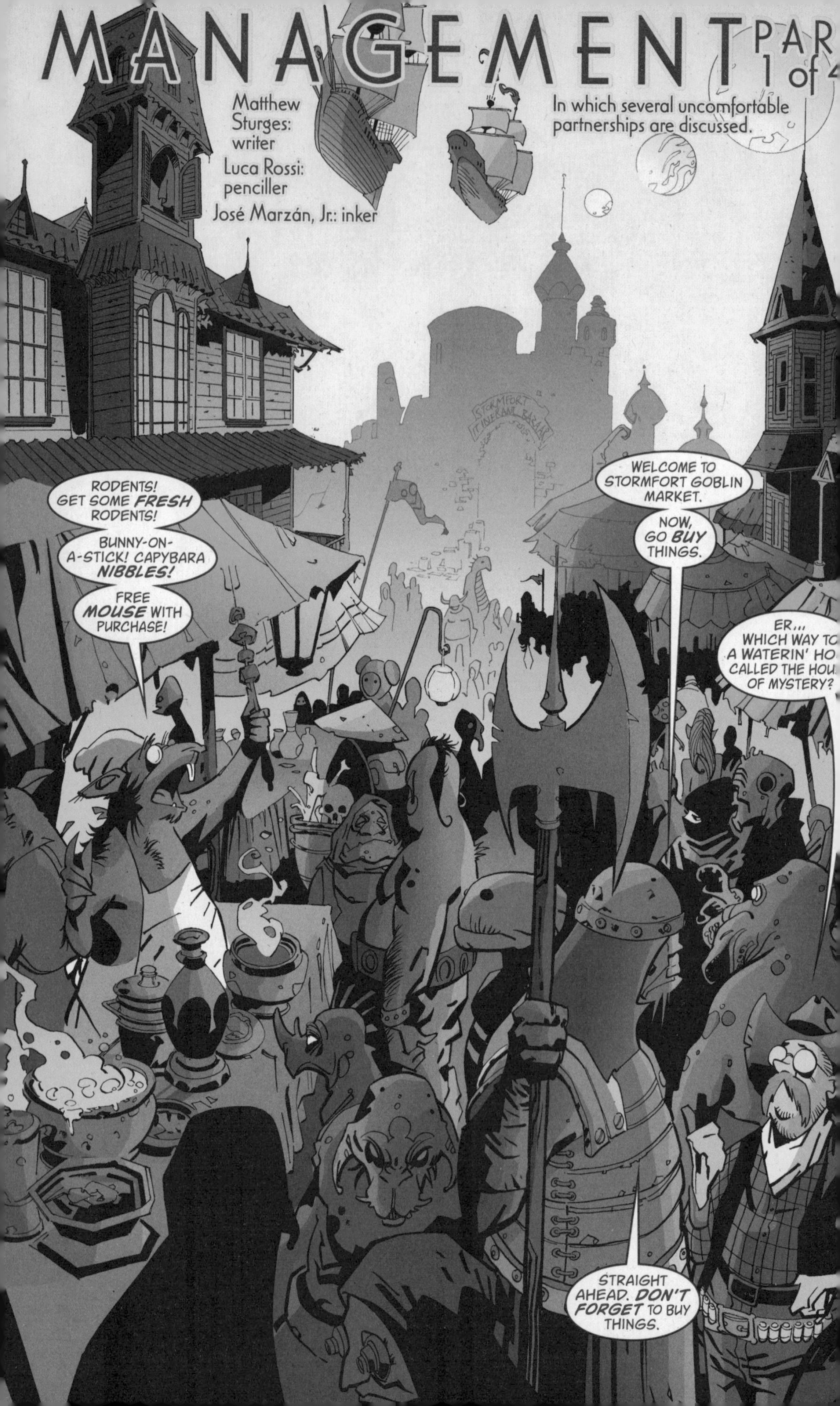
MANAGEMENT PART 1 of 4
Matthew Sturges: writer
Luca Rossi: penciller
José Marzán, Jr.: inker
In which several uncomfortable partnerships are discussed.
STORMFORT ITINERANT BAZAAR
RODENTS! GET SOME *FRESH* RODENTS!
BUNNY-ON-A-STICK! CAPYBARA *NIBBLES!*
FREE *MOUSE* WITH PURCHASE!
WELCOME TO STORMFORT GOBLIN MARKET.
NOW, GO *BUY* THINGS.
ER... WHICH WAY TO A WATERIN' HO CALLED THE HOU OF MYSTERY?
STRAIGHT AHEAD. *DON'T FORGET* TO BUY THINGS.

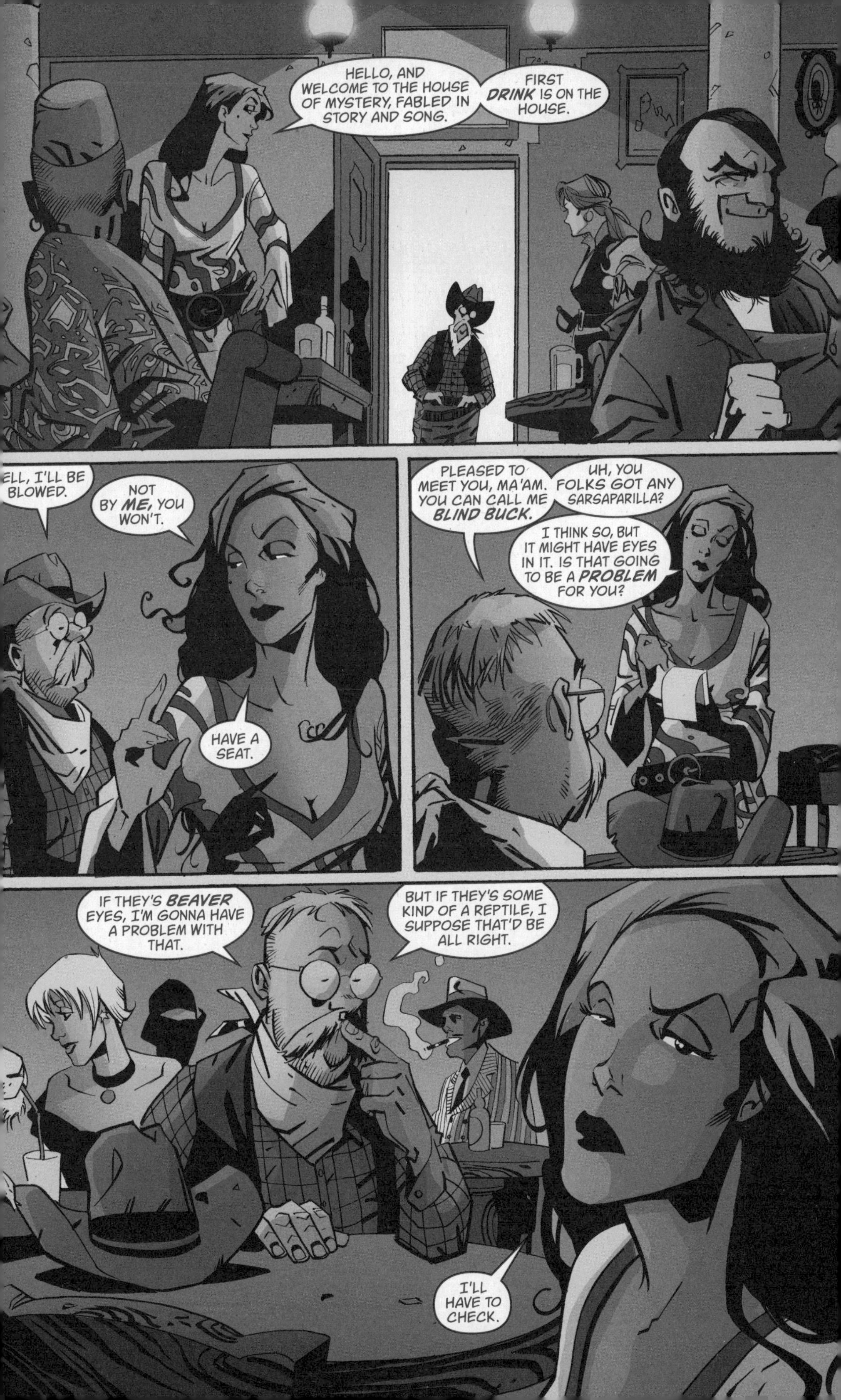
HELLO, AND WELCOME TO THE HOUSE OF MYSTERY, FABLED IN STORY AND SONG.
FIRST DRINK IS ON THE HOUSE.
ELL, I'LL BE BLOWED.
NOT BY ME, YOU WON'T.
HAVE A SEAT.
PLEASED TO MEET YOU, MA'AM. YOU CAN CALL ME BLIND BUCK.
UH, YOU FOLKS GOT ANY SARSAPARILLA?
I THINK SO, BUT IT MIGHT HAVE EYES IN IT. IS THAT GOING TO BE A PROBLEM FOR YOU?
IF THEY'S BEAVER EYES, I'M GONNA HAVE A PROBLEM WITH THAT.
BUT IF THEY'S SOME KIND OF A REPTILE, I SUPPOSE THAT'D BE ALL RIGHT.
I'LL HAVE TO CHECK.

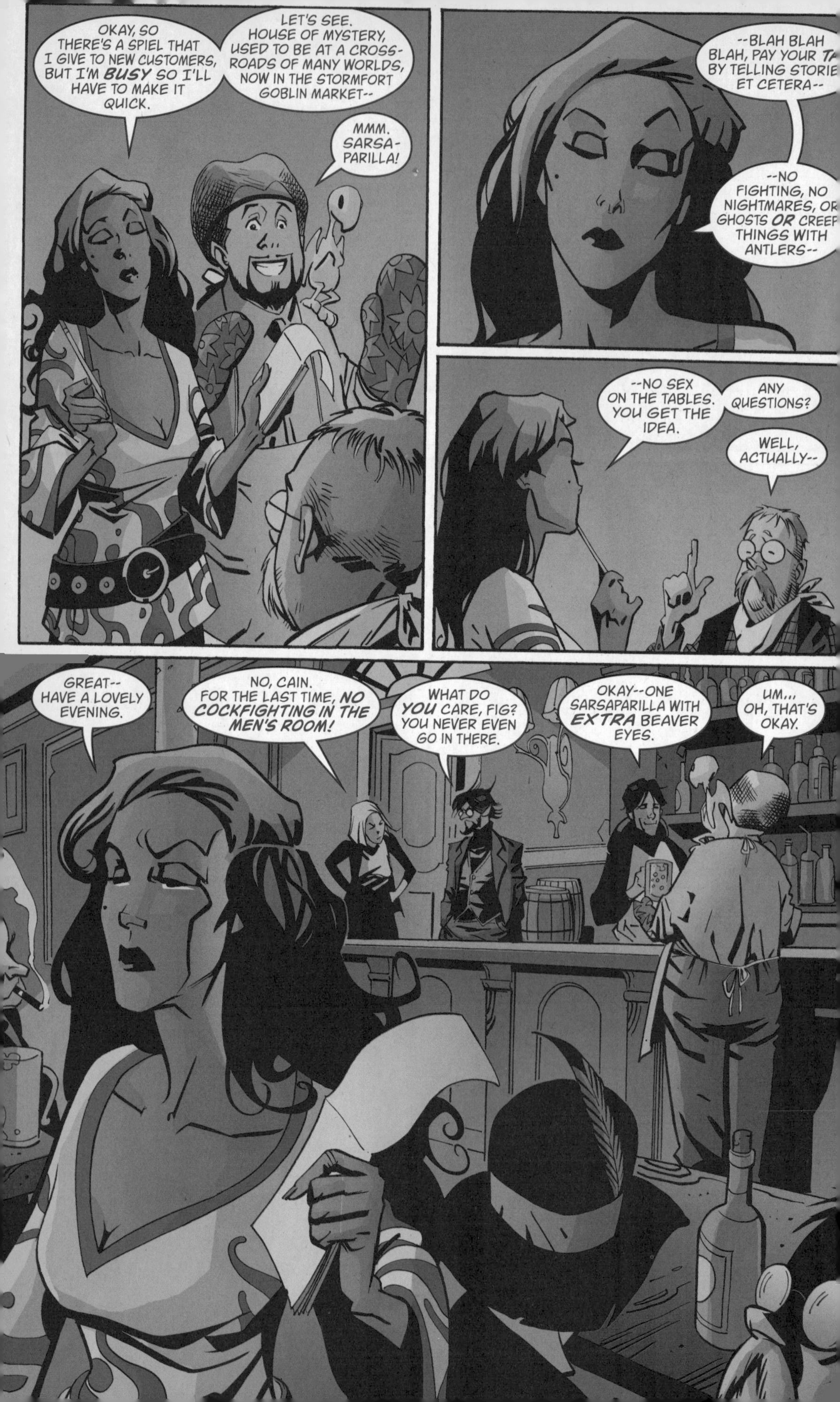
OKAY, SO THERE'S A SPIEL THAT I GIVE TO NEW CUSTOMERS, BUT I'M BUSY SO I'LL HAVE TO MAKE IT QUICK.
LET'S SEE. HOUSE OF MYSTERY, USED TO BE AT A CROSS-ROADS OF MANY WORLDS, NOW IN THE STORMFORT GOBLIN MARKET--
MMM. SARSA-PARILLA!
--BLAH BLAH BLAH, PAY YOUR TA BY TELLING STORIE ET CETERA--
--NO FIGHTING, NO NIGHTMARES, OR GHOSTS OR CREEP THINGS WITH ANTLERS--
--NO SEX ON THE TABLES. YOU GET THE IDEA.
ANY QUESTIONS?
WELL, ACTUALLY--
GREAT-- HAVE A LOVELY EVENING.
NO, CAIN. FOR THE LAST TIME, NO COCKFIGHTING IN THE MEN'S ROOM!
WHAT DO YOU CARE, FIG? YOU NEVER EVEN GO IN THERE.
OKAY--ONE SARSAPARILLA WITH EXTRA BEAVER EYES.
UM... OH, THAT'S OKAY.

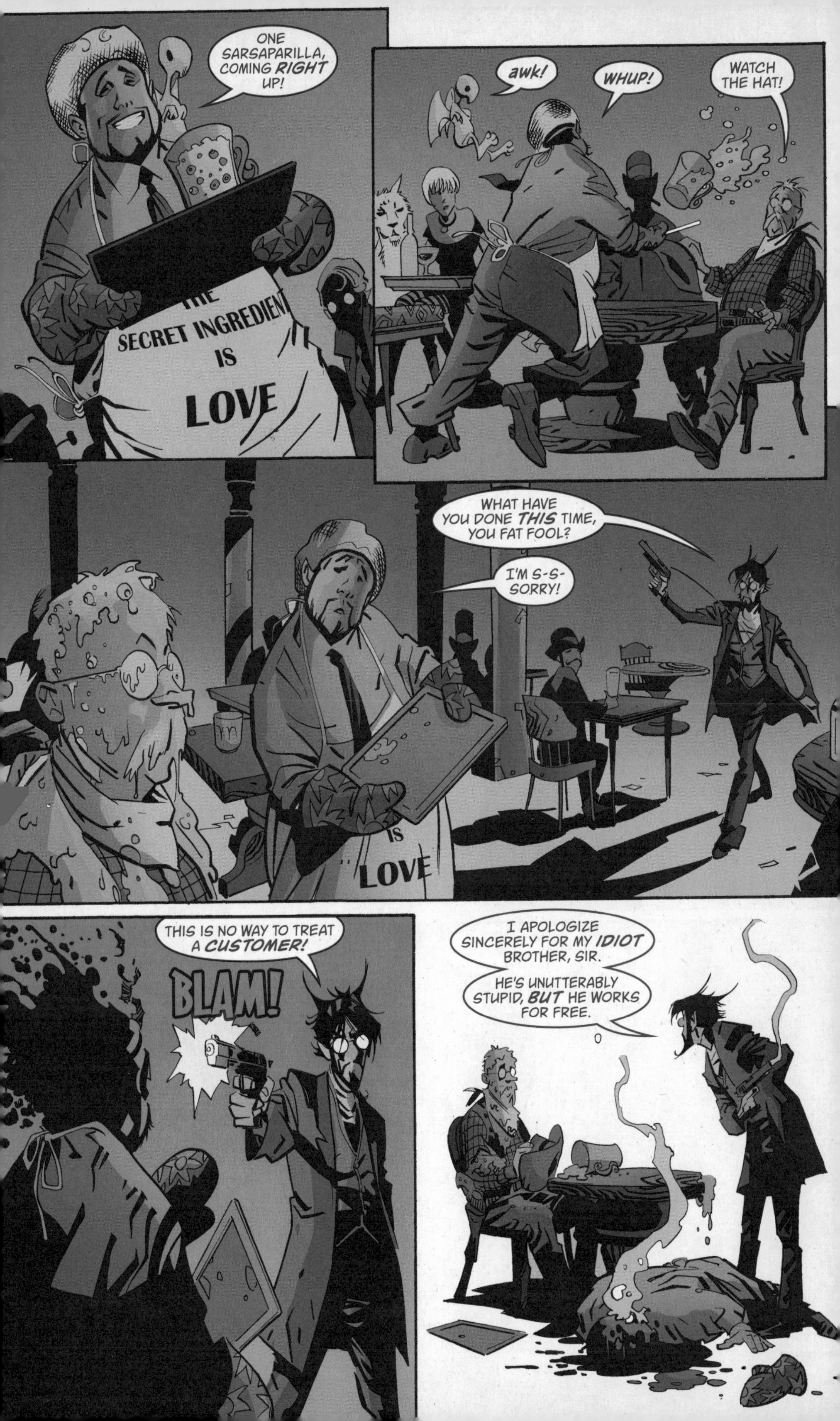
ONE SARSAPARILLA, COMING RIGHT UP!
THE SECRET INGREDIENT IS LOVE
awk!
WHUP!
WATCH THE HAT!
WHAT HAVE YOU DONE THIS TIME, YOU FAT FOOL?
I'M S-S-SORRY!
IS LOVE
THIS IS NO WAY TO TREAT A CUSTOMER!
BLAM!
I APOLOGIZE SINCERELY FOR MY IDIOT BROTHER, SIR.
HE'S UNUTTERABLY STUPID, BUT HE WORKS FOR FREE.

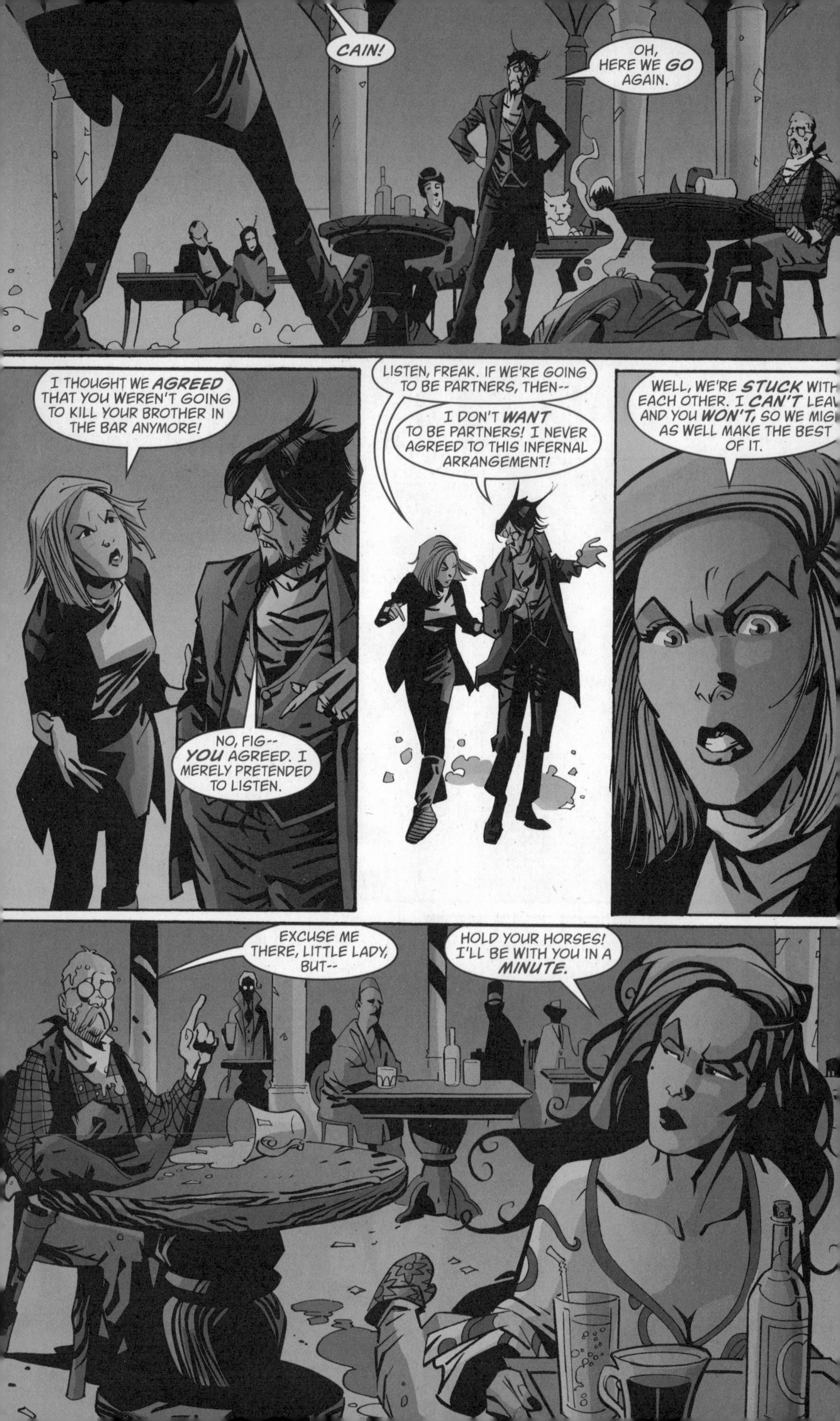
CAIN!
OH, HERE WE GO AGAIN.
I THOUGHT WE AGREED THAT YOU WEREN'T GOING TO KILL YOUR BROTHER IN THE BAR ANYMORE!
NO, FIG-- YOU AGREED. I MERELY PRETENDED TO LISTEN.
LISTEN, FREAK. IF WE'RE GOING TO BE PARTNERS, THEN--
I DON'T WANT TO BE PARTNERS! I NEVER AGREED TO THIS INFERNAL ARRANGEMENT!
WELL, WE'RE STUCK WITH EACH OTHER. I CAN'T LEAV AND YOU WON'T, SO WE MIG AS WELL MAKE THE BEST OF IT.
EXCUSE ME THERE, LITTLE LADY, BUT--
HOLD YOUR HORSES! I'LL BE WITH YOU IN A MINUTE.

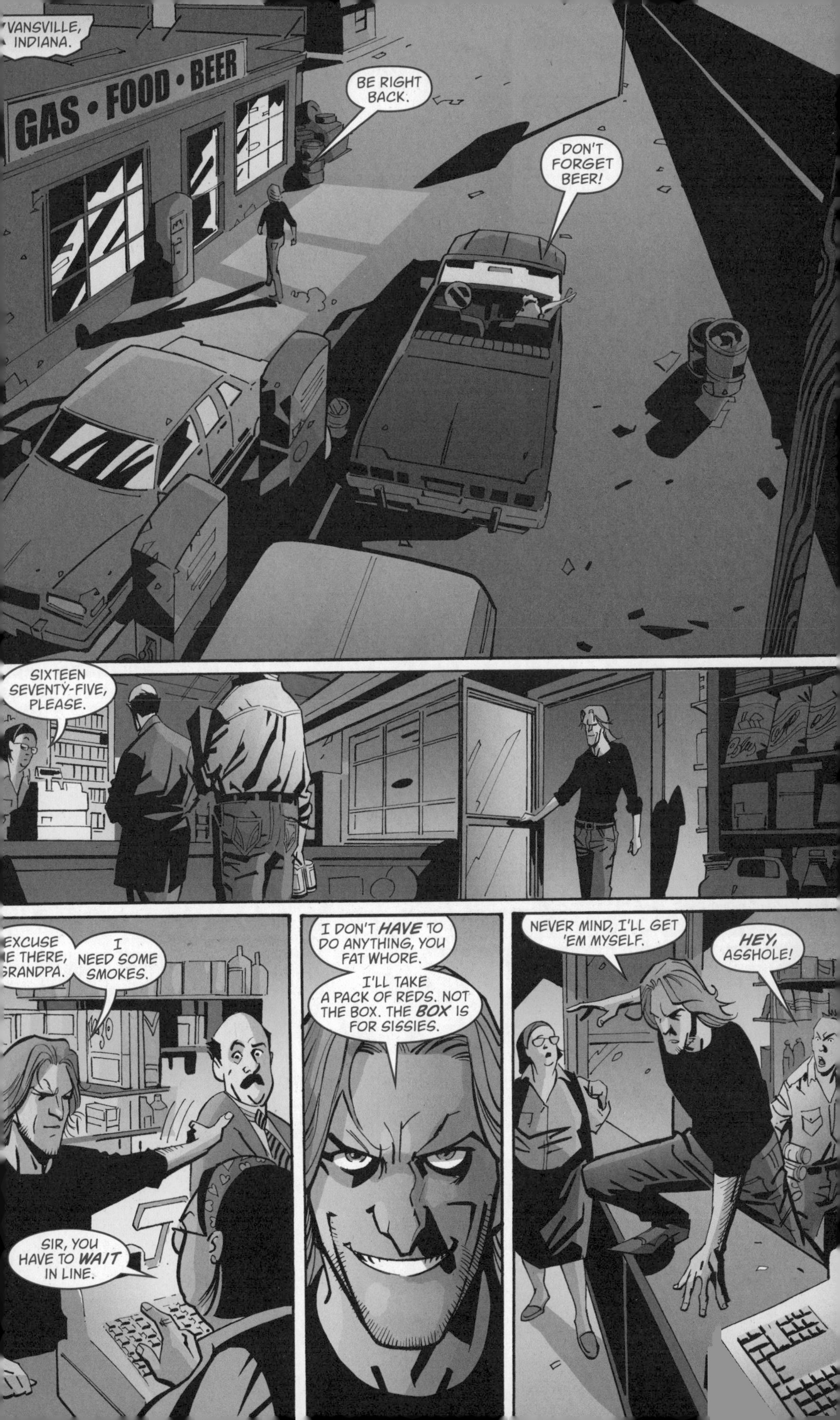
VANSVILLE, INDIANA.
GAS • FOOD • BEER
BE RIGHT BACK.
DON'T FORGET BEER!
SIXTEEN SEVENTY-FIVE, PLEASE.
EXCUSE E THERE, GRANDPA.
I NEED SOME SMOKES.
SIR, YOU HAVE TO **WAIT** IN LINE.
I DON'T **HAVE** TO DO ANYTHING, YOU FAT WHORE.
I'LL TAKE A PACK OF REDS. NOT THE BOX. THE **BOX** IS FOR SISSIES.
NEVER MIND, I'LL GET 'EM MYSELF.
HEY, ASSHOLE!

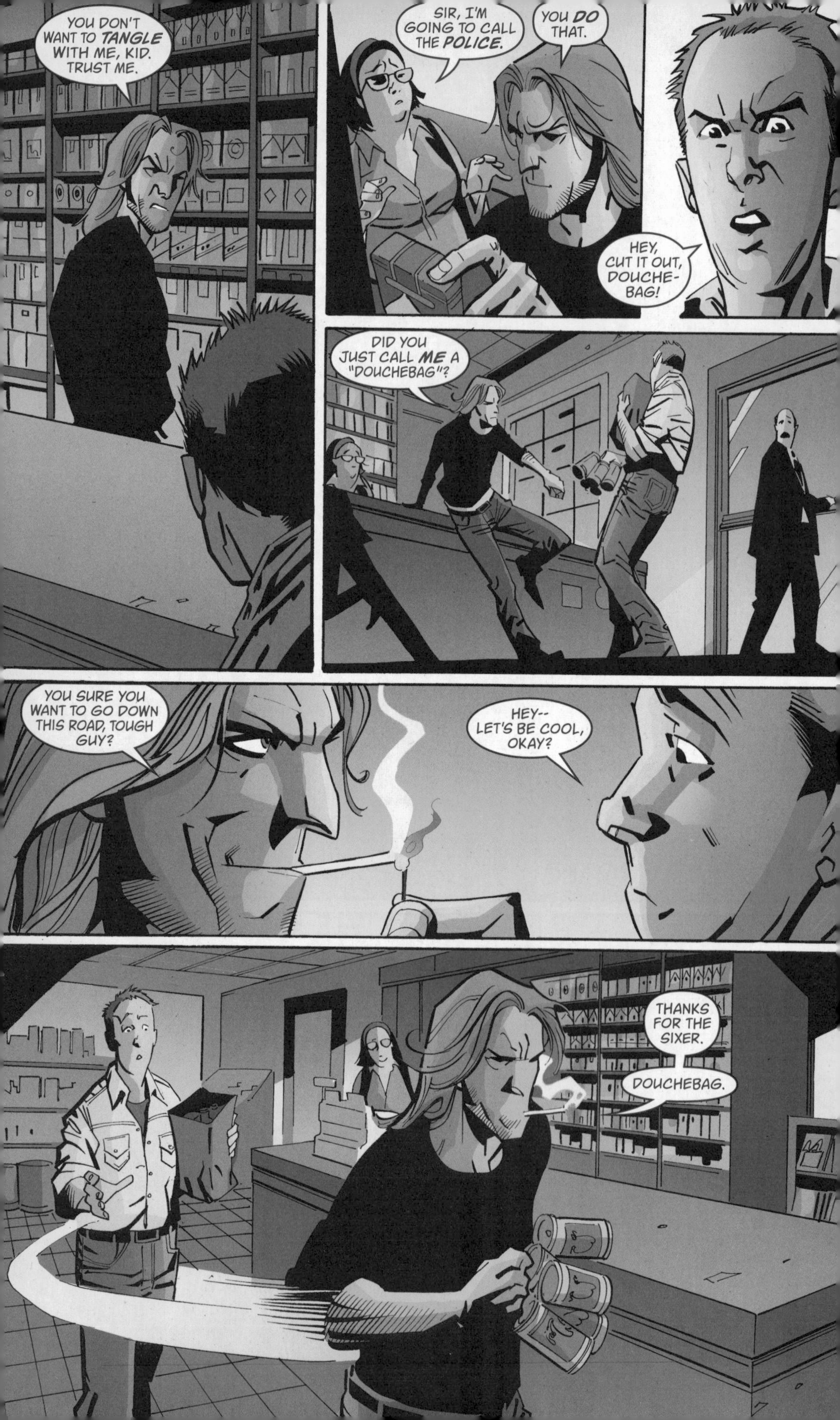
YOU DON'T WANT TO TANGLE WITH ME, KID. TRUST ME.
SIR, I'M GOING TO CALL THE POLICE.
YOU DO THAT.
HEY, CUT IT OUT, DOUCHE-BAG!
DID YOU JUST CALL ME A "DOUCHEBAG"?
YOU SURE YOU WANT TO GO DOWN THIS ROAD, TOUGH GUY?
HEY-- LET'S BE COOL, OKAY?
THANKS FOR THE SIXER.
DOUCHEBAG.

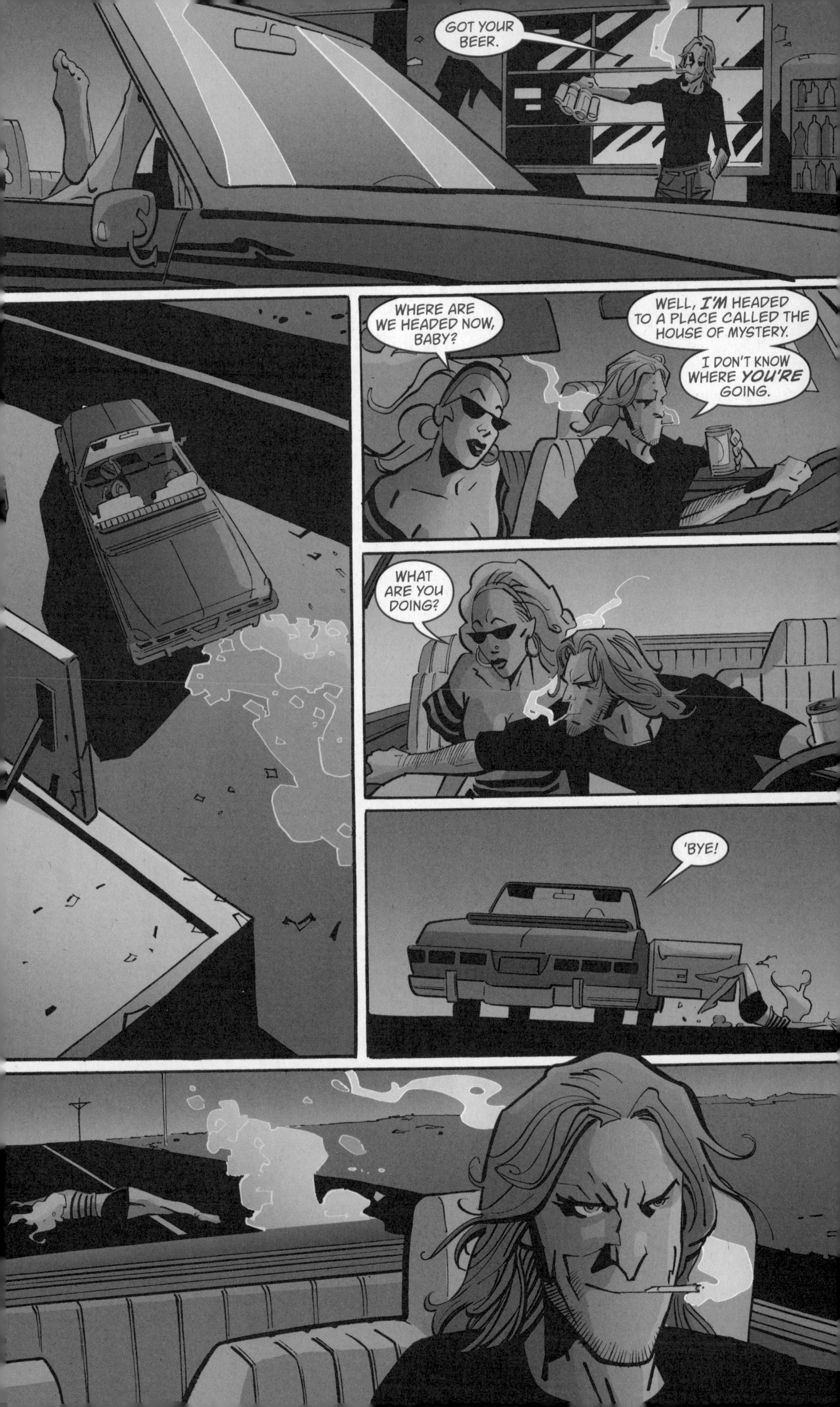
GOT YOUR BEER.
WHERE ARE WE HEADED NOW, BABY?
WELL, I'M HEADED TO A PLACE CALLED THE HOUSE OF MYSTERY.
I DON'T KNOW WHERE YOU'RE GOING.
WHAT ARE YOU DOING?
'BYE!

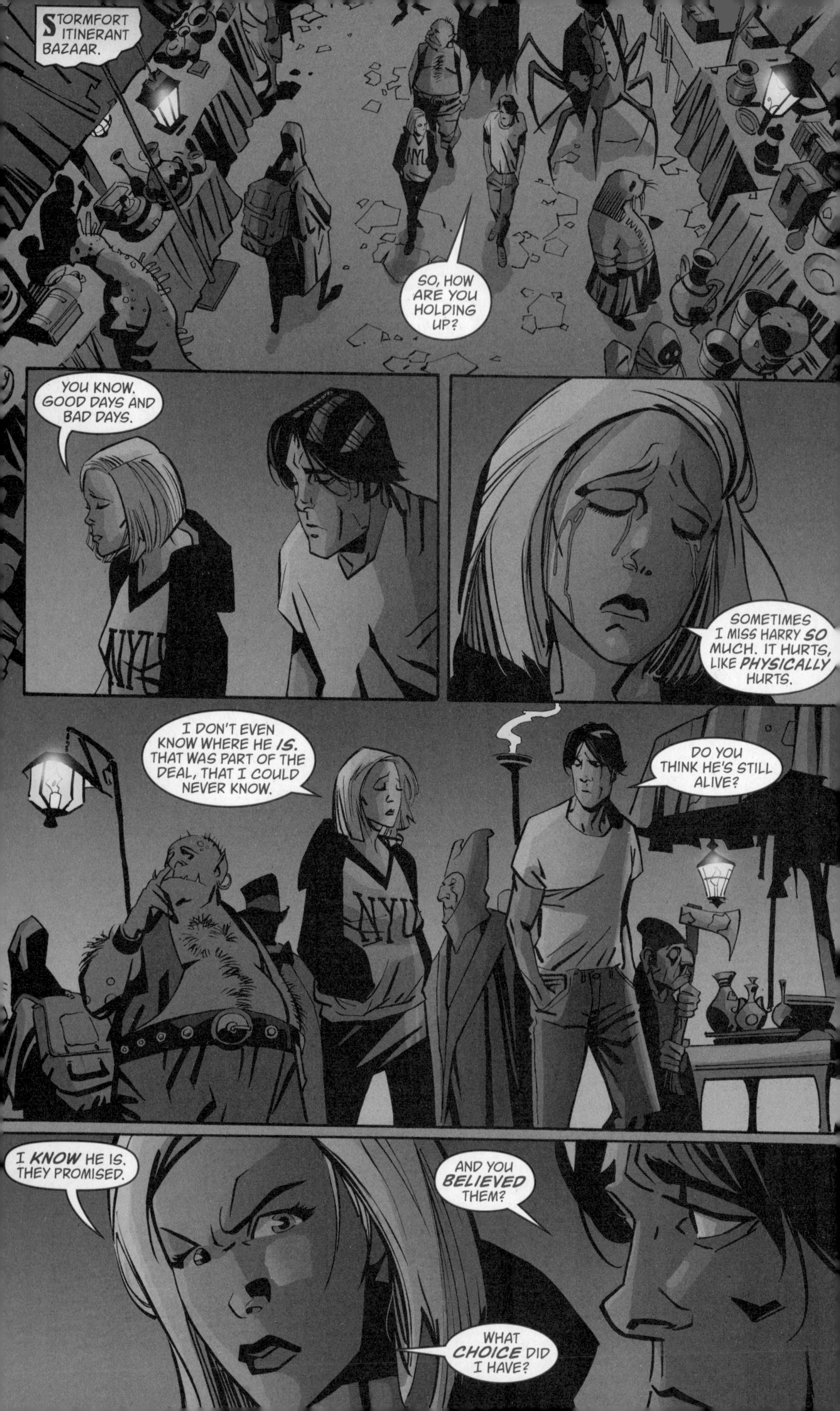
STORMFORT ITINERANT BAZAAR.
SO, HOW ARE YOU HOLDING UP?
YOU KNOW. GOOD DAYS AND BAD DAYS.
SOMETIMES I MISS HARRY SO MUCH. IT HURTS, LIKE PHYSICALLY HURTS.
I DON'T EVEN KNOW WHERE HE IS. THAT WAS PART OF THE DEAL, THAT I COULD NEVER KNOW.
DO YOU THINK HE'S STILL ALIVE?
I KNOW HE IS. THEY PROMISED.
AND YOU BELIEVED THEM?
WHAT CHOICE DID I HAVE?

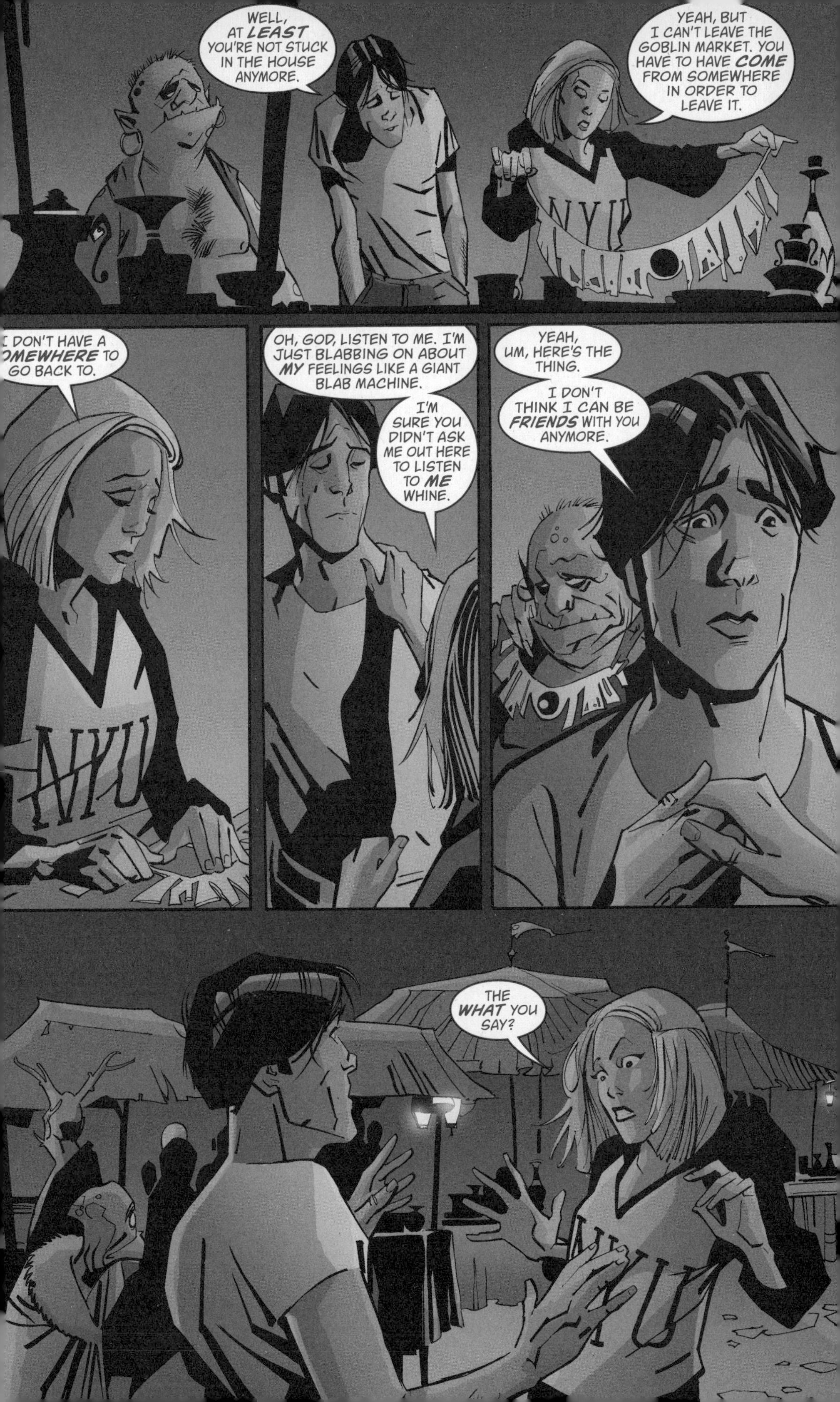
WELL, AT LEAST YOU'RE NOT STUCK IN THE HOUSE ANYMORE.
YEAH, BUT I CAN'T LEAVE THE GOBLIN MARKET. YOU HAVE TO HAVE COME FROM SOMEWHERE IN ORDER TO LEAVE IT.
I DON'T HAVE A SOMEWHERE TO GO BACK TO.
OH, GOD, LISTEN TO ME. I'M JUST BLABBING ON ABOUT MY FEELINGS LIKE A GIANT BLAB MACHINE.
I'M SURE YOU DIDN'T ASK ME OUT HERE TO LISTEN TO ME WHINE.
YEAH, UM, HERE'S THE THING.
I DON'T THINK I CAN BE FRIENDS WITH YOU ANYMORE.
THE WHAT YOU SAY?

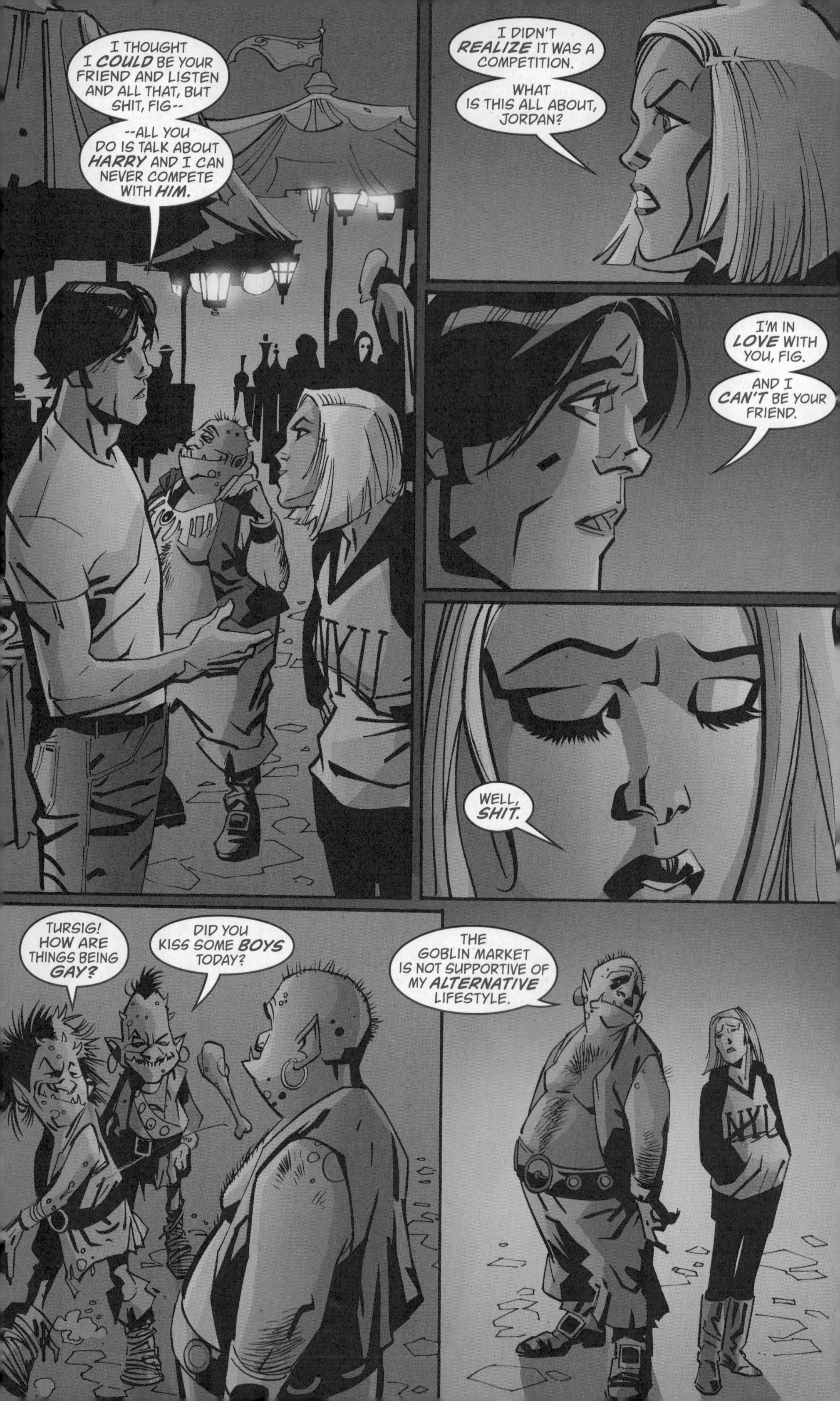
I THOUGHT I COULD BE YOUR FRIEND AND LISTEN AND ALL THAT, BUT SHIT, FIG--
--ALL YOU DO IS TALK ABOUT HARRY AND I CAN NEVER COMPETE WITH HIM.
I DIDN'T REALIZE IT WAS A COMPETITION.
WHAT IS THIS ALL ABOUT, JORDAN?
I'M IN LOVE WITH YOU, FIG.
AND I CAN'T BE YOUR FRIEND.
WELL, SHIT.
TURSIG! HOW ARE THINGS BEING GAY?
DID YOU KISS SOME BOYS TODAY?
THE GOBLIN MARKET IS NOT SUPPORTIVE OF MY ALTERNATIVE LIFESTYLE.
NYU

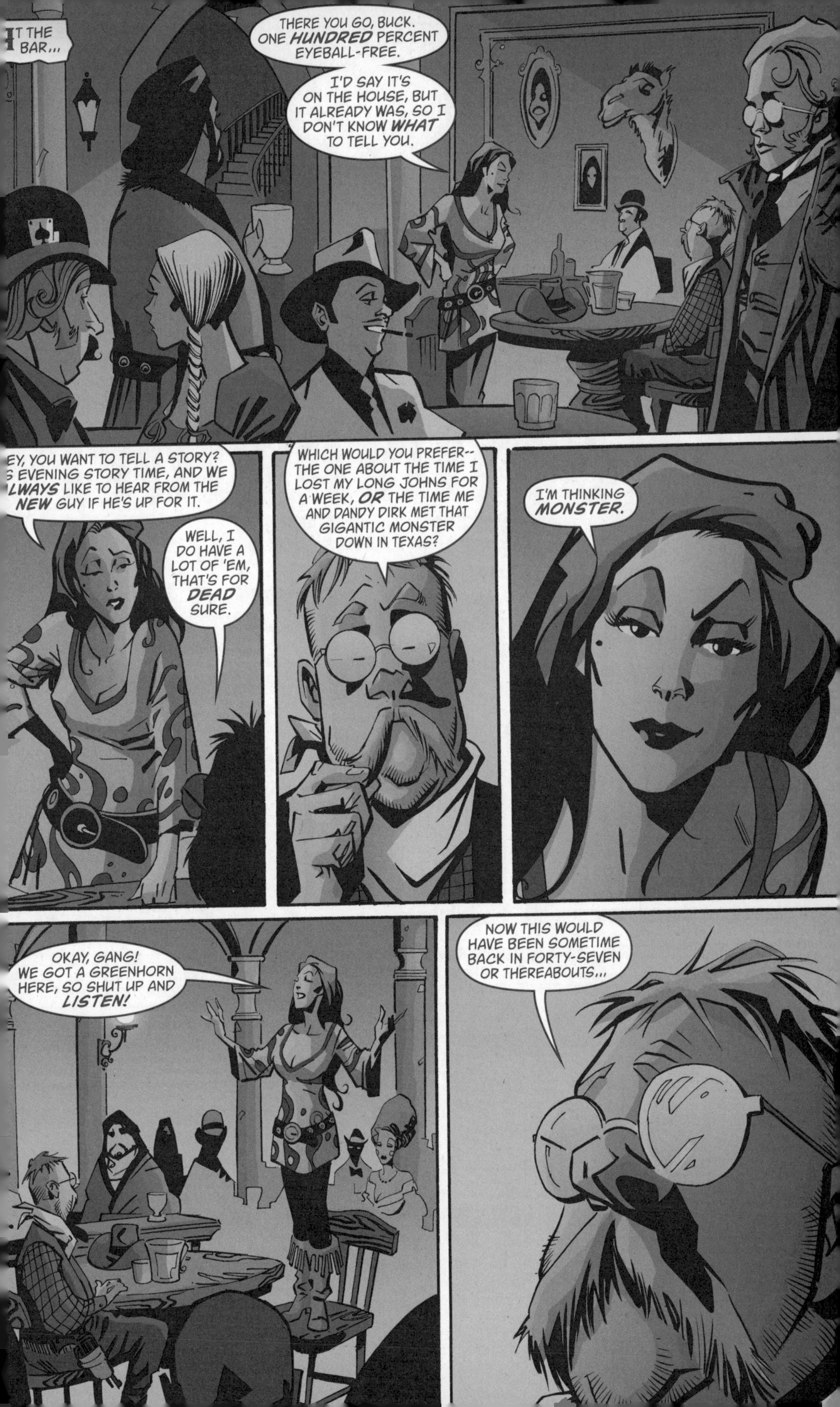

T THE BAR...
THERE YOU GO, BUCK. ONE HUNDRED PERCENT EYEBALL-FREE.
I'D SAY IT'S ON THE HOUSE, BUT IT ALREADY WAS, SO I DON'T KNOW WHAT TO TELL YOU.
EY, YOU WANT TO TELL A STORY? S EVENING STORY TIME, AND WE LWAYS LIKE TO HEAR FROM THE NEW GUY IF HE'S UP FOR IT.
WELL, I DO HAVE A LOT OF 'EM, THAT'S FOR DEAD SURE.
WHICH WOULD YOU PREFER-- THE ONE ABOUT THE TIME I LOST MY LONG JOHNS FOR A WEEK, OR THE TIME ME AND DANDY DIRK MET THAT GIGANTIC MONSTER DOWN IN TEXAS?
I'M THINKING MONSTER.
OKAY, GANG! WE GOT A GREENHORN HERE, SO SHUT UP AND LISTEN!
NOW THIS WOULD HAVE BEEN SOMETIME BACK IN FORTY-SEVEN OR THEREABOUTS...

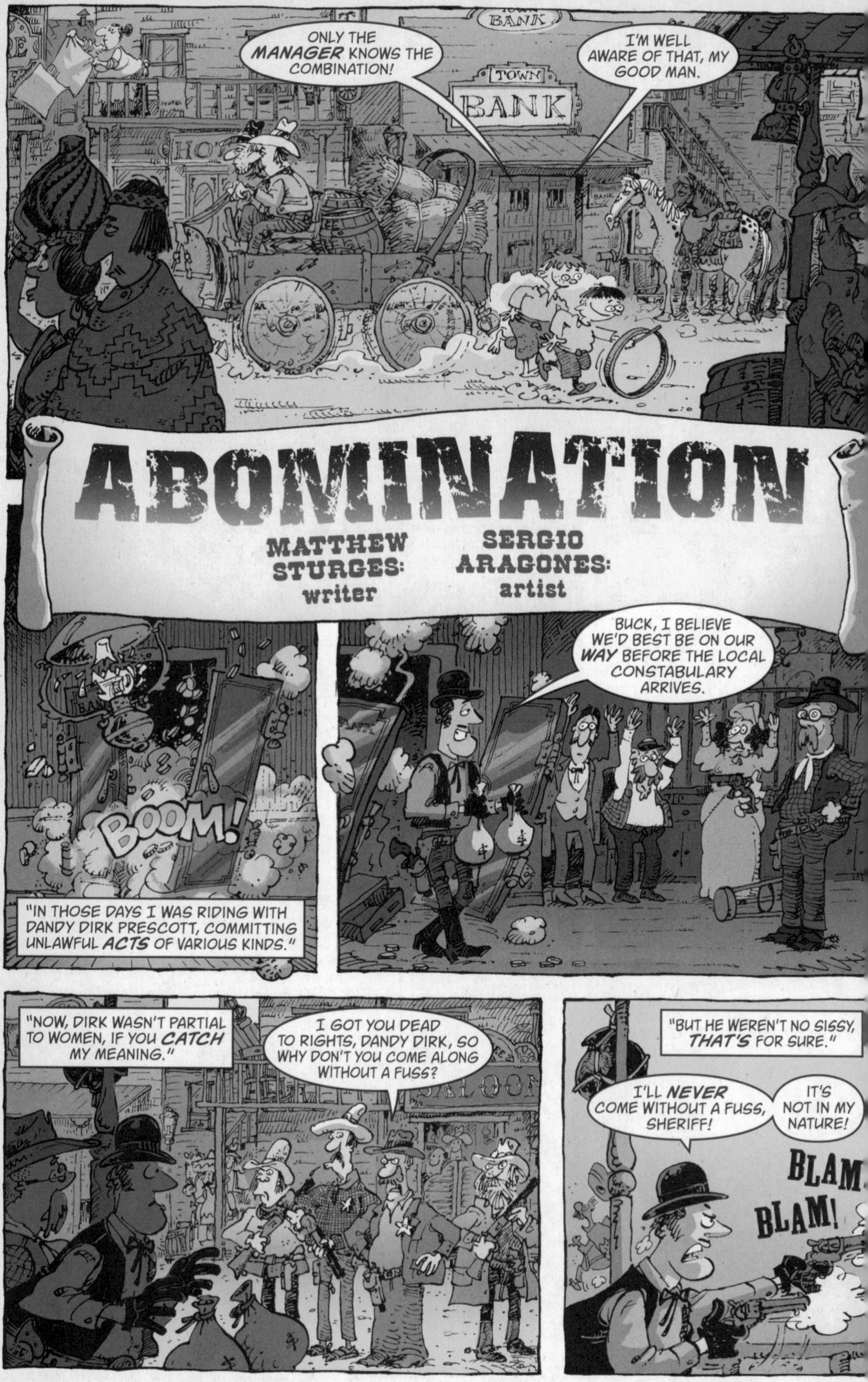

ONLY THE *MANAGER* KNOWS THE COMBINATION!
I'M WELL AWARE OF THAT, MY GOOD MAN.
TOWN BANK
ABOMINATION
MATTHEW STURGES: writer
SERGIO ARAGONES: artist
BOOM!
"IN THOSE DAYS I WAS RIDING WITH DANDY DIRK PRESCOTT, COMMITTING UNLAWFUL *ACTS* OF VARIOUS KINDS."
BUCK, I BELIEVE WE'D BEST BE ON OUR *WAY* BEFORE THE LOCAL CONSTABULARY ARRIVES.
"NOW, DIRK WASN'T PARTIAL TO WOMEN, IF YOU *CATCH* MY MEANING."
I GOT YOU DEAD TO RIGHTS, DANDY DIRK, SO WHY DON'T YOU COME ALONG WITHOUT A FUSS?
"BUT HE WEREN'T NO SISSY, *THAT'S* FOR SURE."
I'LL *NEVER* COME WITHOUT A FUSS, SHERIFF!
IT'S NOT IN MY NATURE!
BLAM!
BLAM!

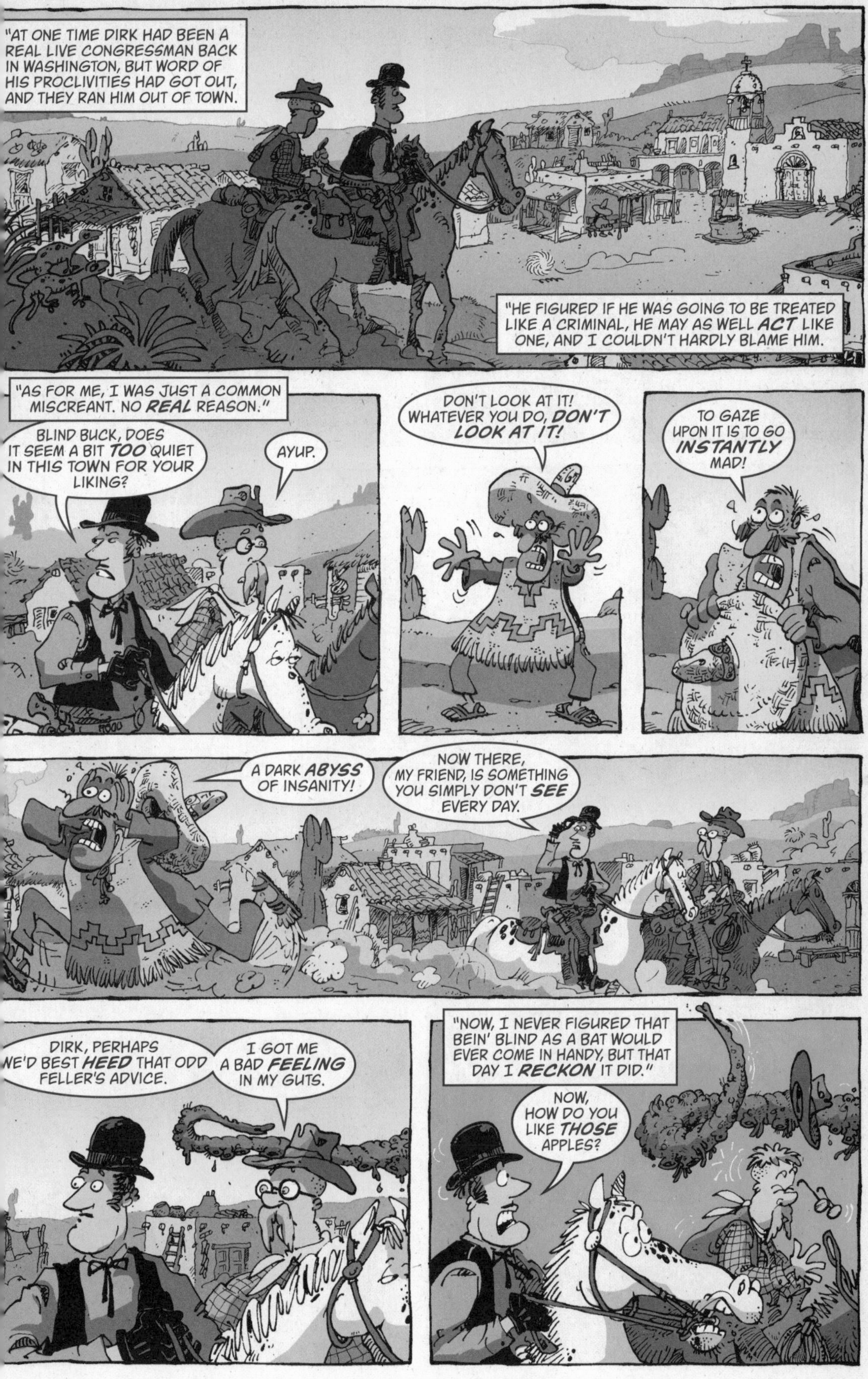
"AT ONE TIME DIRK HAD BEEN A REAL LIVE CONGRESSMAN BACK IN WASHINGTON, BUT WORD OF HIS PROCLIVITIES HAD GOT OUT, AND THEY RAN HIM OUT OF TOWN.
"HE FIGURED IF HE WAS GOING TO BE TREATED LIKE A CRIMINAL, HE MAY AS WELL ACT LIKE ONE, AND I COULDN'T HARDLY BLAME HIM.
"AS FOR ME, I WAS JUST A COMMON MISCREANT. NO REAL REASON."
BLIND BUCK, DOES IT SEEM A BIT TOO QUIET IN THIS TOWN FOR YOUR LIKING?
AYUP.
DON'T LOOK AT IT! WHATEVER YOU DO, DON'T LOOK AT IT!
TO GAZE UPON IT IS TO GO INSTANTLY MAD!
A DARK ABYSS OF INSANITY!
NOW THERE, MY FRIEND, IS SOMETHING YOU SIMPLY DON'T SEE EVERY DAY.
DIRK, PERHAPS WE'D BEST HEED THAT ODD FELLER'S ADVICE.
I GOT ME A BAD FEELING IN MY GUTS.
"NOW, I NEVER FIGURED THAT BEIN' BLIND AS A BAT WOULD EVER COME IN HANDY, BUT THAT DAY I RECKON IT DID."
NOW, HOW DO YOU LIKE THOSE APPLES?

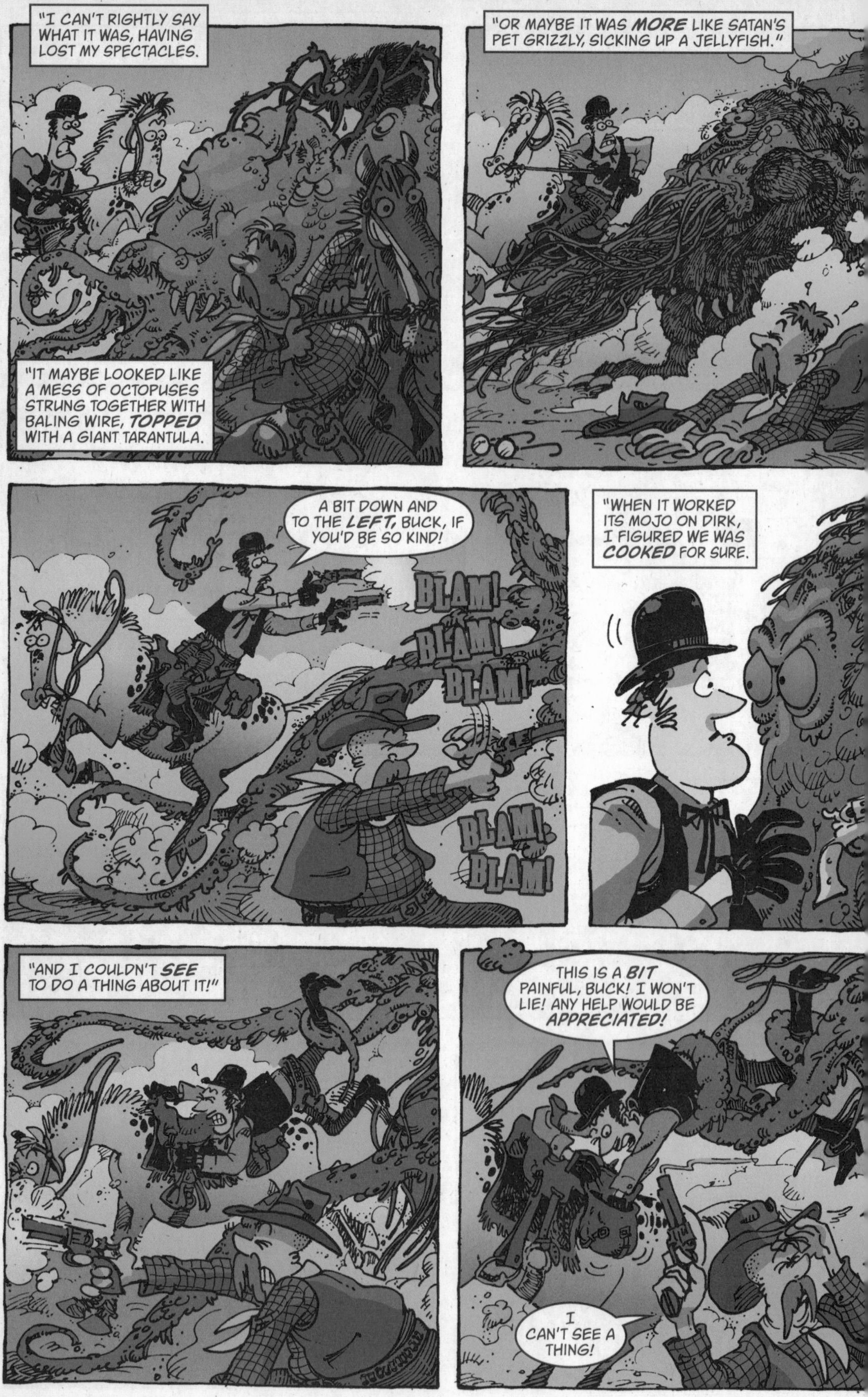
"I CAN'T RIGHTLY SAY WHAT IT WAS, HAVING LOST MY SPECTACLES.
"IT MAYBE LOOKED LIKE A MESS OF OCTOPUSES STRUNG TOGETHER WITH BALING WIRE, *TOPPED* WITH A GIANT TARANTULA.
"OR MAYBE IT WAS *MORE* LIKE SATAN'S PET GRIZZLY, SICKING UP A JELLYFISH."
A BIT DOWN AND TO THE *LEFT,* BUCK, IF YOU'D BE SO KIND!
BLAM! BLAM! BLAM!
BLAM! BLAM!
"WHEN IT WORKED ITS MOJO ON DIRK, I FIGURED WE WAS *COOKED* FOR SURE.
"AND I COULDN'T *SEE* TO DO A THING ABOUT IT!"
THIS IS A *BIT* PAINFUL, BUCK! I WON'T LIE! ANY HELP WOULD BE *APPRECIATED!*
I CAN'T SEE A THING!

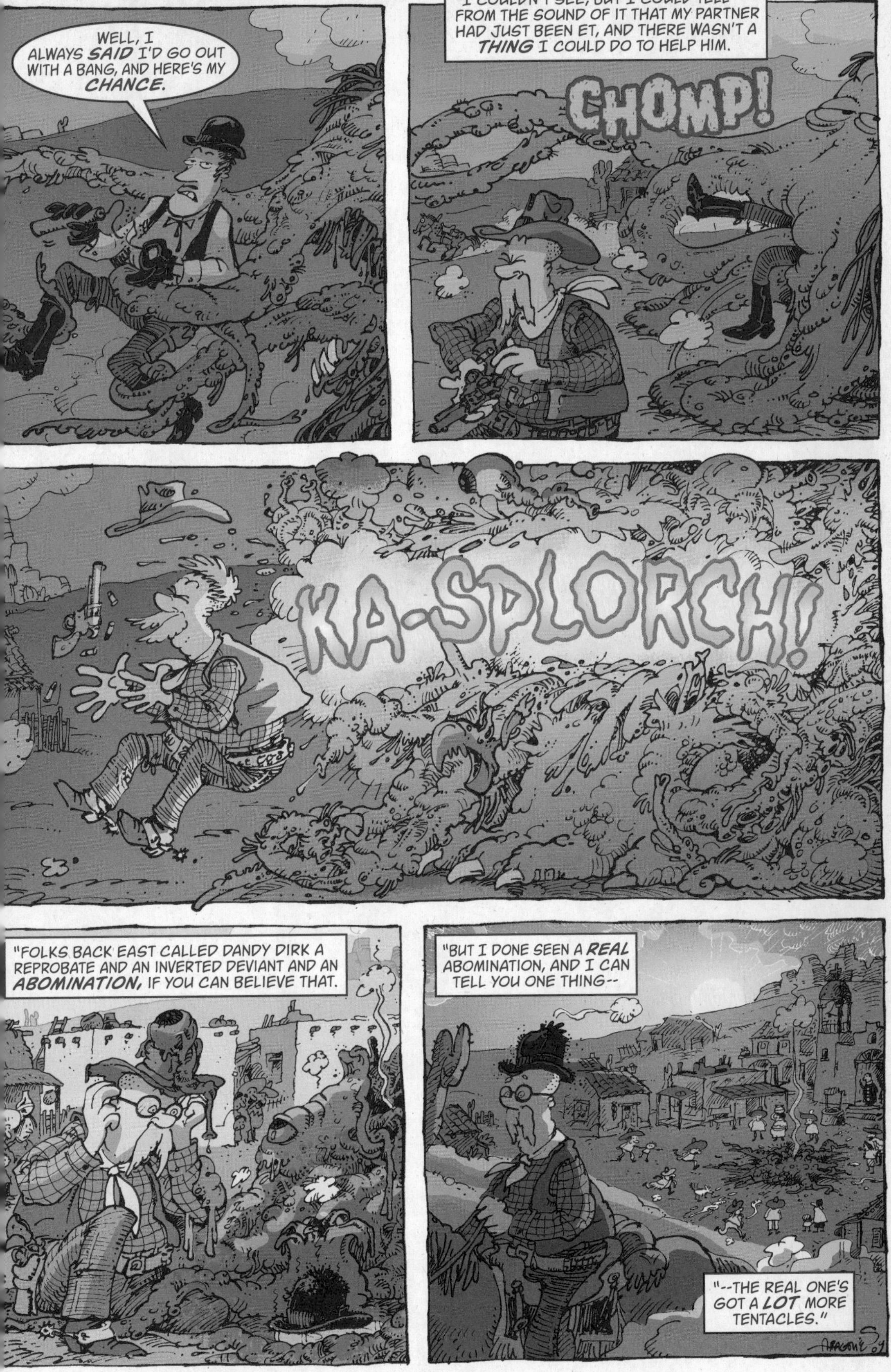
WELL, I ALWAYS SAID I'D GO OUT WITH A BANG, AND HERE'S MY CHANCE.
"I COULDN'T SEE, BUT I COULD TELL FROM THE SOUND OF IT THAT MY PARTNER HAD JUST BEEN ET, AND THERE WASN'T A THING I COULD DO TO HELP HIM.
CHOMP!
KA-SPLORCH!
"FOLKS BACK EAST CALLED DANDY DIRK A REPROBATE AND AN INVERTED DEVIANT AND AN ABOMINATION, IF YOU CAN BELIEVE THAT.
"BUT I DONE SEEN A REAL ABOMINATION, AND I CAN TELL YOU ONE THING--
"--THE REAL ONE'S GOT A LOT MORE TENTACLES."

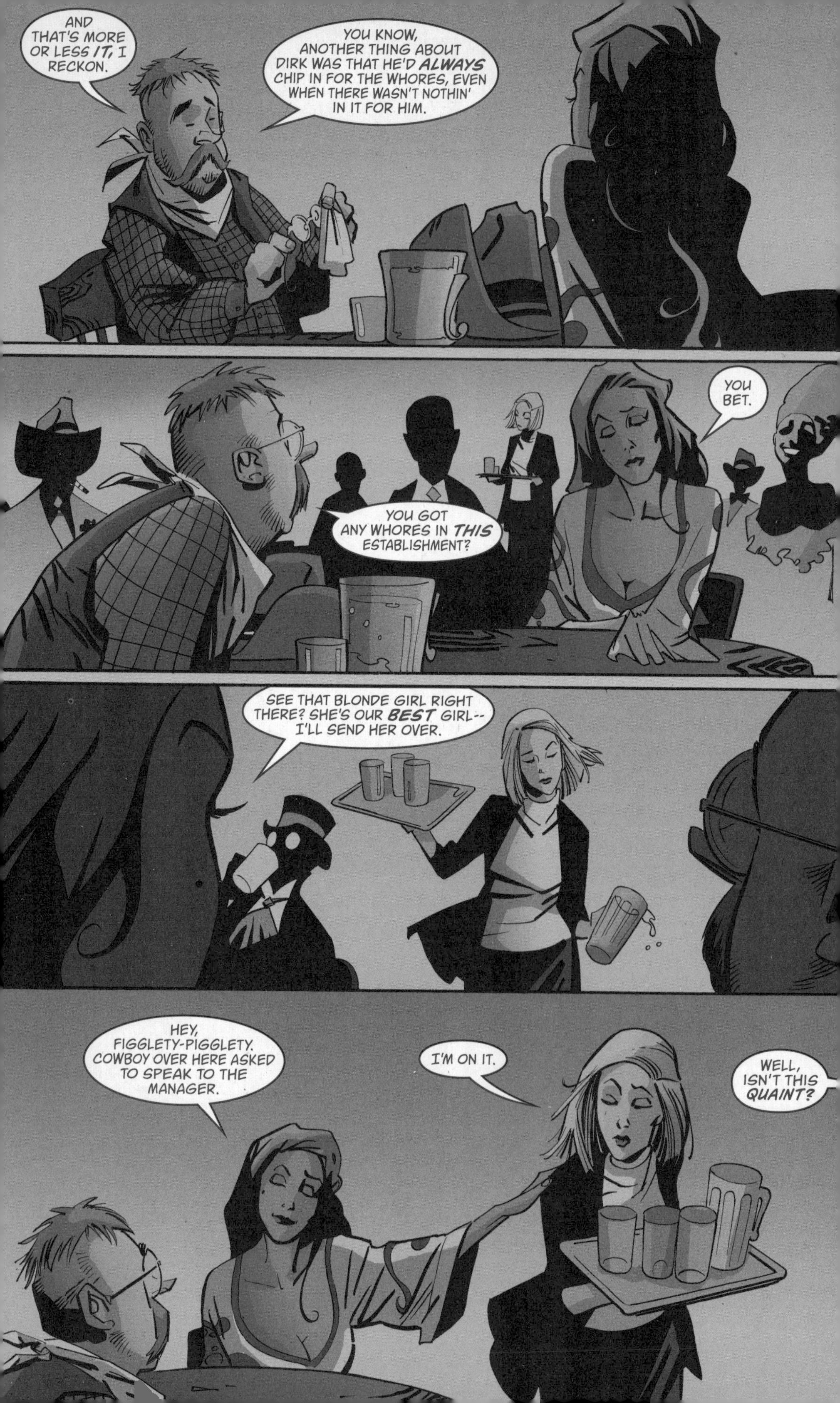
AND THAT'S MORE OR LESS IT, I RECKON.
YOU KNOW, ANOTHER THING ABOUT DIRK WAS THAT HE'D ALWAYS CHIP IN FOR THE WHORES, EVEN WHEN THERE WASN'T NOTHIN' IN IT FOR HIM.
YOU GOT ANY WHORES IN THIS ESTABLISHMENT?
YOU BET.
SEE THAT BLONDE GIRL RIGHT THERE? SHE'S OUR BEST GIRL-- I'LL SEND HER OVER.
HEY, FIGGLETY-PIGGLETY. COWBOY OVER HERE ASKED TO SPEAK TO THE MANAGER.
I'M ON IT.
WELL, ISN'T THIS QUAINT?

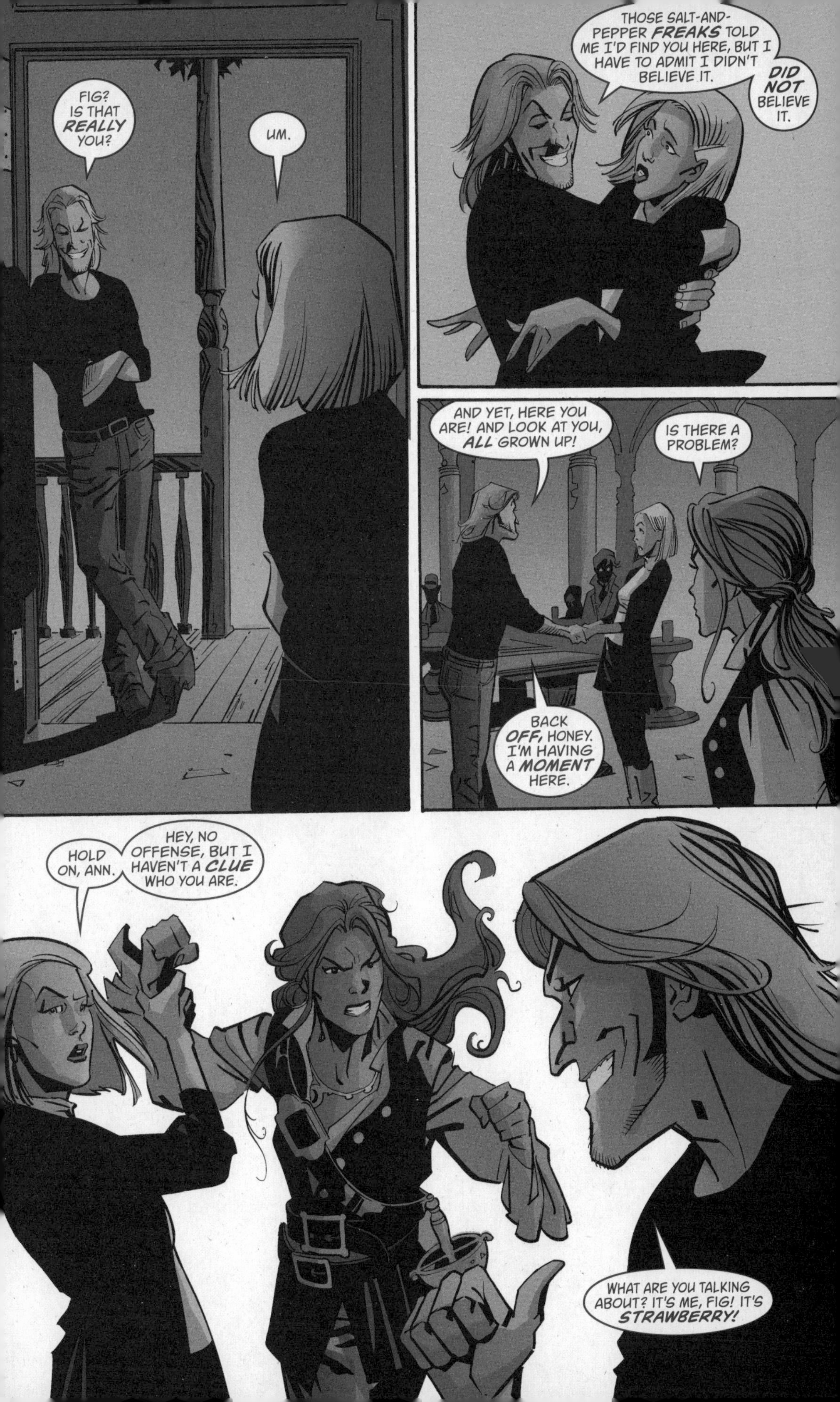
FIG? IS THAT REALLY YOU?
UM.
THOSE SALT-AND-PEPPER FREAKS TOLD ME I'D FIND YOU HERE, BUT I HAVE TO ADMIT I DIDN'T BELIEVE IT.
DID NOT BELIEVE IT.
AND YET, HERE YOU ARE! AND LOOK AT YOU, ALL GROWN UP!
IS THERE A PROBLEM?
BACK OFF, HONEY. I'M HAVING A MOMENT HERE.
HOLD ON, ANN.
HEY, NO OFFENSE, BUT I HAVEN'T A CLUE WHO YOU ARE.
WHAT ARE YOU TALKING ABOUT? IT'S ME, FIG! IT'S STRAWBERRY!

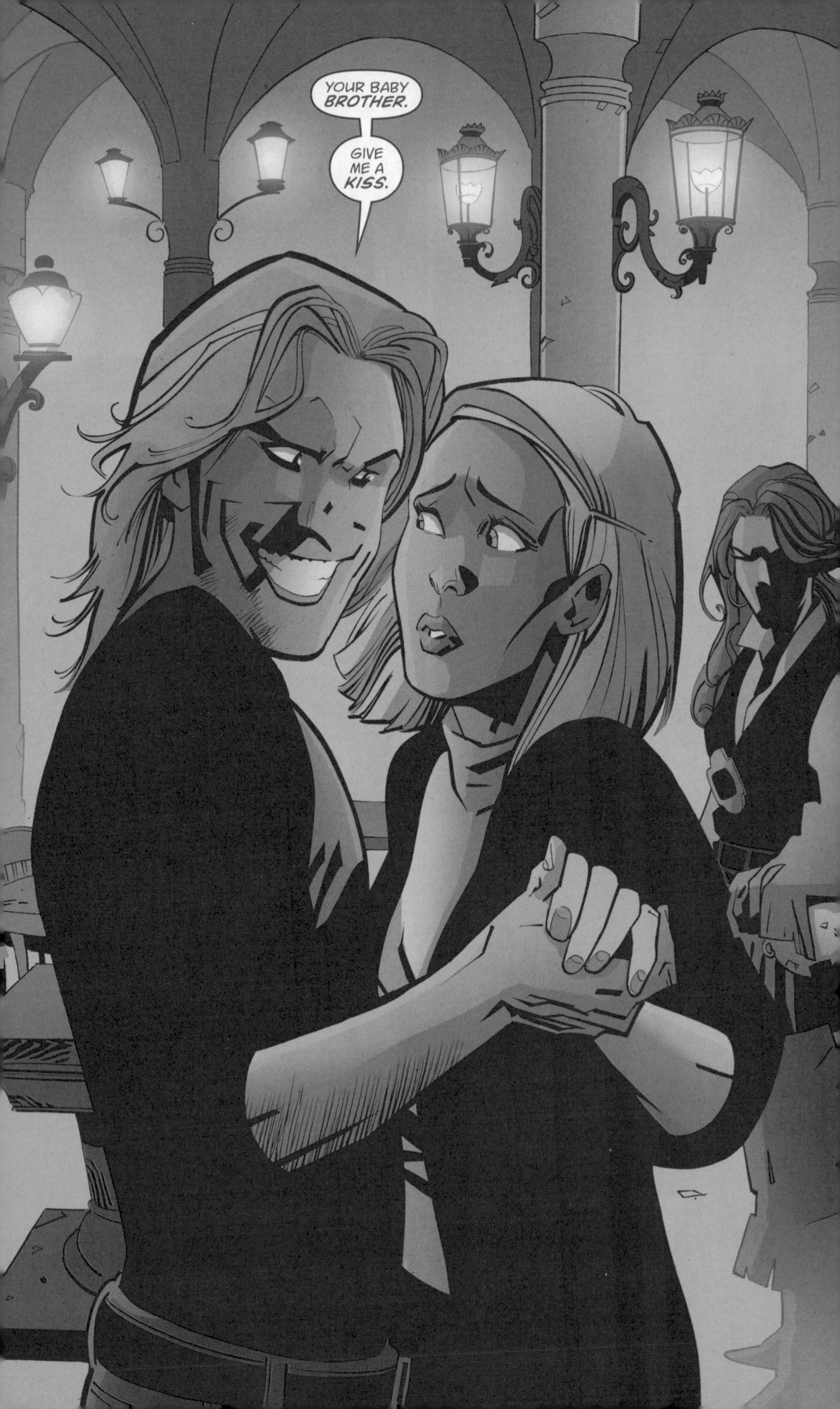
YOUR BABY BROTHER.
GIVE ME A KISS.

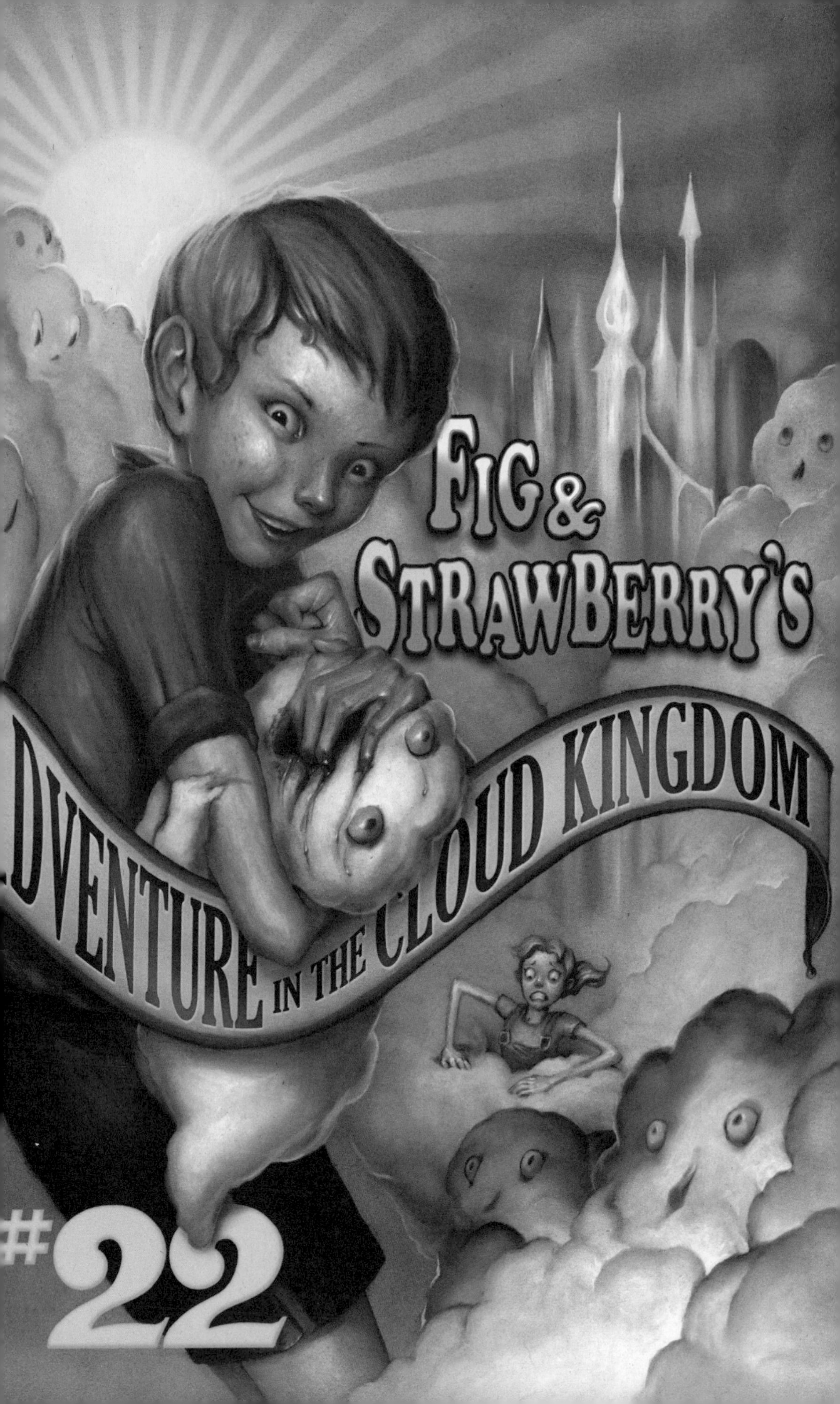
FIG &
STRAWBERRY'S
DVENTURE IN THE CLOUD KINGDOM
#22

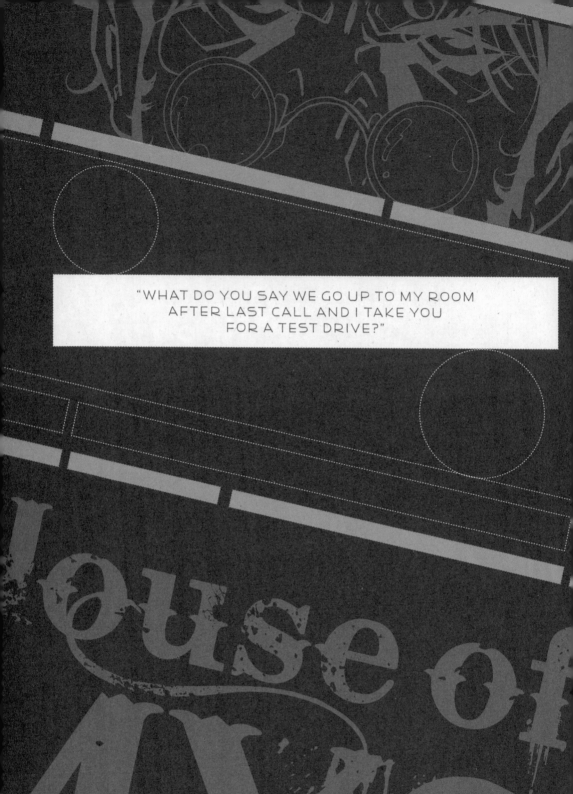

"WHAT DO YOU SAY WE GO UP TO MY ROOM
AFTER LAST CALL AND I TAKE YOU
FOR A TEST DRIVE?"

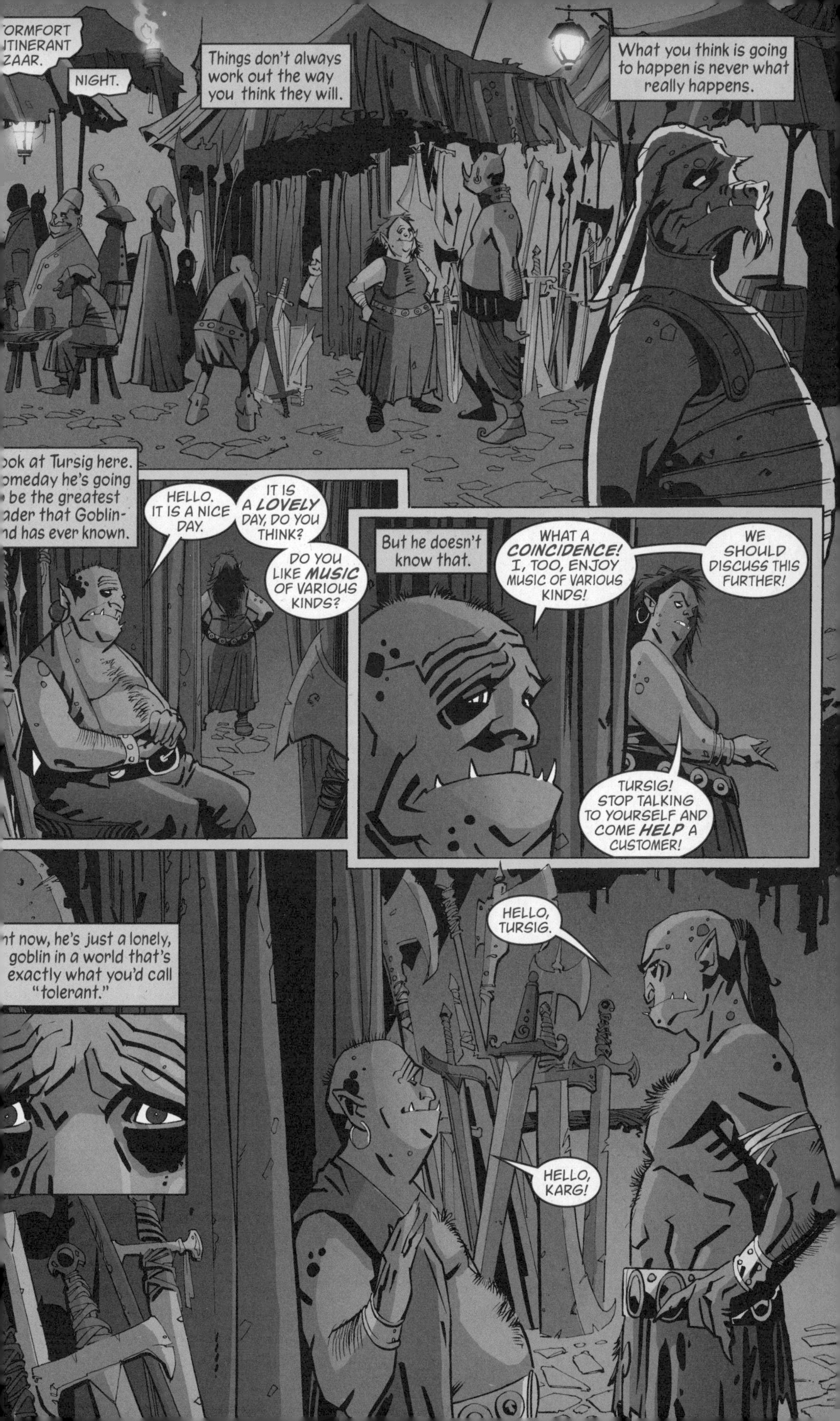

TORMFORT
ITINERANT
ZAAR.
NIGHT.
Things don't always work out the way you think they will.
What you think is going to happen is never what really happens.
ook at Tursig here. omeday he's going be the greatest ader that Goblin- nd has ever known.
HELLO. IT IS A NICE DAY.
IT IS A LOVELY DAY, DO YOU THINK?
DO YOU LIKE MUSIC OF VARIOUS KINDS?
But he doesn't know that.
WHAT A COINCIDENCE! I, TOO, ENJOY MUSIC OF VARIOUS KINDS!
WE SHOULD DISCUSS THIS FURTHER!
TURSIG! STOP TALKING TO YOURSELF AND COME HELP A CUSTOMER!
nt now, he's just a lonely, goblin in a world that's exactly what you'd call "tolerant."
HELLO, TURSIG.
HELLO, KARG!

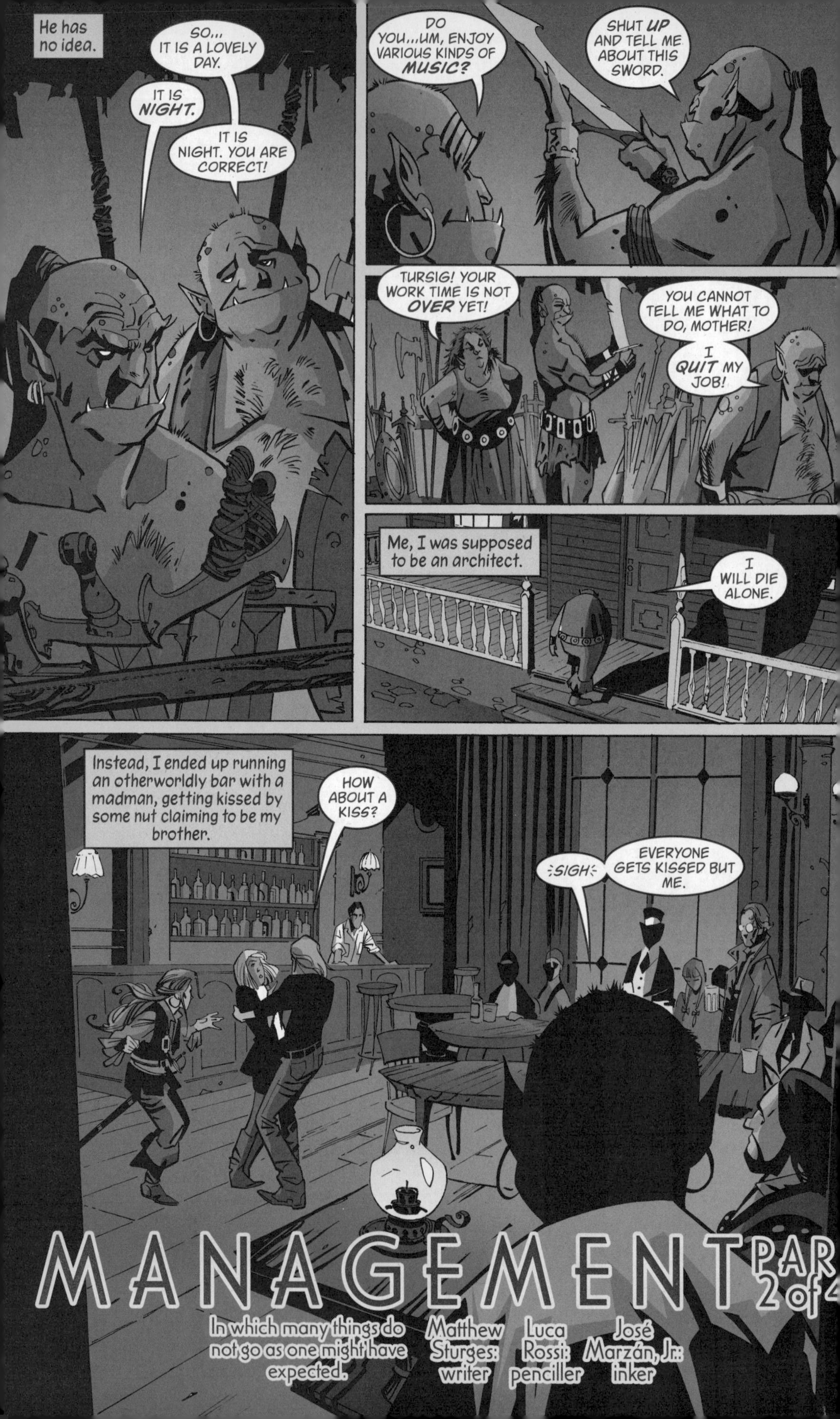
He has no idea.
SO... IT IS A LOVELY DAY.
IT IS NIGHT.
IT IS NIGHT. YOU ARE CORRECT!
DO YOU...UM, ENJOY VARIOUS KINDS OF MUSIC?
SHUT UP AND TELL ME ABOUT THIS SWORD.
TURSIG! YOUR WORK TIME IS NOT OVER YET!
YOU CANNOT TELL ME WHAT TO DO, MOTHER!
I QUIT MY JOB!
Me, I was supposed to be an architect.
I WILL DIE ALONE.
Instead, I ended up running an otherworldly bar with a madman, getting kissed by some nut claiming to be my brother.
HOW ABOUT A KISS?
SIGH
EVERYONE GETS KISSED BUT ME.
MANAGEMENT PART 2 of 4
In which many things do not go as one might have expected.
Matthew Sturges: writer
Luca Rossi: penciller
José Marzán, Jr.: inker

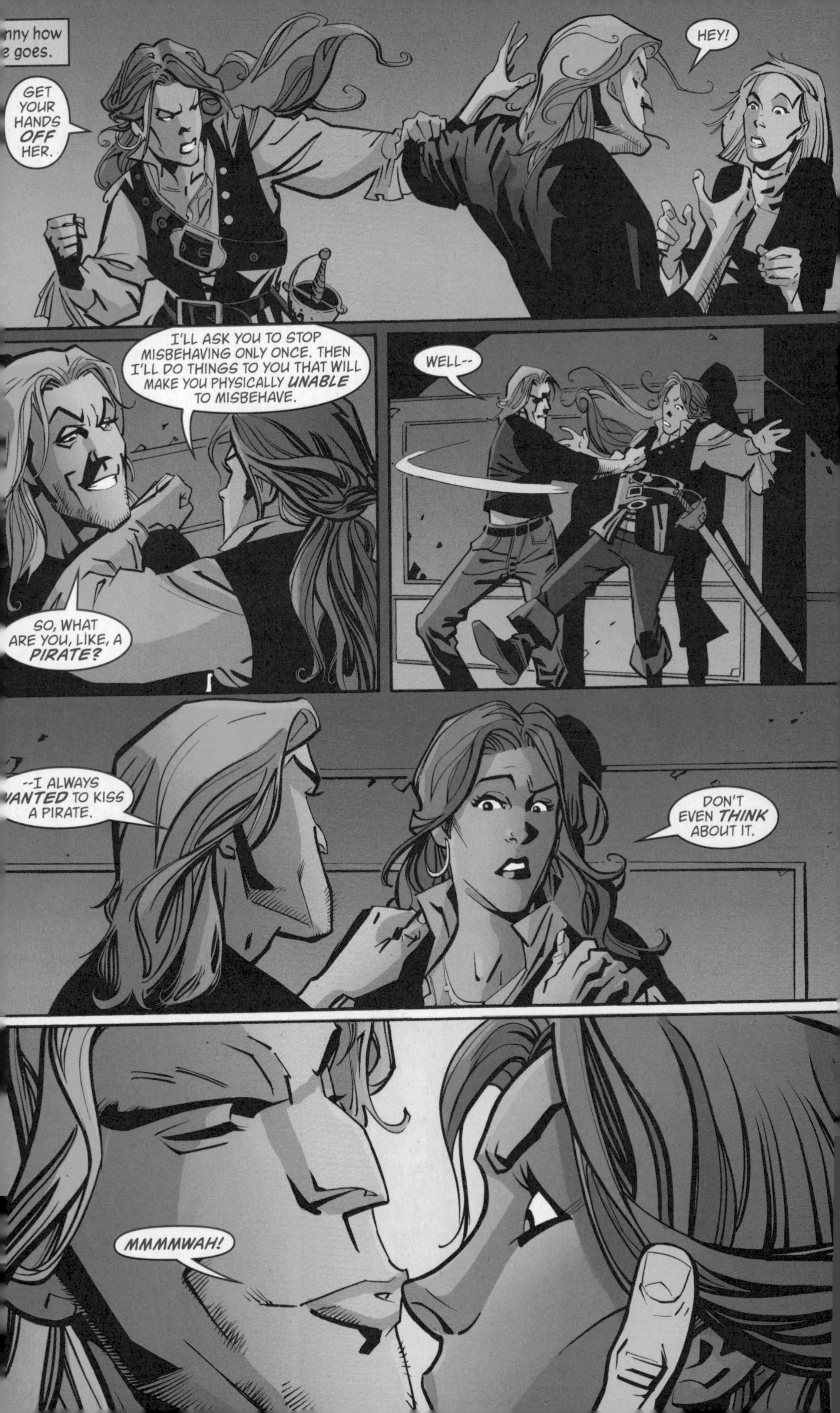

nny how
e goes.
GET YOUR HANDS OFF HER.
HEY!
I'LL ASK YOU TO STOP MISBEHAVING ONLY ONCE. THEN I'LL DO THINGS TO YOU THAT WILL MAKE YOU PHYSICALLY UNABLE TO MISBEHAVE.
SO, WHAT ARE YOU, LIKE, A PIRATE?
WELL--
--I ALWAYS WANTED TO KISS A PIRATE.
DON'T EVEN THINK ABOUT IT.
MMMMWAH!

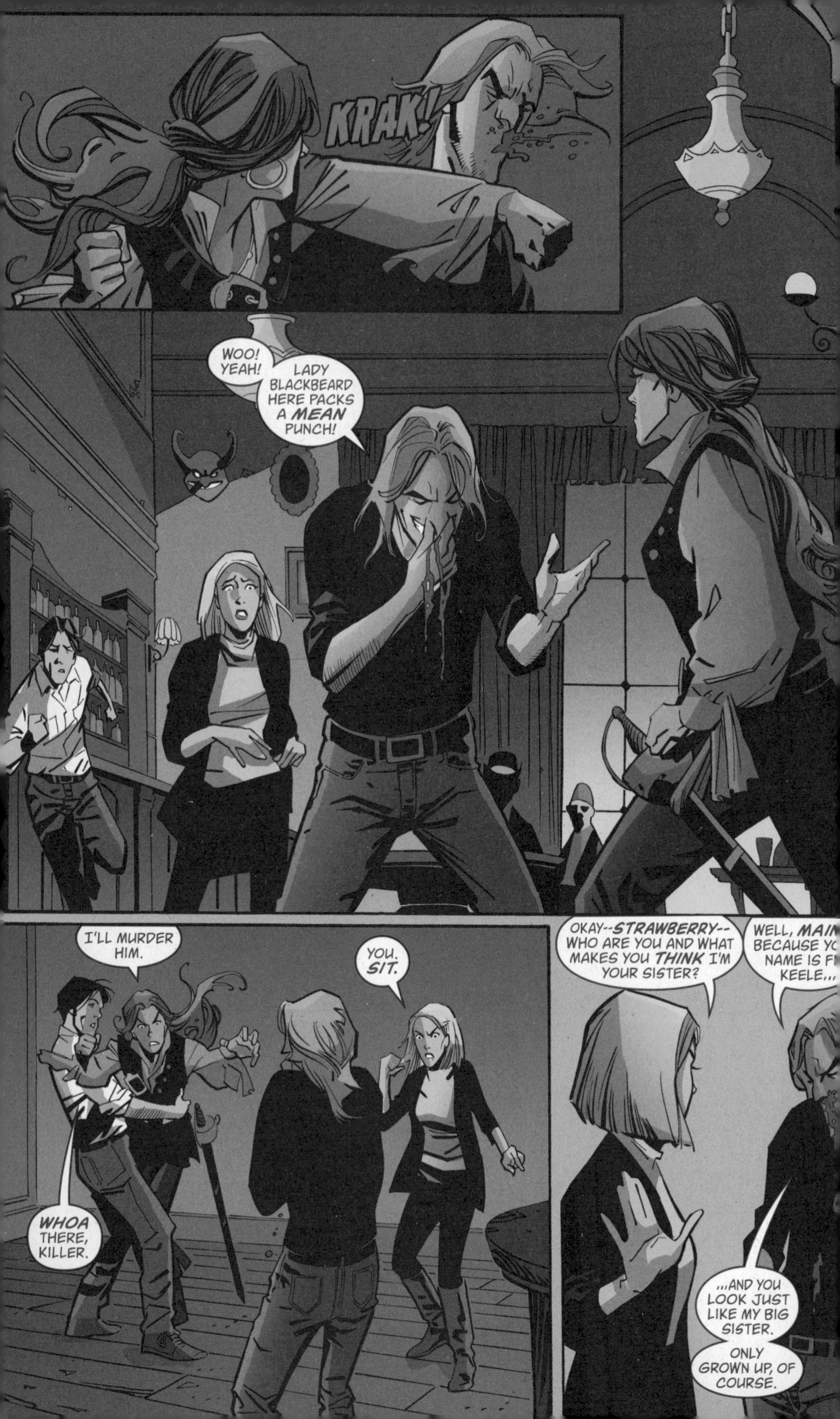
KRAK!
WOO! YEAH!
LADY BLACKBEARD HERE PACKS A MEAN PUNCH!
I'LL MURDER HIM.
WHOA THERE, KILLER.
YOU. SIT.
OKAY--STRAWBERRY-- WHO ARE YOU AND WHAT MAKES YOU THINK I'M YOUR SISTER?
...AND YOU LOOK JUST LIKE MY BIG SISTER.
ONLY GROWN UP, OF COURSE.

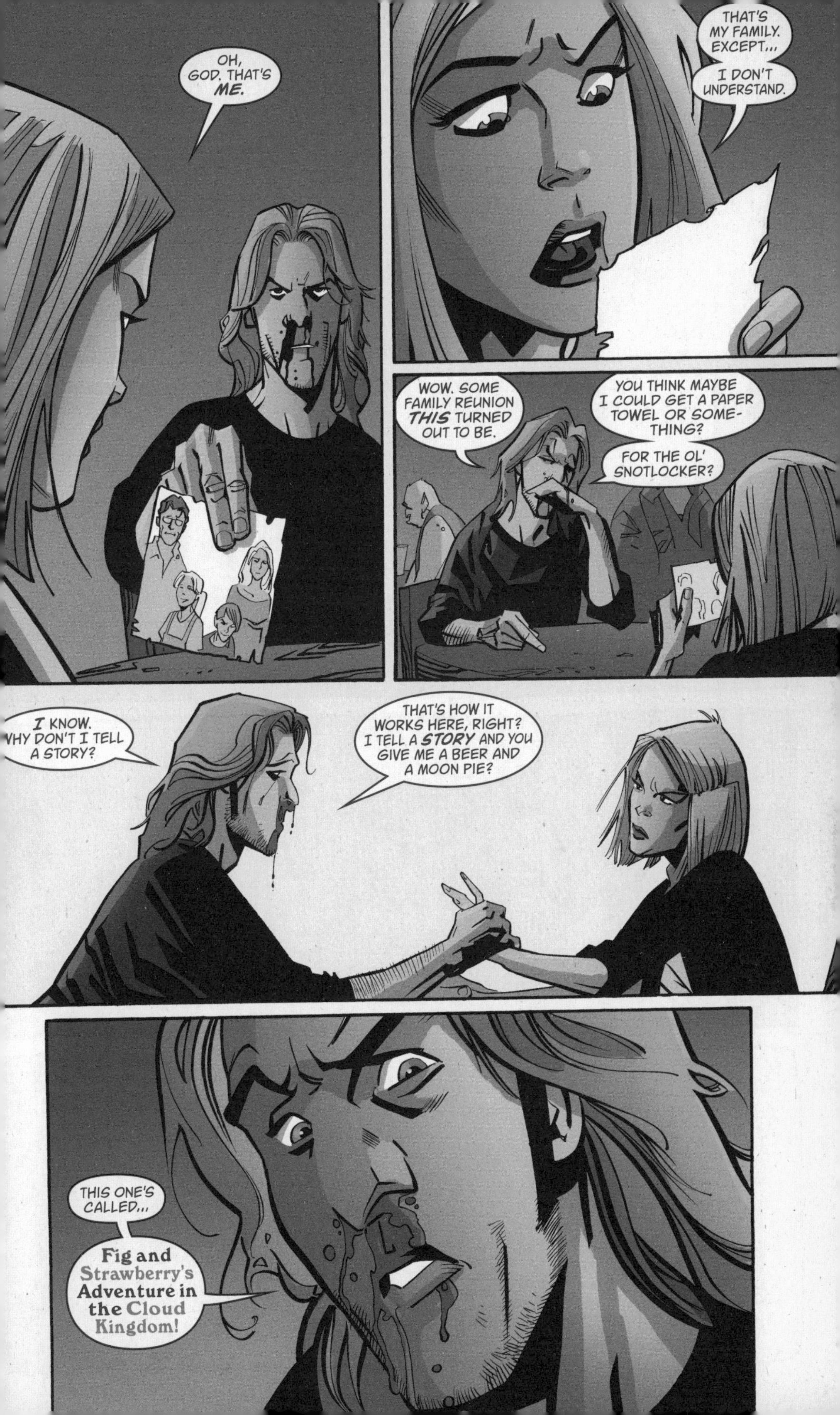
OH, GOD. THAT'S ME.
THAT'S MY FAMILY. EXCEPT...
I DON'T UNDERSTAND.
WOW. SOME FAMILY REUNION THIS TURNED OUT TO BE.
YOU THINK MAYBE I COULD GET A PAPER TOWEL OR SOMETHING?
FOR THE OL' SNOTLOCKER?
I KNOW. WHY DON'T I TELL A STORY?
THAT'S HOW IT WORKS HERE, RIGHT? I TELL A STORY AND YOU GIVE ME A BEER AND A MOON PIE?
THIS ONE'S CALLED...
Fig and Strawberry's Adventure in the Cloud Kingdom!

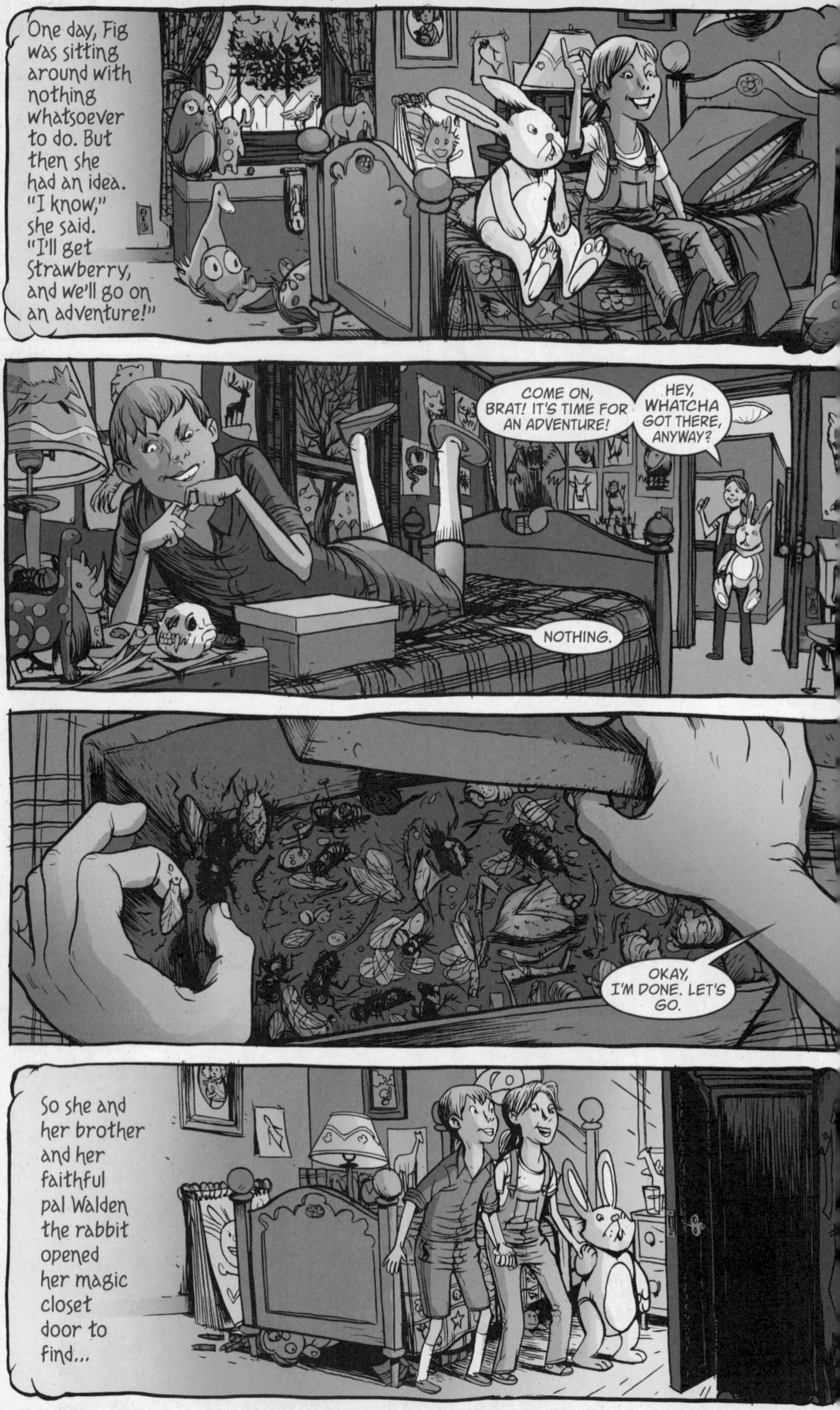
One day, Fig was sitting around with nothing whatsoever to do. But then she had an idea. "I know," she said. "I'll get Strawberry, and we'll go on an adventure!"
COME ON, BRAT! IT'S TIME FOR AN ADVENTURE!
HEY, WHATCHA GOT THERE, ANYWAY?
NOTHING.
OKAY, I'M DONE. LET'S GO.
So she and her brother and her faithful pal Walden the rabbit opened her magic closet door to find...

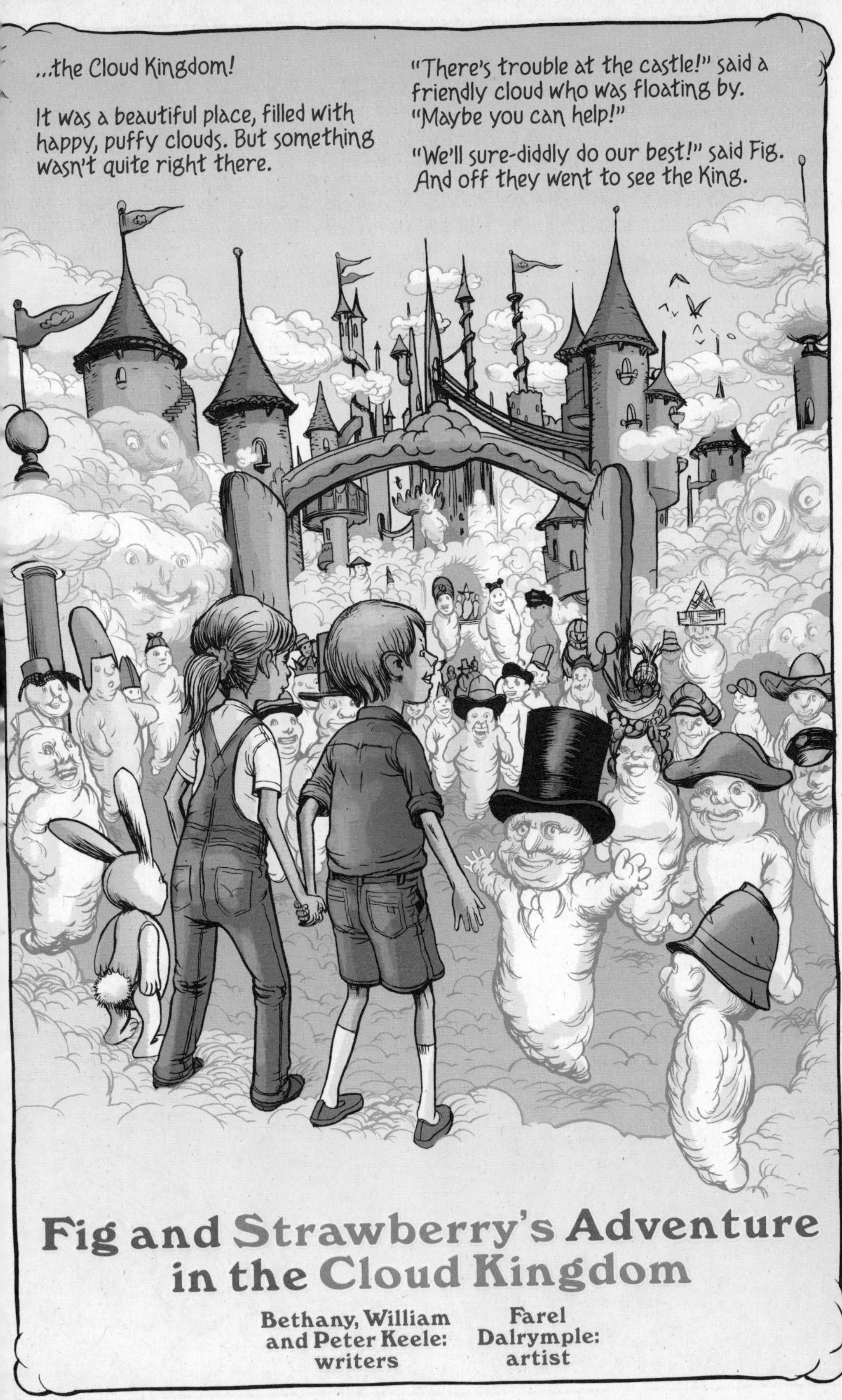
...the Cloud Kingdom!
It was a beautiful place, filled with happy, puffy clouds. But something wasn't quite right there.
"There's trouble at the castle!" said a friendly cloud who was floating by. "Maybe you can help!"
"We'll sure-diddly do our best!" said Fig. And off they went to see the King.
Fig and Strawberry's Adventure in the Cloud Kingdom
Bethany, William and Peter Keele: writers
Farel Dalrymple: artist

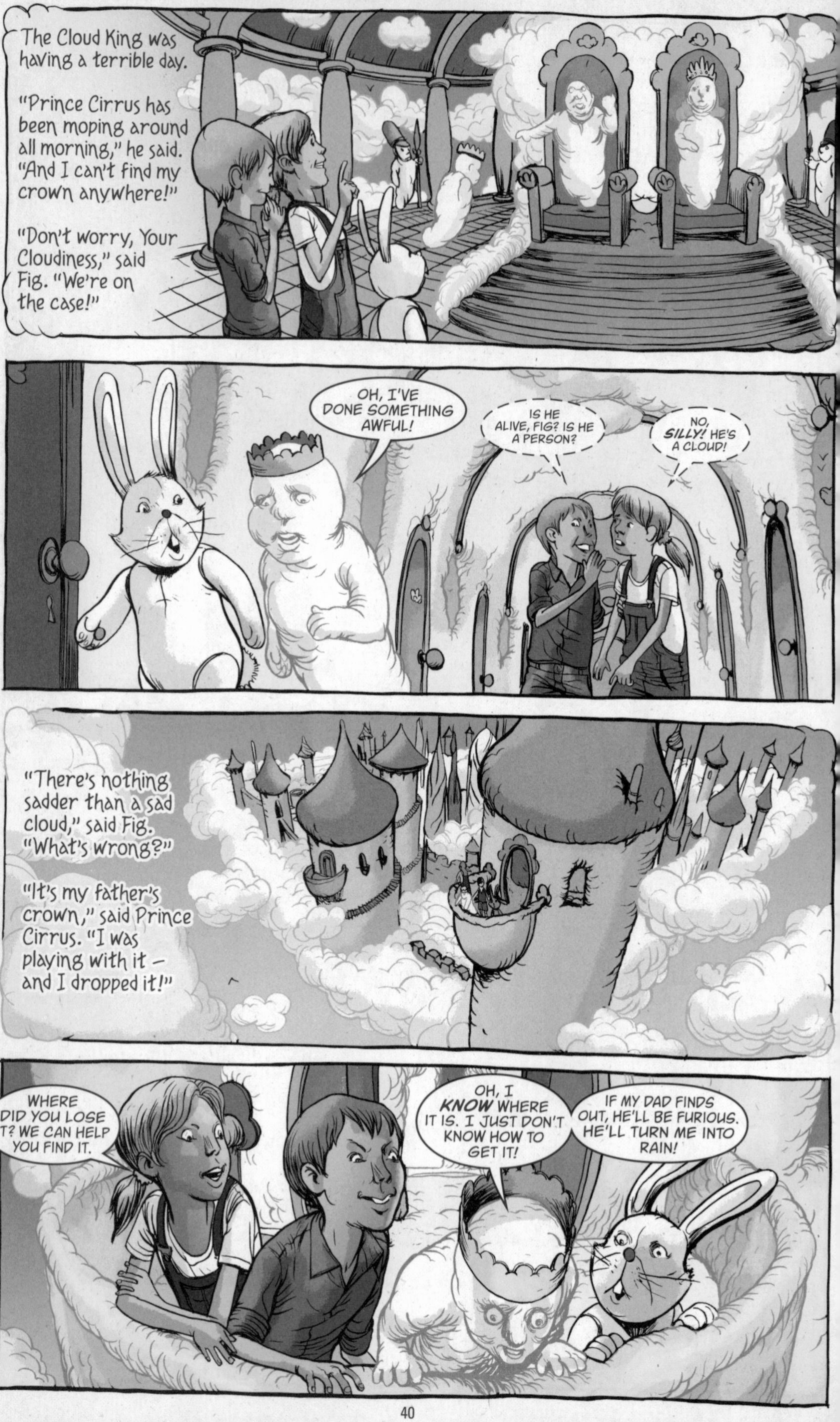

The Cloud King was having a terrible day.
"Prince Cirrus has been moping around all morning," he said. "And I can't find my crown anywhere!"
"Don't worry, Your Cloudiness," said Fig. "We're on the case!"
OH, I'VE DONE SOMETHING AWFUL!
IS HE ALIVE, FIG? IS HE A PERSON?
NO, SILLY! HE'S A CLOUD!
"There's nothing sadder than a sad cloud," said Fig. "What's wrong?"
"It's my father's crown," said Prince Cirrus. "I was playing with it – and I dropped it!"
WHERE DID YOU LOSE IT? WE CAN HELP YOU FIND IT.
OH, I KNOW WHERE IT IS. I JUST DON'T KNOW HOW TO GET IT!
IF MY DAD FINDS OUT, HE'LL BE FURIOUS. HE'LL TURN ME INTO RAIN!

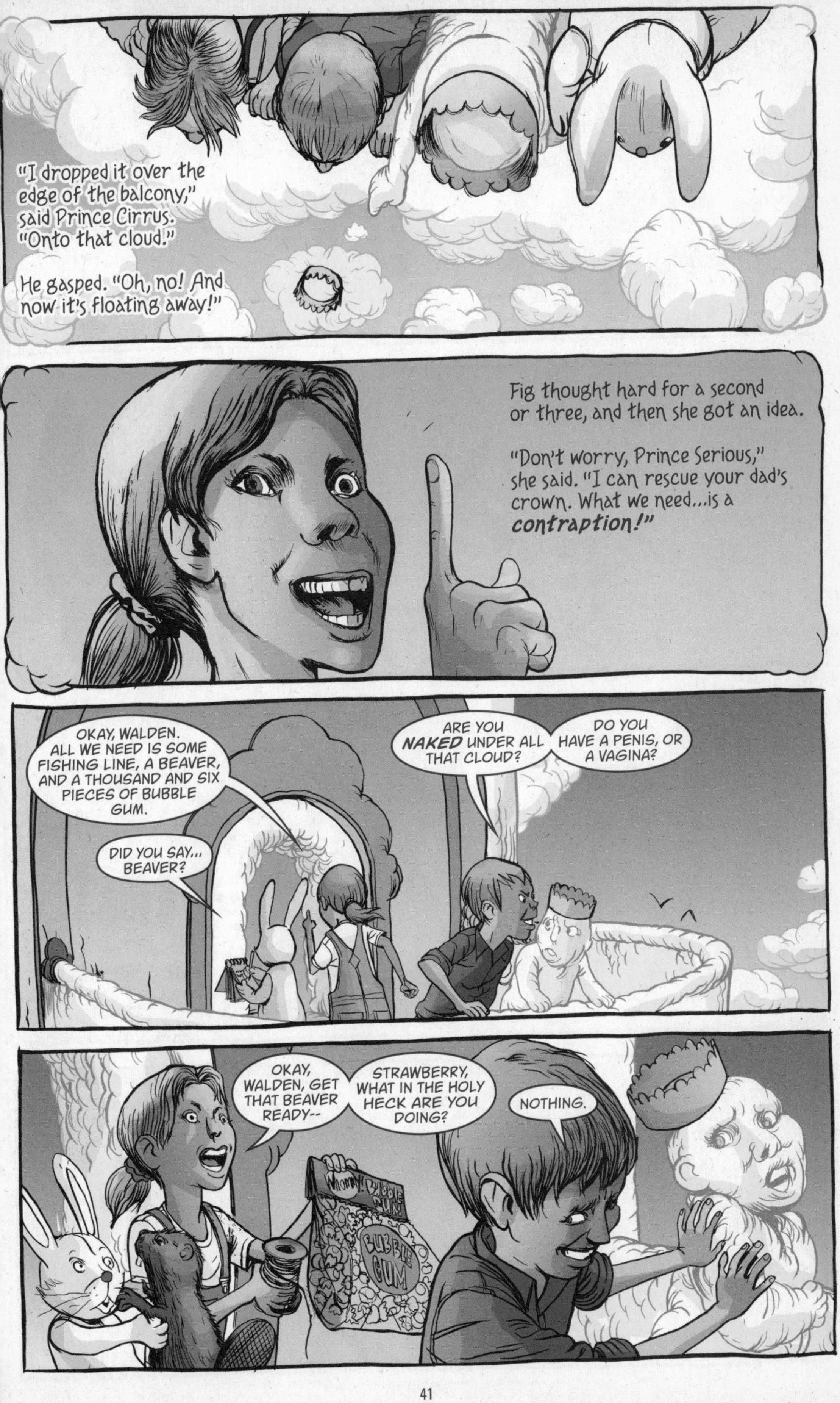
"I dropped it over the edge of the balcony," said Prince Cirrus. "Onto that cloud."
He gasped. "Oh, no! And now it's floating away!"
Fig thought hard for a second or three, and then she got an idea.
"Don't worry, Prince Serious," she said. "I can rescue your dad's crown. What we need...is a *contraption!*"
OKAY, WALDEN. ALL WE NEED IS SOME FISHING LINE, A BEAVER, AND A THOUSAND AND SIX PIECES OF BUBBLE GUM.
DID YOU SAY... BEAVER?
ARE YOU ***NAKED*** UNDER ALL THAT CLOUD?
DO YOU HAVE A PENIS, OR A VAGINA?
OKAY, WALDEN, GET THAT BEAVER READY--
STRAWBERRY, WHAT IN THE HOLY HECK ARE YOU DOING?
NOTHING.
BUBBLE GUM

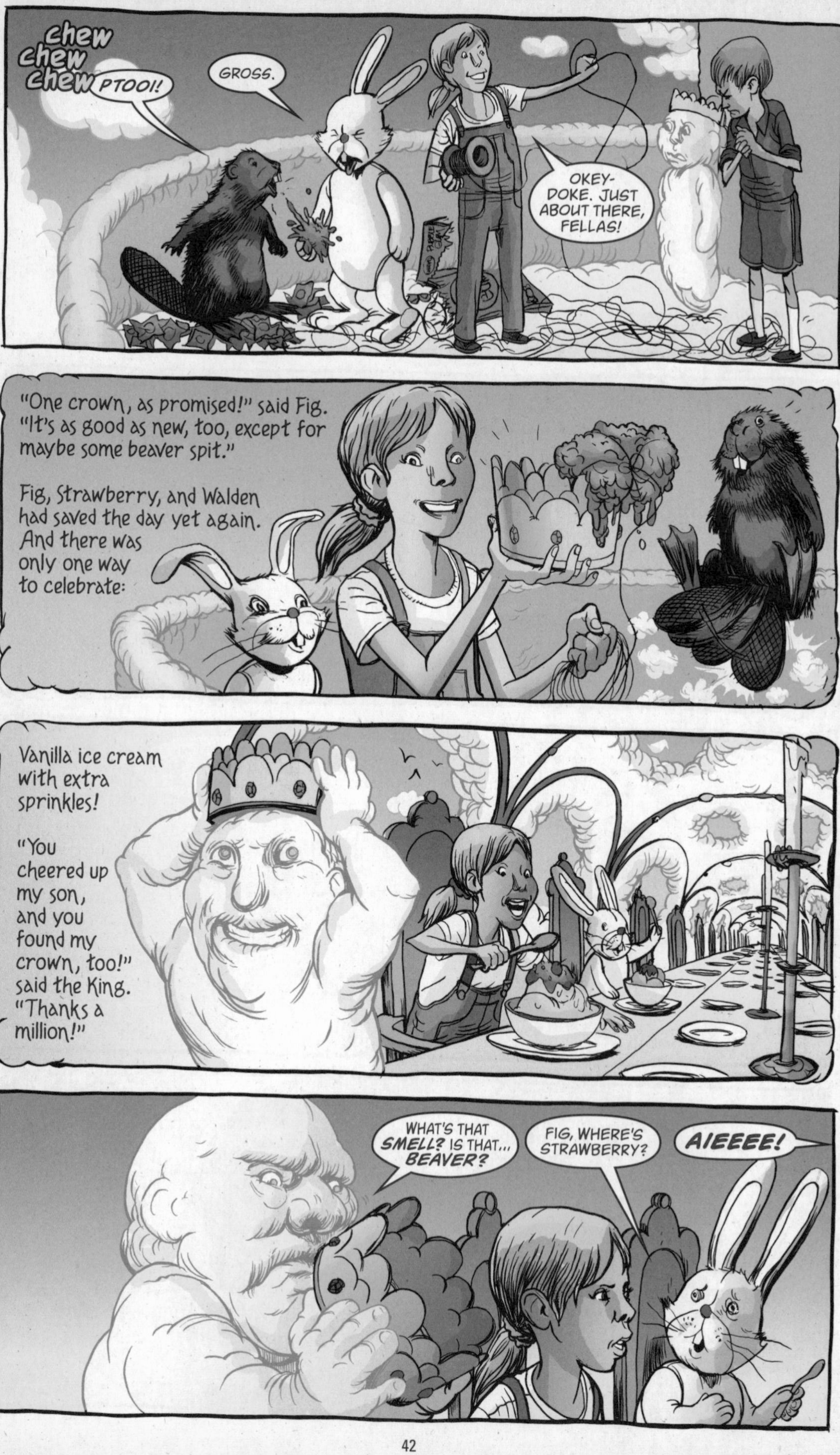
chew chew chew
PTOOI!
GROSS.
OKEY-DOKE. JUST ABOUT THERE, FELLAS!
"One crown, as promised!" said Fig. "It's as good as new, too, except for maybe some beaver spit."
Fig, Strawberry, and Walden had saved the day yet again. And there was only one way to celebrate:
Vanilla ice cream with extra sprinkles!
"You cheered up my son, and you found my crown, too!" said the King. "Thanks a million!"
WHAT'S THAT SMELL? IS THAT... BEAVER?
FIG, WHERE'S STRAWBERRY?
AIEEEE!

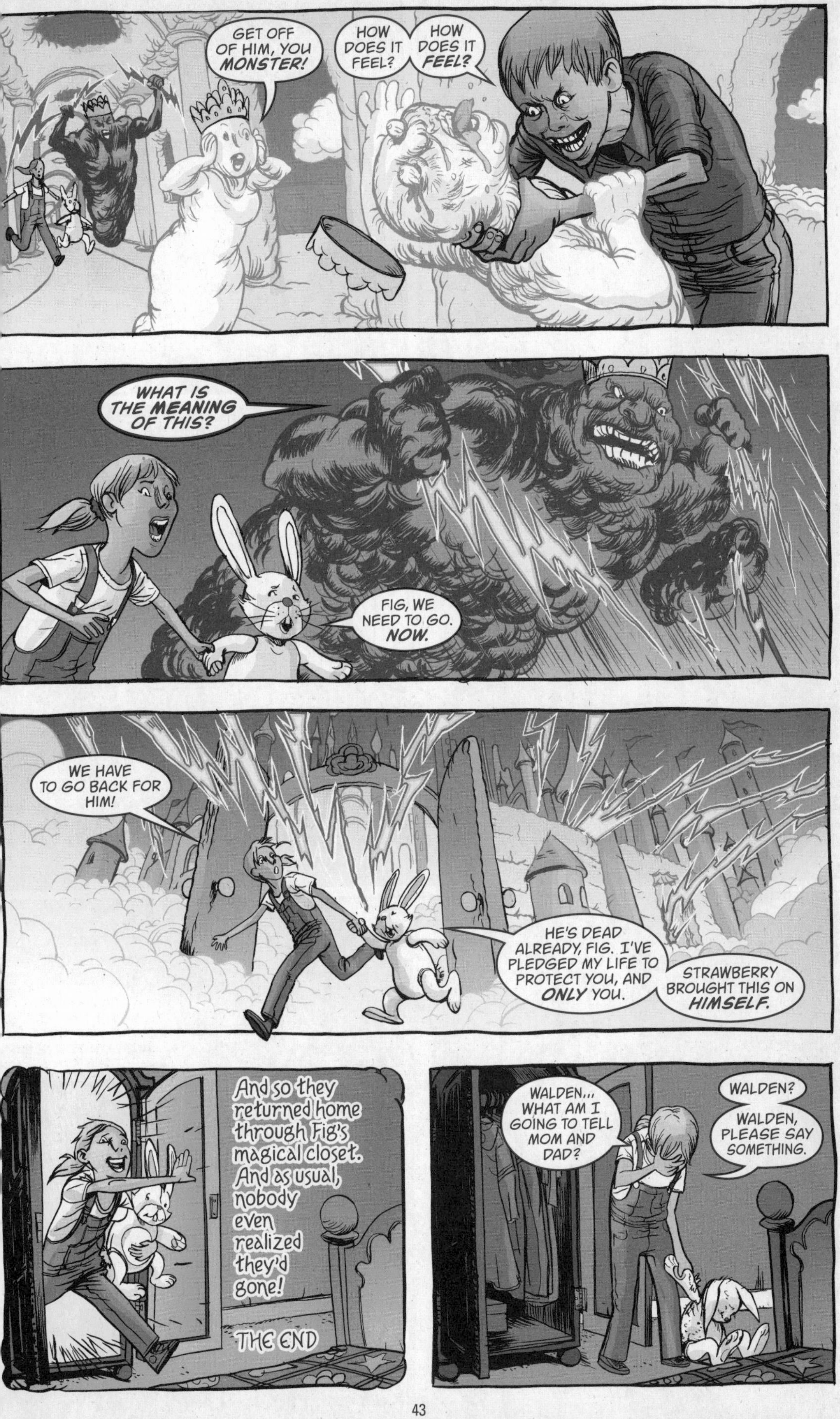
GET OFF OF HIM, YOU MONSTER!
HOW DOES IT FEEL?
HOW DOES IT FEEL?
WHAT IS THE MEANING OF THIS?
FIG, WE NEED TO GO. NOW.
WE HAVE TO GO BACK FOR HIM!
HE'S DEAD ALREADY, FIG. I'VE PLEDGED MY LIFE TO PROTECT YOU, AND ONLY YOU.
STRAWBERRY BROUGHT THIS ON HIMSELF.
And so they returned home through Fig's magical closet. And as usual, nobody even realized they'd gone!
THE END
WALDEN... WHAT AM I GOING TO TELL MOM AND DAD?
WALDEN?
WALDEN, PLEASE SAY SOMETHING.

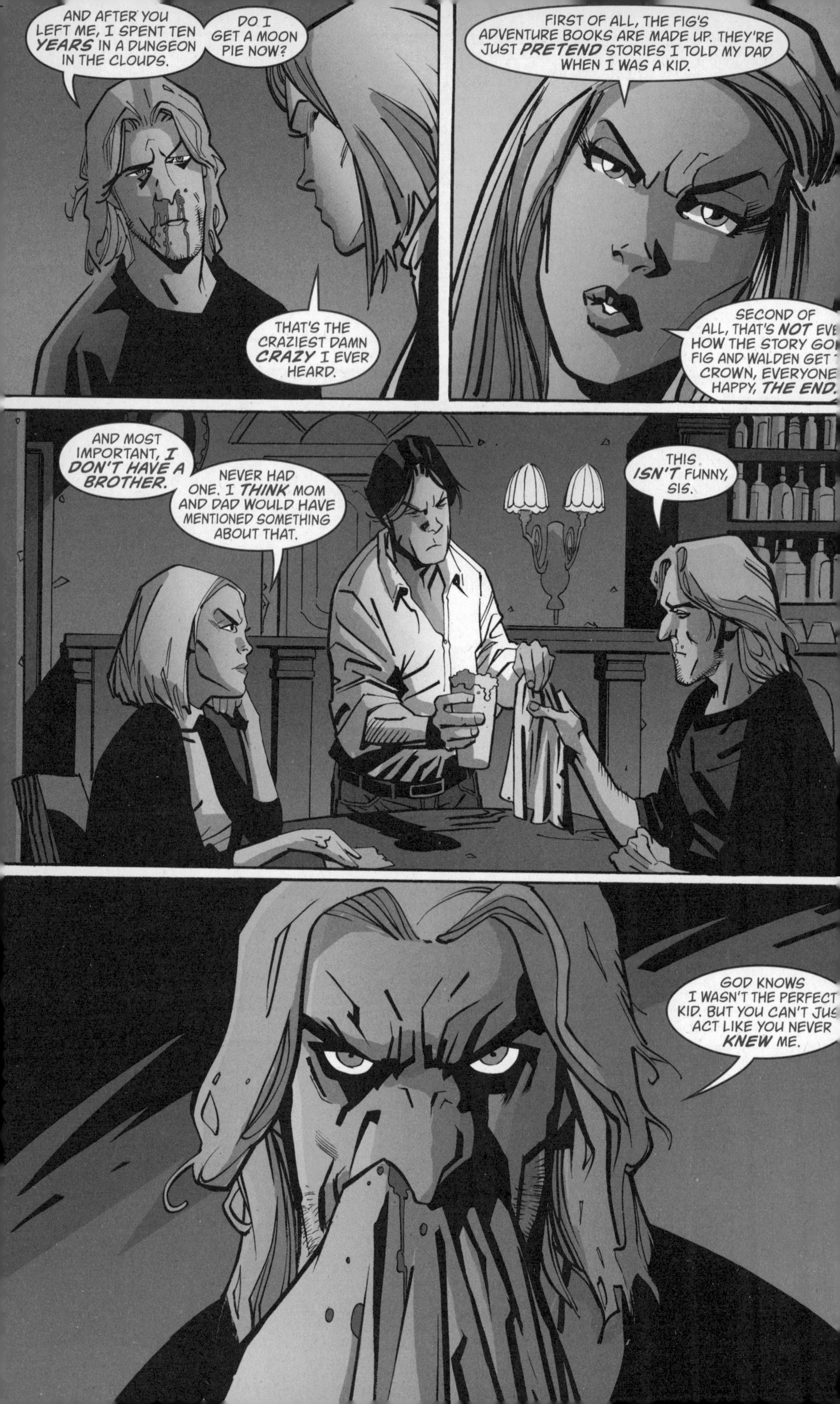
AND AFTER YOU LEFT ME, I SPENT TEN YEARS IN A DUNGEON IN THE CLOUDS.
DO I GET A MOON PIE NOW?
THAT'S THE CRAZIEST DAMN CRAZY I EVER HEARD.
FIRST OF ALL, THE FIG'S ADVENTURE BOOKS ARE MADE UP. THEY'RE JUST PRETEND STORIES I TOLD MY DAD WHEN I WAS A KID.
SECOND OF ALL, THAT'S NOT EVE HOW THE STORY GO FIG AND WALDEN GET CROWN, EVERYONE HAPPY, THE END.
AND MOST IMPORTANT, I DON'T HAVE A BROTHER.
NEVER HAD ONE. I THINK MOM AND DAD WOULD HAVE MENTIONED SOMETHING ABOUT THAT.
THIS ISN'T FUNNY, SIS.
GOD KNOWS I WASN'T THE PERFECT KID. BUT YOU CAN'T JUS ACT LIKE YOU NEVER KNEW ME.

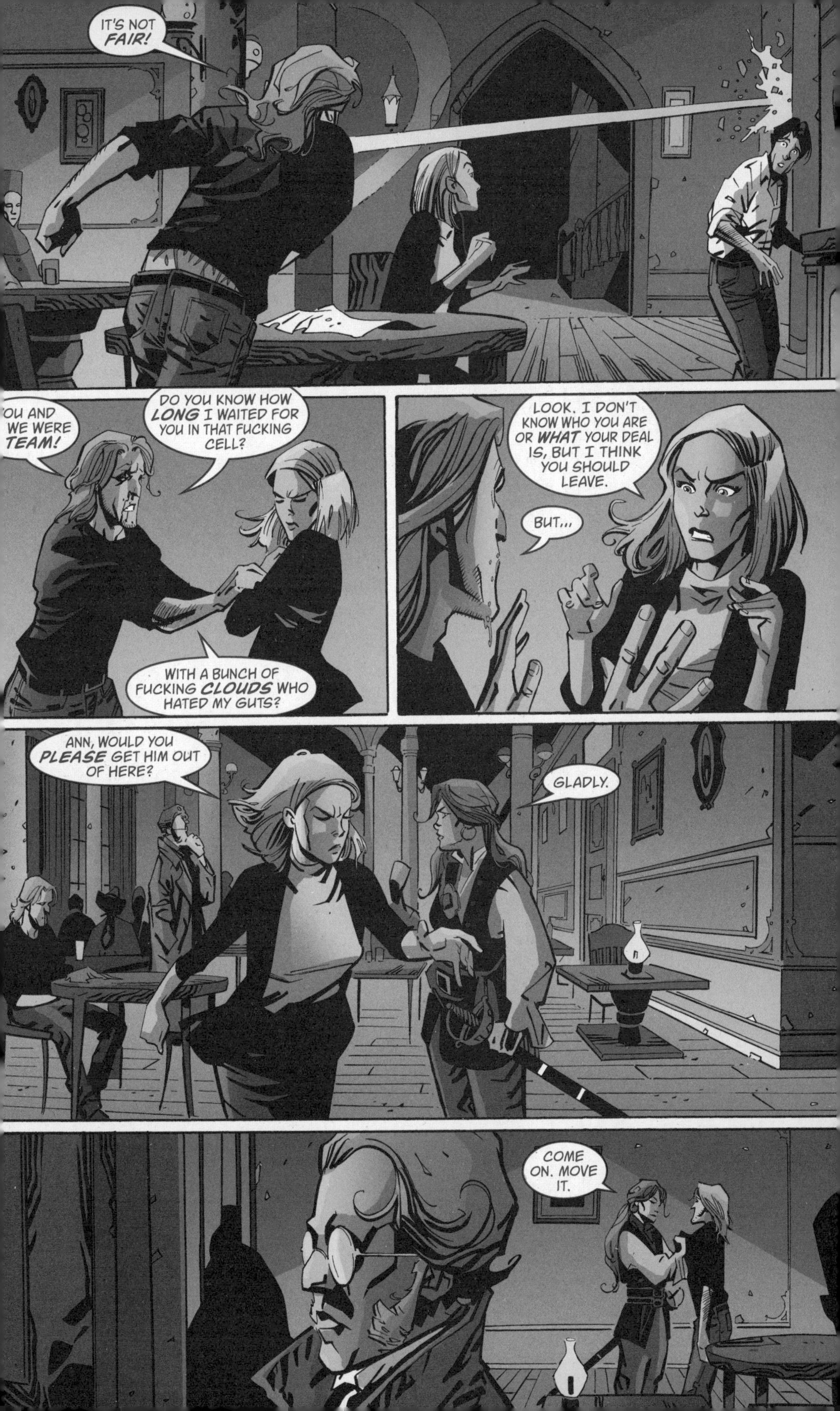
IT'S NOT FAIR!
OU AND WE WERE TEAM!
DO YOU KNOW HOW LONG I WAITED FOR YOU IN THAT FUCKING CELL?
WITH A BUNCH OF FUCKING CLOUDS WHO HATED MY GUTS?
LOOK. I DON'T KNOW WHO YOU ARE OR WHAT YOUR DEAL IS, BUT I THINK YOU SHOULD LEAVE.
BUT...
ANN, WOULD YOU PLEASE GET HIM OUT OF HERE?
GLADLY.
COME ON. MOVE IT.

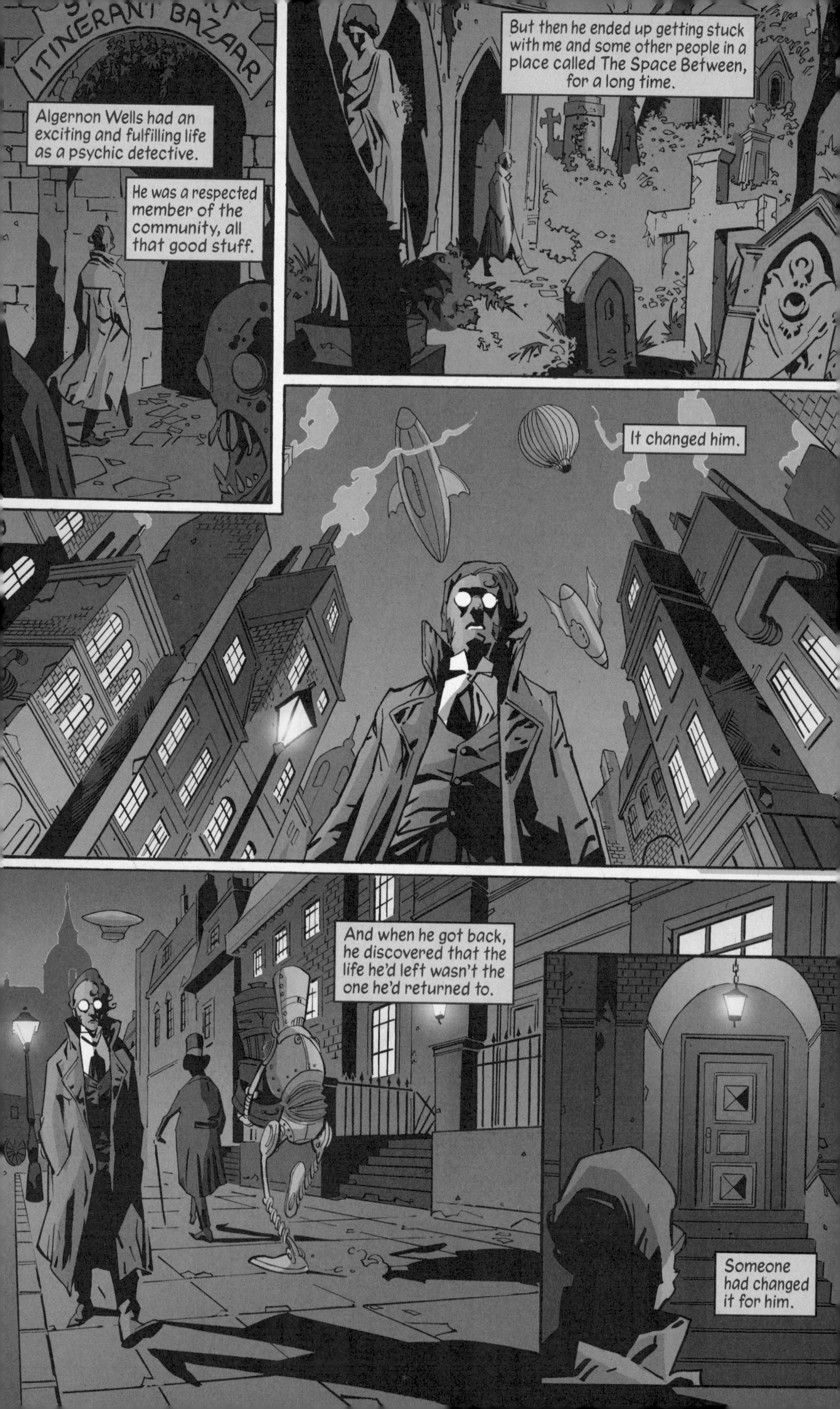
ITINERANT BAZAAR
Algernon Wells had an exciting and fulfilling life as a psychic detective.
He was a respected member of the community, all that good stuff.
But then he ended up getting stuck with me and some other people in a place called The Space Between, for a long time.
It changed him.
And when he got back, he discovered that the life he'd left wasn't the one he'd returned to.
Someone had changed it for him.

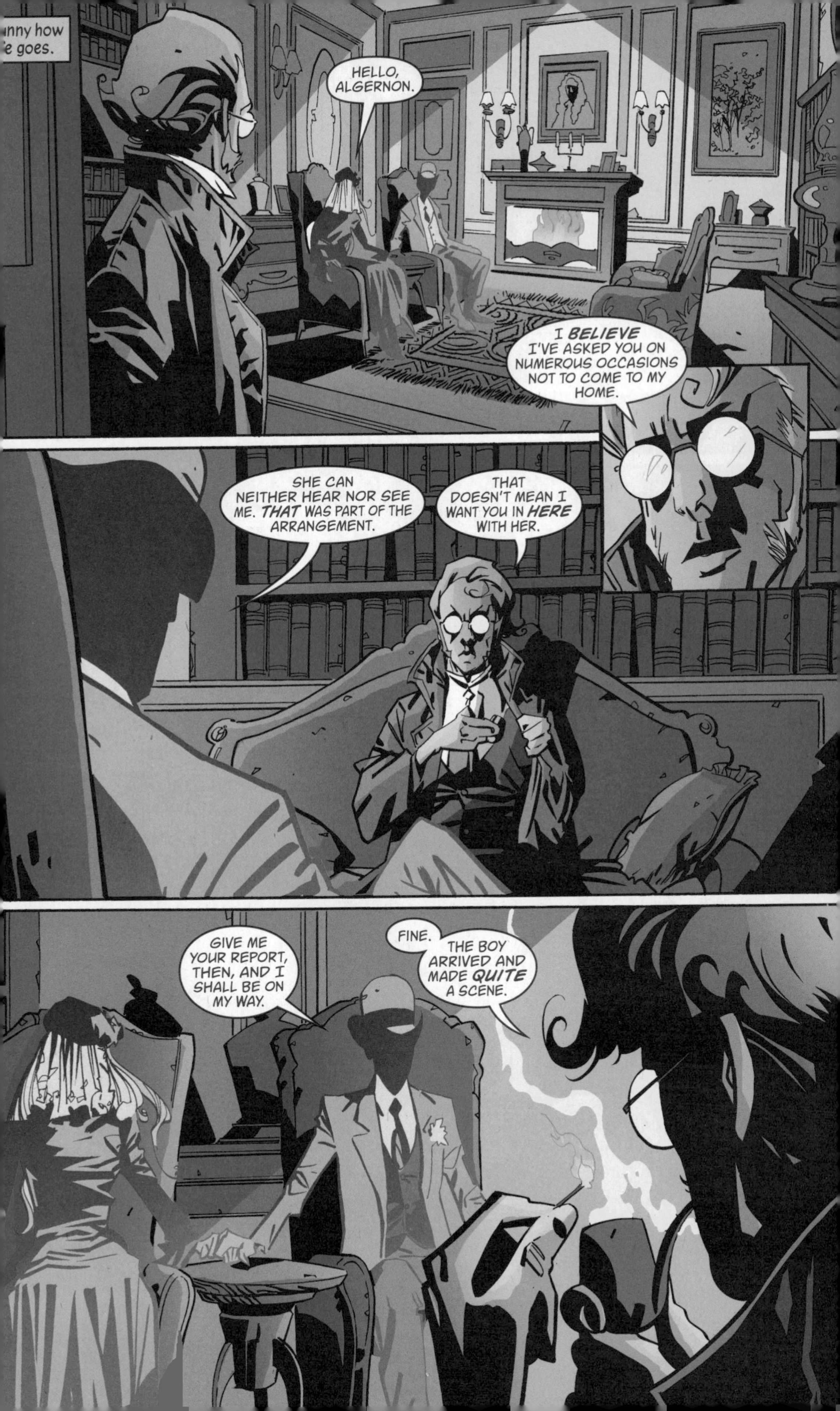
...nny how
...e goes.
HELLO, ALGERNON.
I *BELIEVE* I'VE ASKED YOU ON NUMEROUS OCCASIONS NOT TO COME TO MY HOME.
SHE CAN NEITHER HEAR NOR SEE ME. *THAT* WAS PART OF THE ARRANGEMENT.
THAT DOESN'T MEAN I WANT YOU IN *HERE* WITH HER.
GIVE ME YOUR REPORT, THEN, AND I SHALL BE ON MY WAY.
FINE.
THE BOY ARRIVED AND MADE *QUITE* A SCENE.

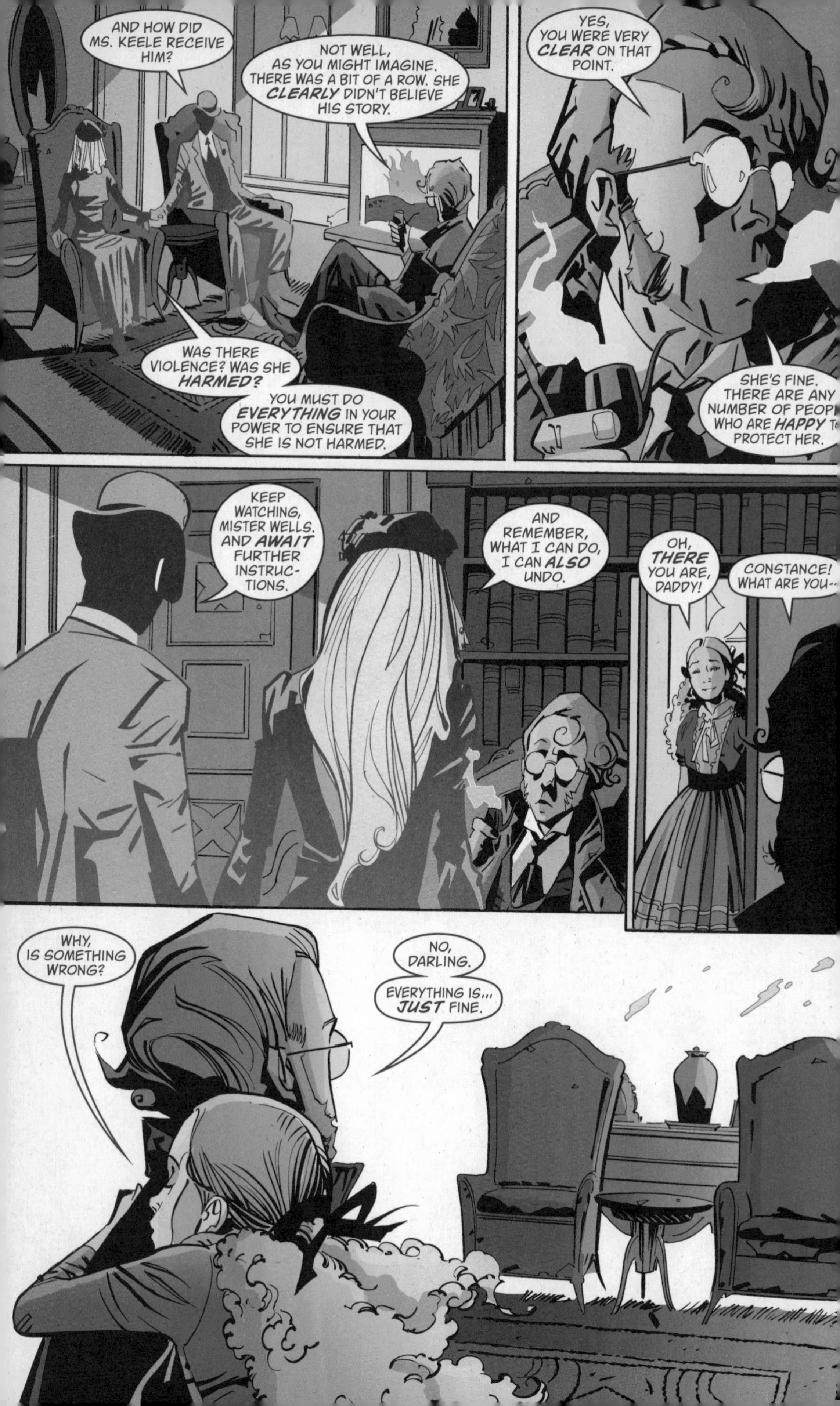

AND HOW DID MS. KEELE RECEIVE HIM?
NOT WELL, AS YOU MIGHT IMAGINE. THERE WAS A BIT OF A ROW. SHE *CLEARLY* DIDN'T BELIEVE HIS STORY.
WAS THERE VIOLENCE? WAS SHE *HARMED?*
YOU MUST DO *EVERYTHING* IN YOUR POWER TO ENSURE THAT SHE IS NOT HARMED.
YES, YOU WERE VERY *CLEAR* ON THAT POINT.
SHE'S FINE. THERE ARE ANY NUMBER OF PEOP WHO ARE *HAPPY* T PROTECT HER.
KEEP WATCHING, MISTER WELLS. AND *AWAIT* FURTHER INSTRUC- TIONS.
AND REMEMBER, WHAT I CAN DO, I CAN *ALSO* UNDO.
OH, *THERE* YOU ARE, DADDY!
CONSTANCE! WHAT ARE YOU--
WHY, IS SOMETHING WRONG?
NO, DARLING.
EVERYTHING IS... *JUST* FINE.

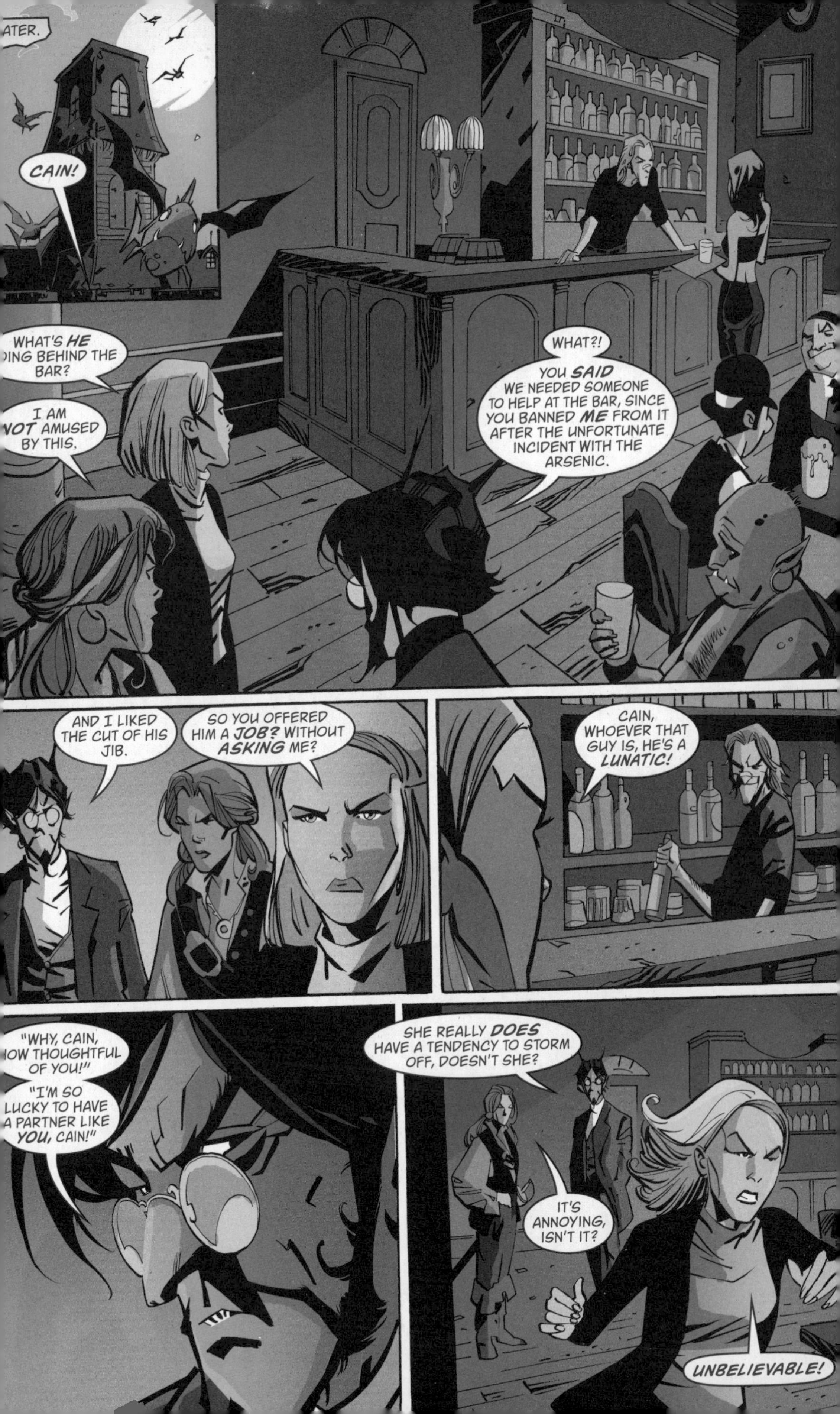

ATER.
CAIN!
WHAT'S HE
DING BEHIND THE BAR?
I AM NOT AMUSED BY THIS.
WHAT?!
YOU SAID WE NEEDED SOMEONE TO HELP AT THE BAR, SINCE YOU BANNED ME FROM IT AFTER THE UNFORTUNATE INCIDENT WITH THE ARSENIC.
AND I LIKED THE CUT OF HIS JIB.
SO YOU OFFERED HIM A JOB? WITHOUT ASKING ME?
CAIN, WHOEVER THAT GUY IS, HE'S A LUNATIC!
"WHY, CAIN, HOW THOUGHTFUL OF YOU!"
"I'M SO LUCKY TO HAVE A PARTNER LIKE YOU, CAIN!"
SHE REALLY DOES HAVE A TENDENCY TO STORM OFF, DOESN'T SHE?
IT'S ANNOYING, ISN'T IT?
UNBELIEVABLE!

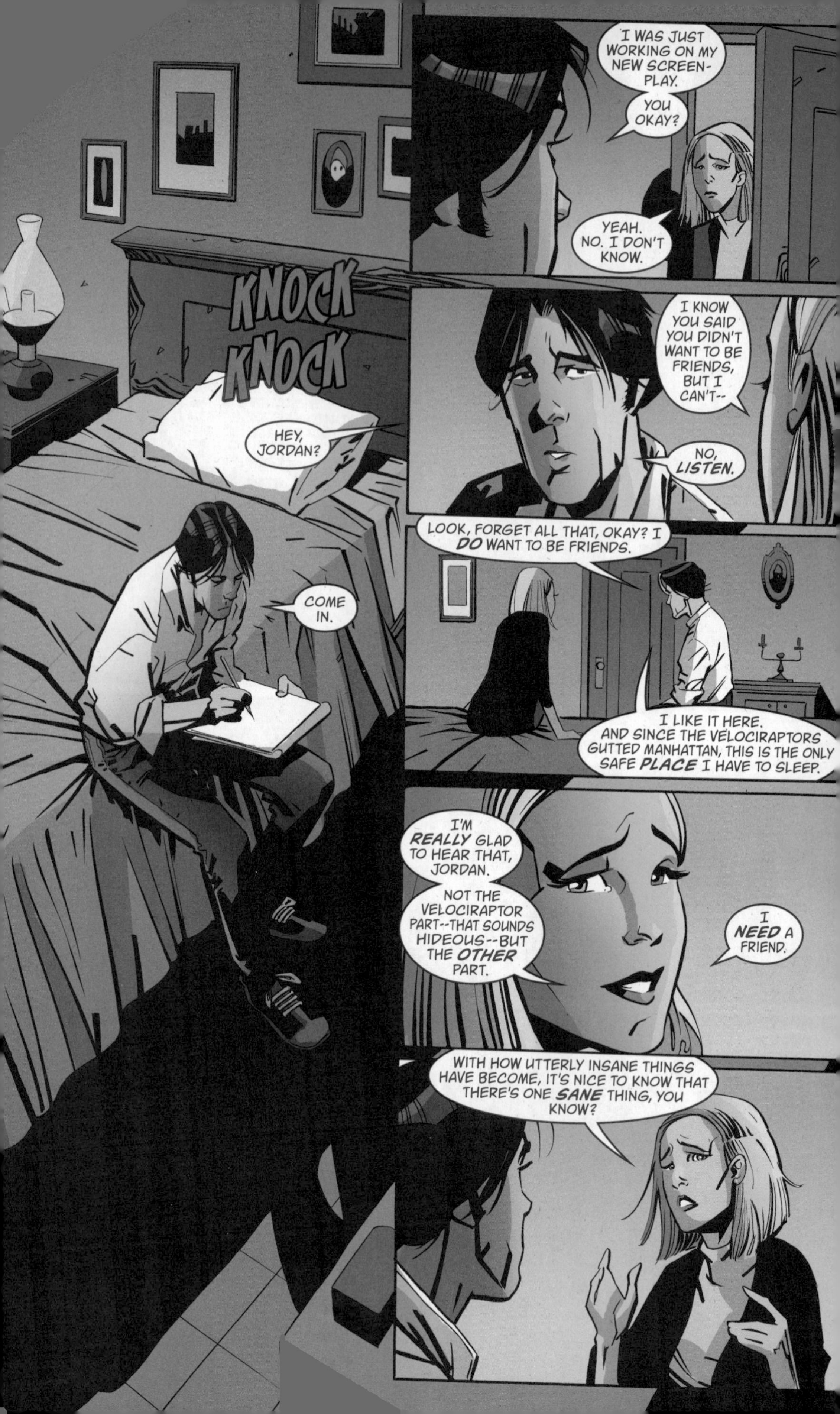
KNOCK KNOCK
HEY, JORDAN?
COME IN.
I WAS JUST WORKING ON MY NEW SCREEN-PLAY.
YOU OKAY?
YEAH. NO. I DON'T KNOW.
I KNOW YOU SAID YOU DIDN'T WANT TO BE FRIENDS, BUT I CAN'T--
NO, LISTEN.
LOOK, FORGET ALL THAT, OKAY? I DO WANT TO BE FRIENDS.
I LIKE IT HERE. AND SINCE THE VELOCIRAPTORS GUTTED MANHATTAN, THIS IS THE ONLY SAFE PLACE I HAVE TO SLEEP.
I'M REALLY GLAD TO HEAR THAT, JORDAN.
NOT THE VELOCIRAPTOR PART--THAT SOUNDS HIDEOUS--BUT THE OTHER PART.
I NEED A FRIEND.
WITH HOW UTTERLY INSANE THINGS HAVE BECOME, IT'S NICE TO KNOW THAT THERE'S ONE SANE THING, YOU KNOW?

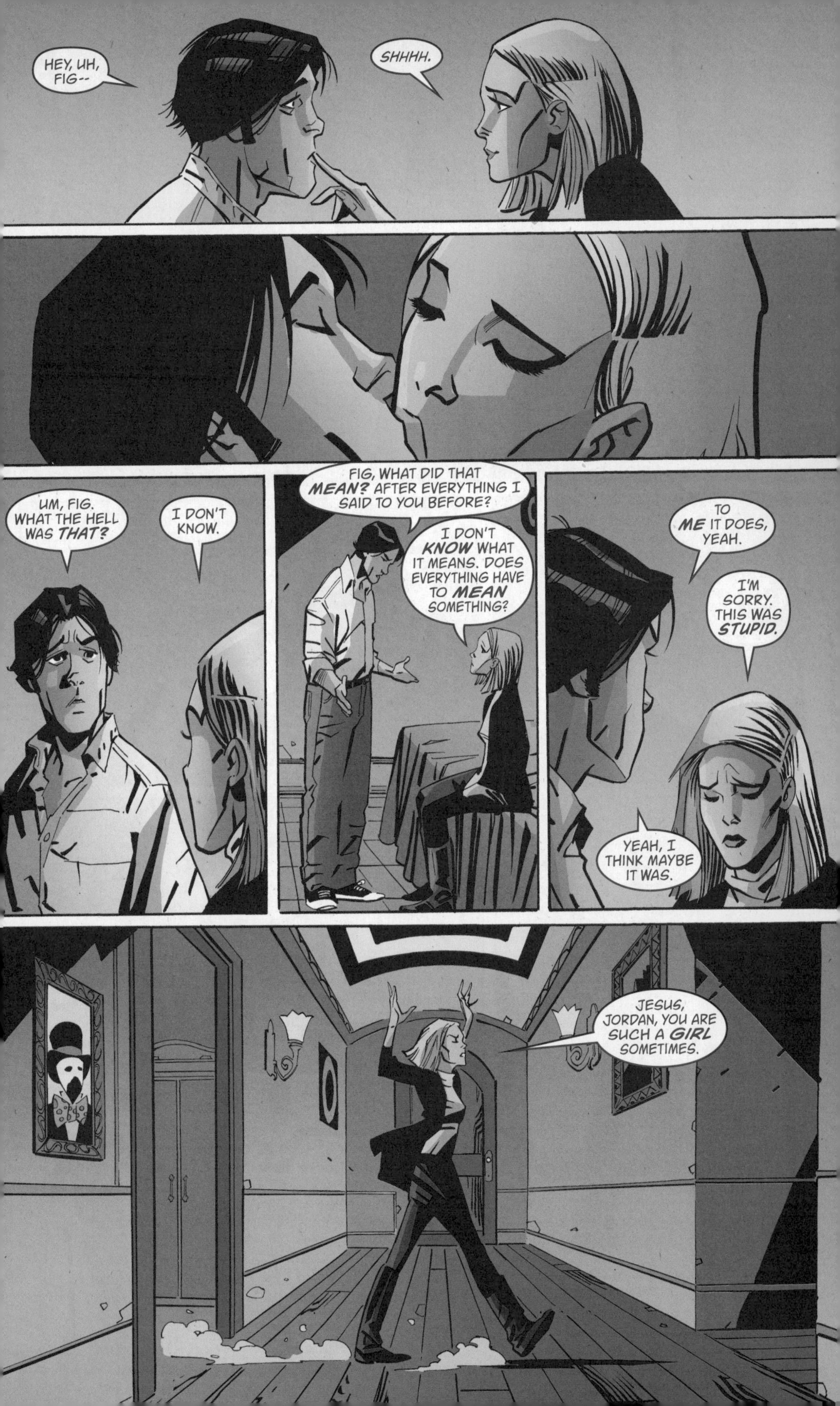
HEY, UH, FIG--
SHHHH.
UM, FIG. WHAT THE HELL WAS THAT?
I DON'T KNOW.
FIG, WHAT DID THAT MEAN? AFTER EVERYTHING I SAID TO YOU BEFORE?
I DON'T KNOW WHAT IT MEANS. DOES EVERYTHING HAVE TO MEAN SOMETHING?
TO ME IT DOES, YEAH.
I'M SORRY. THIS WAS STUPID.
YEAH, I THINK MAYBE IT WAS.
JESUS, JORDAN, YOU ARE SUCH A GIRL SOMETIMES.

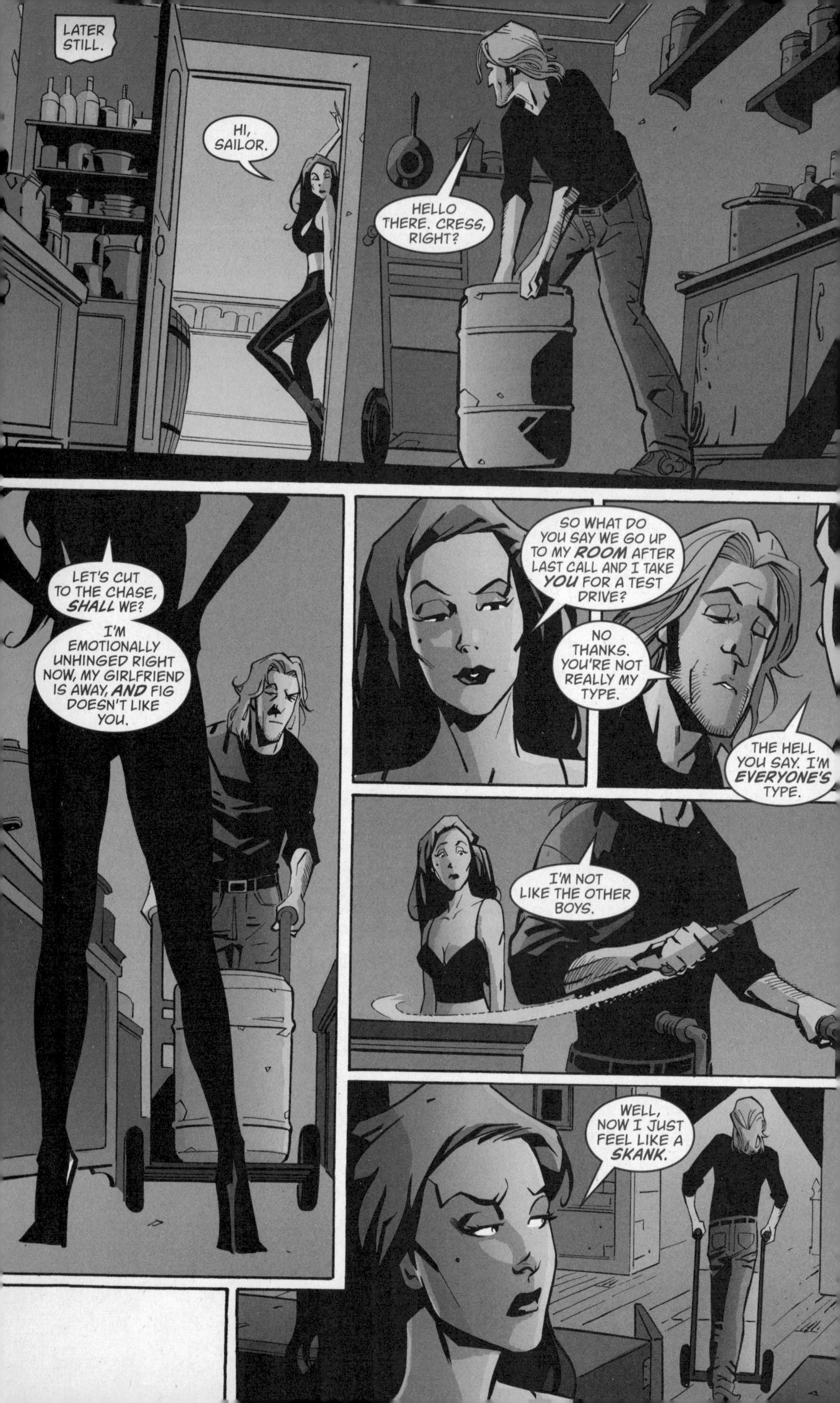

LATER STILL.
HI, SAILOR.
HELLO THERE. CRESS, RIGHT?
LET'S CUT TO THE CHASE, SHALL WE?
I'M EMOTIONALLY UNHINGED RIGHT NOW, MY GIRLFRIEND IS AWAY, AND FIG DOESN'T LIKE YOU.
SO WHAT DO YOU SAY WE GO UP TO MY ROOM AFTER LAST CALL AND I TAKE YOU FOR A TEST DRIVE?
NO THANKS. YOU'RE NOT REALLY MY TYPE.
THE HELL YOU SAY. I'M EVERYONE'S TYPE.
I'M NOT LIKE THE OTHER BOYS.
WELL, NOW I JUST FEEL LIKE A SKANK.

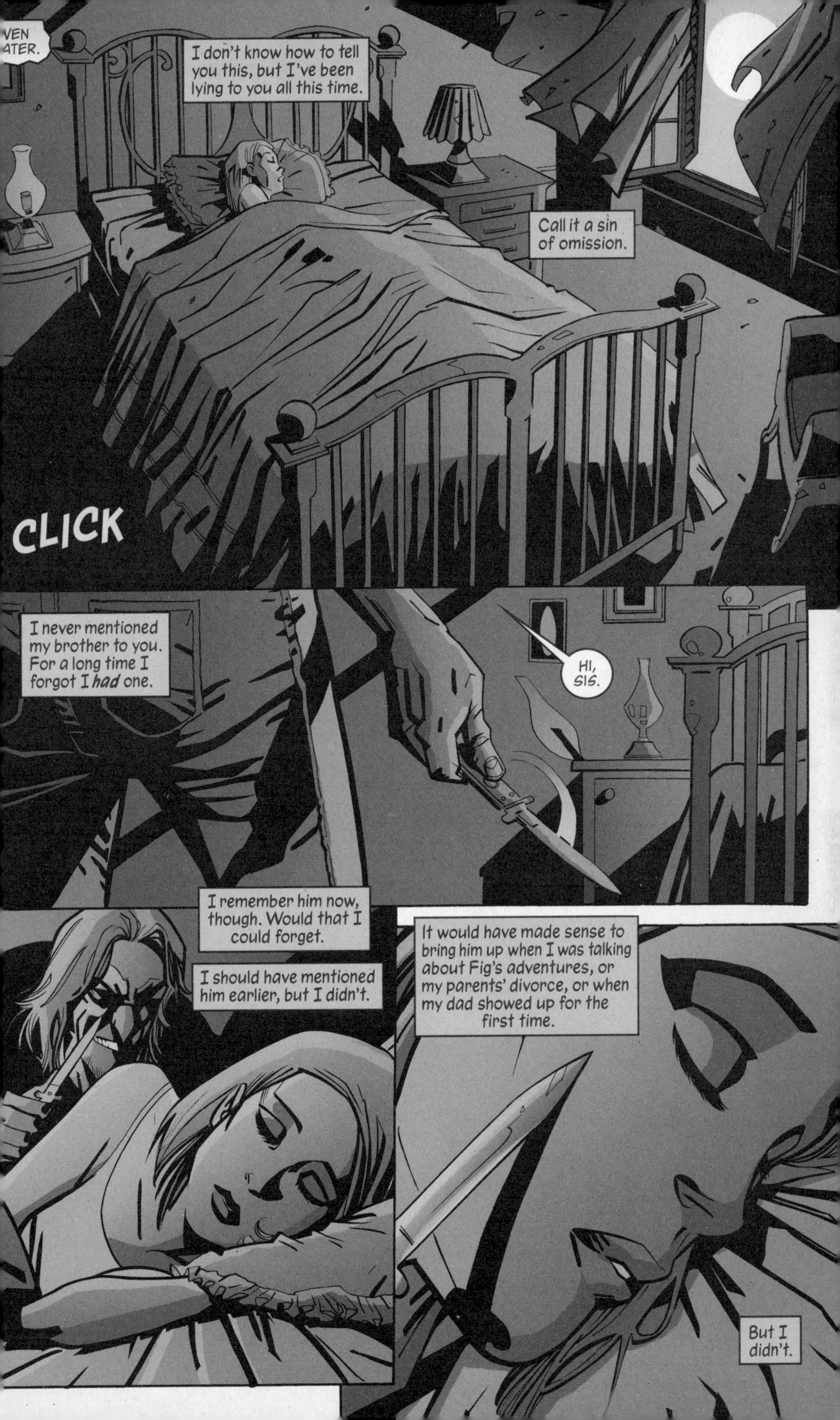
VEN
ATER.
I don't know how to tell you this, but I've been lying to you all this time.
Call it a sin of omission.
CLICK
I never mentioned my brother to you. For a long time I forgot I *had* one.
HI, SIS.
I remember him now, though. Would that I could forget.
I should have mentioned him earlier, but I didn't.
It would have made sense to bring him up when I was talking about Fig's adventures, or my parents' divorce, or when my dad showed up for the first time.
But I didn't.

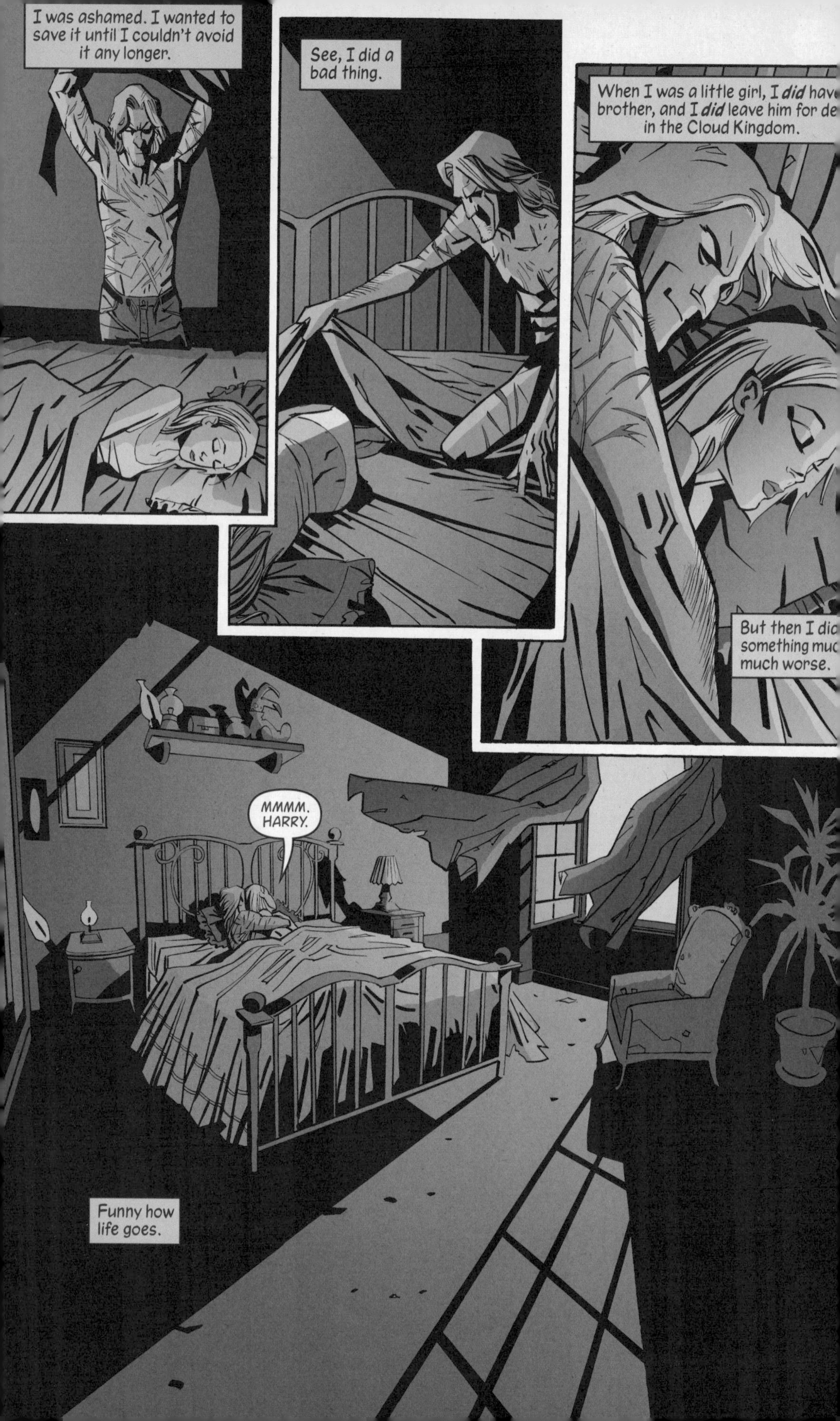
I was ashamed. I wanted to save it until I couldn't avoid it any longer.
See, I did a bad thing.
When I was a little girl, I *did* have a brother, and I *did* leave him for de in the Cloud Kingdom.
But then I did something muc much worse.
MMMM. HARRY.
Funny how life goes.

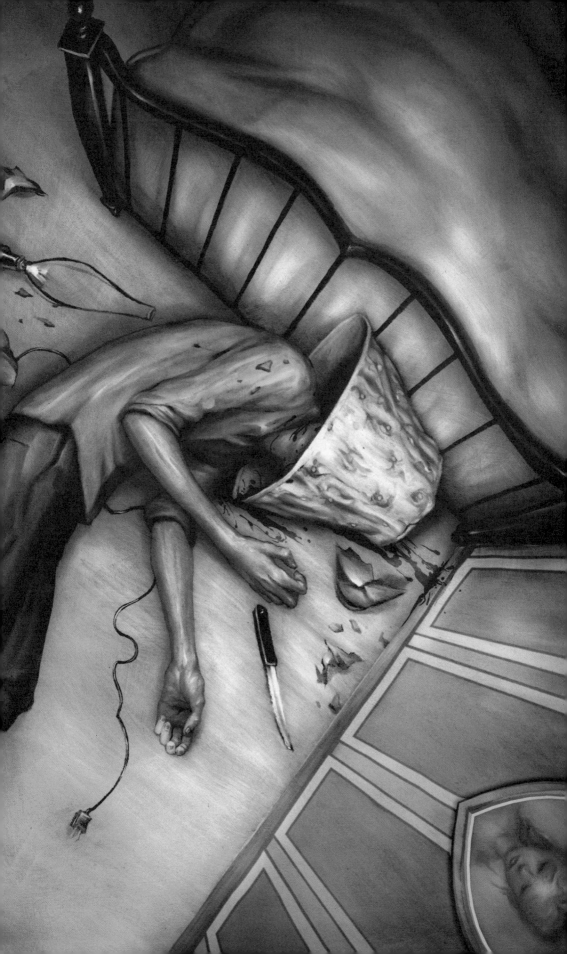

"GRIEF MAKES LIARS OF US ALL."

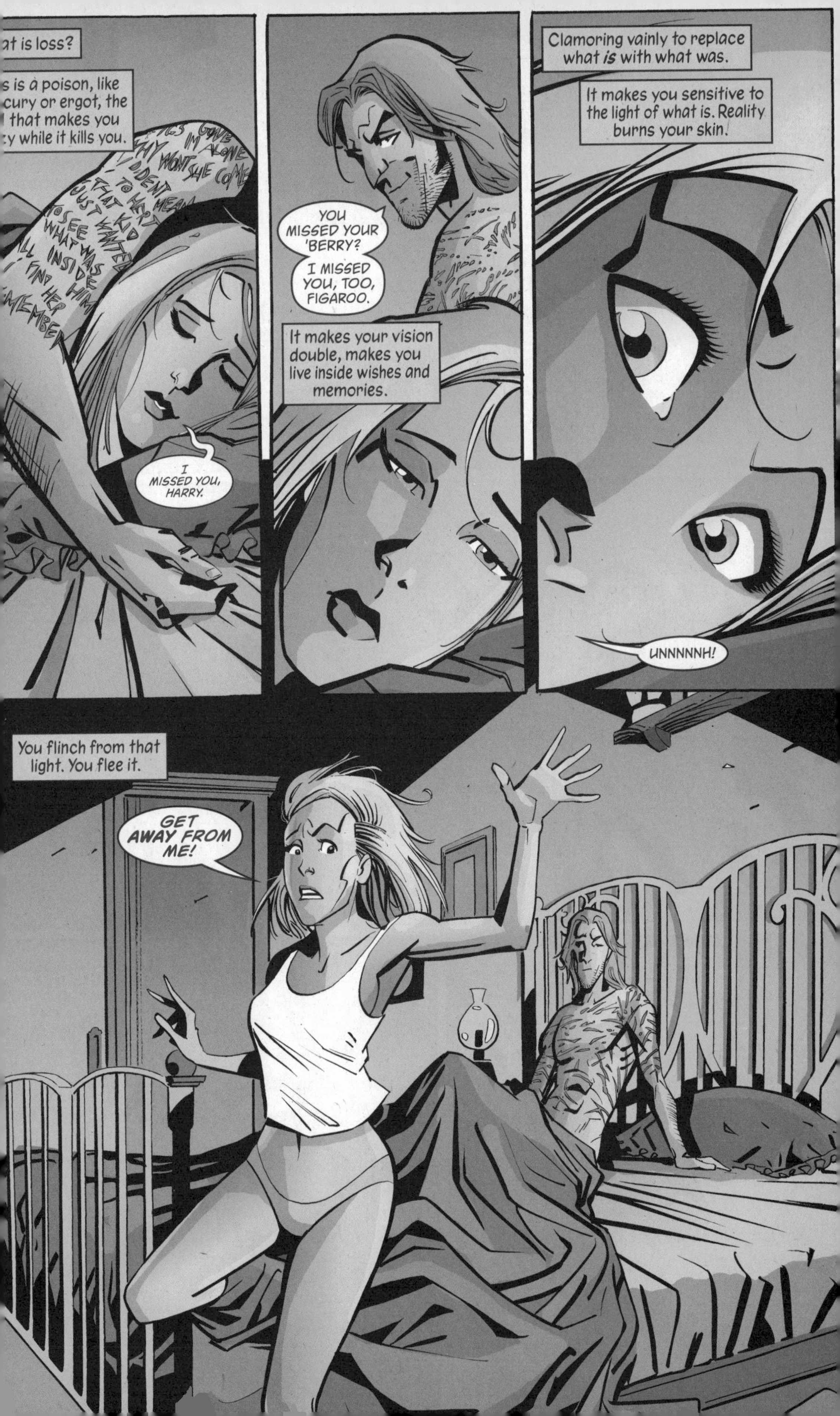
at is loss?
s is a poison, like
cury or ergot, the
that makes you
y while it kills you.
I MISSED YOU, HARRY.
YOU MISSED YOUR 'BERRY?
I MISSED YOU, TOO, FIGAROO.
It makes your vision double, makes you live inside wishes and memories.
Clamoring vainly to replace what *is* with what was.
It makes you sensitive to the light of what is. Reality burns your skin.
UNNNNNH!
You flinch from that light. You flee it.
GET AWAY FROM ME!

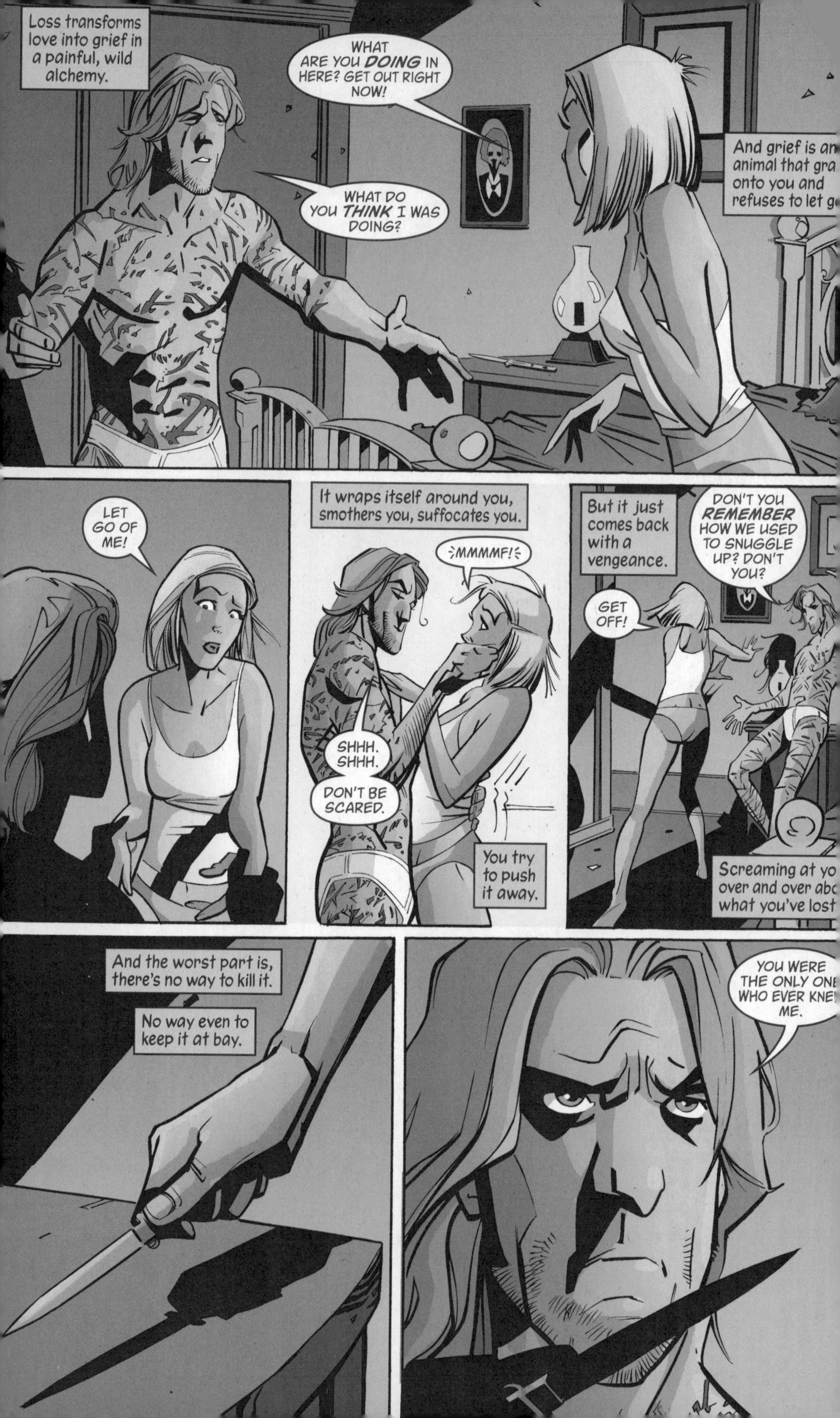
Loss transforms love into grief in a painful, wild alchemy.
WHAT ARE YOU DOING IN HERE? GET OUT RIGHT NOW!
WHAT DO YOU THINK I WAS DOING?
And grief is an animal that gra onto you and refuses to let g
LET GO OF ME!
It wraps itself around you, smothers you, suffocates you.
MMMMF!
SHHH. SHHH.
DON'T BE SCARED.
You try to push it away.
But it just comes back with a vengeance.
DON'T YOU REMEMBER HOW WE USED TO SNUGGLE UP? DON'T YOU?
GET OFF!
Screaming at yo over and over abo what you've lost
And the worst part is, there's no way to kill it.
No way even to keep it at bay.
YOU WERE THE ONLY ONE WHO EVER KNE ME.

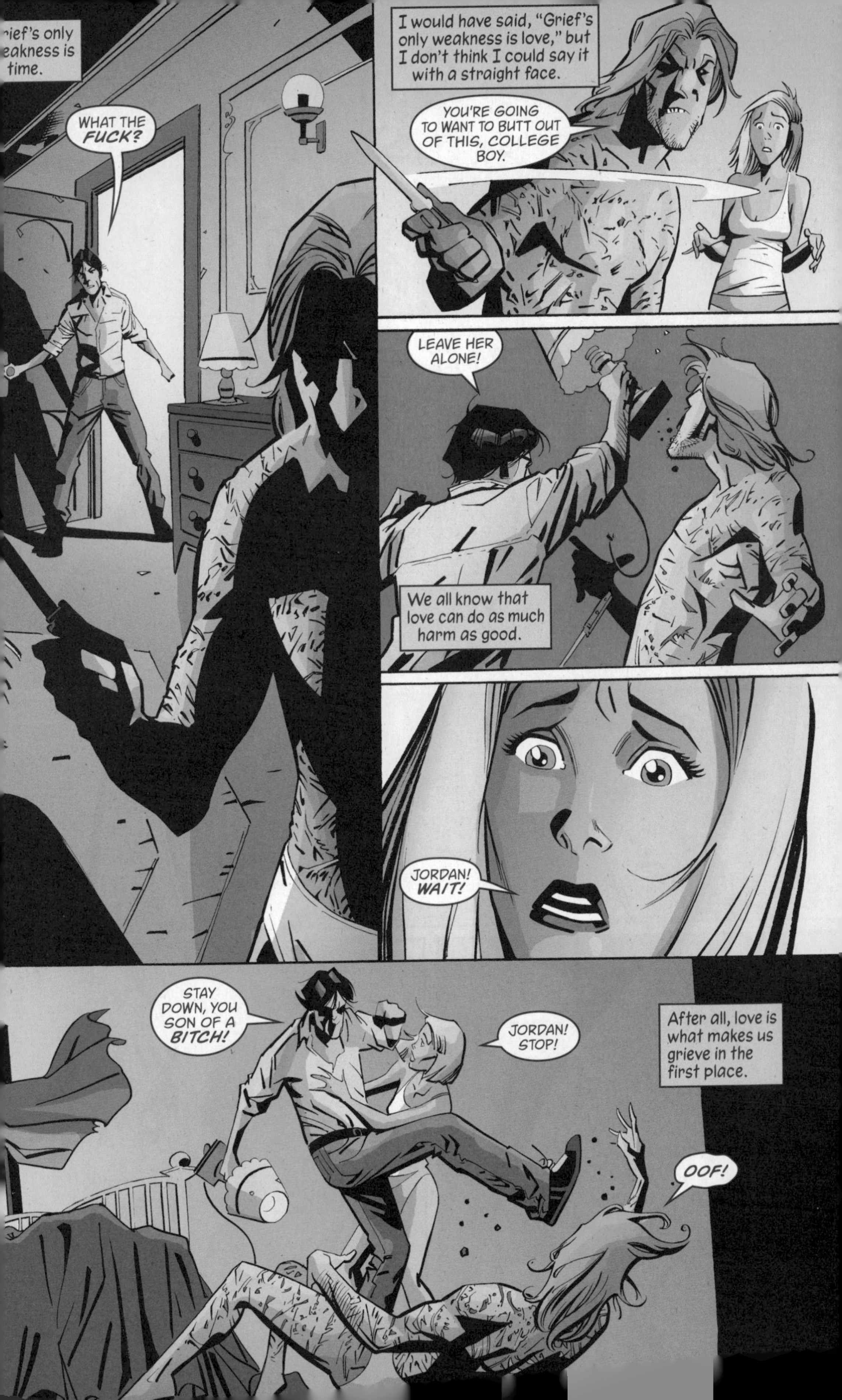

rief's only
eakness is
time.
WHAT THE FUCK?
I would have said, "Grief's only weakness is love," but I don't think I could say it with a straight face.
YOU'RE GOING TO WANT TO BUTT OUT OF THIS, COLLEGE BOY.
LEAVE HER ALONE!
We all know that love can do as much harm as good.
JORDAN! WAIT!
STAY DOWN, YOU SON OF A BITCH!
JORDAN! STOP!
After all, love is what makes us grieve in the first place.
OOF!

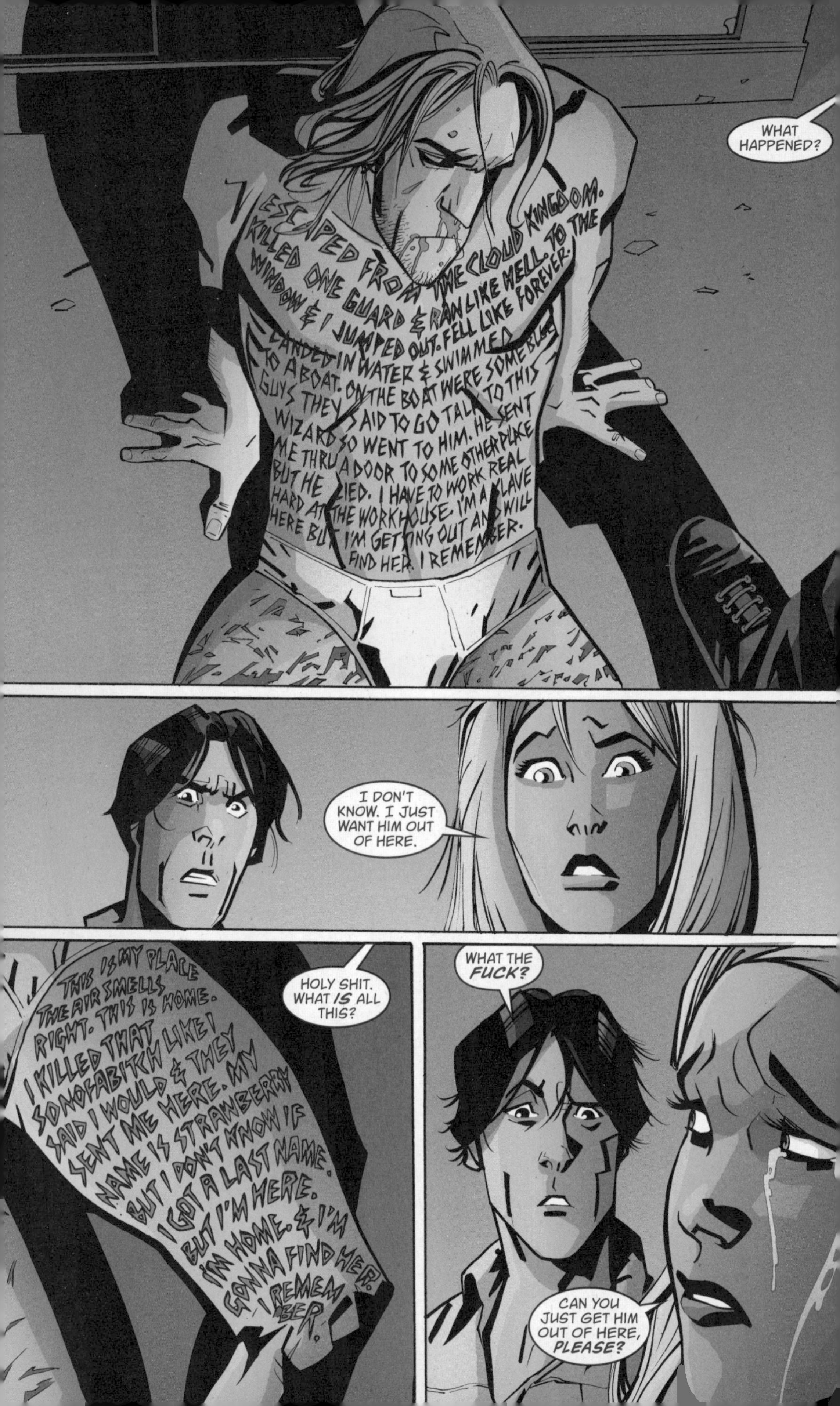
WHAT HAPPENED?
ESCAPED FROM THE CLOUD KINGDOM.
KILLED ONE GUARD & RAN LIKE HELL. TO THE
WINDOW & I JUMPED OUT. FELL LIKE FOREVER.
LANDED IN WATER & SWIMMED
TO A BOAT. ON THE BOAT WERE SOME BL
GUYS THEY AID TO GO TAL TO THIS
WIZARD SO WENT TO HIM. HE SENT
ME THRU A DOOR TO SOME OTHER PLACE
BUT HE IED. I HAVE TO WORK REAL
HARD AT THE WORKHOUSE. I'M A LAVE
HERE BU I'M GET ING OUT AN WILL
FIND HER. I REMEMBER.
I DON'T KNOW. I JUST WANT HIM OUT OF HERE.
THIS IS MY PLACE
THE AIR SMELLS
RIGHT. THIS IS HOME.
I KILLED THAT
SONOFABITCH LIKE I
SAID I WOULD & THEY
SENT ME HERE. MY
NAME IS STRAWBERRY
BUT I DON'T KNOW IF
I GOT A LAST NAME.
BUT I'M HERE.
I'M HOME. & I'M
GONNA FIND HER.
I REMEMBER.
HOLY SHIT. WHAT *IS* ALL THIS?
WHAT THE *FUCK?*
CAN YOU JUST GET HIM OUT OF HERE, *PLEASE?*

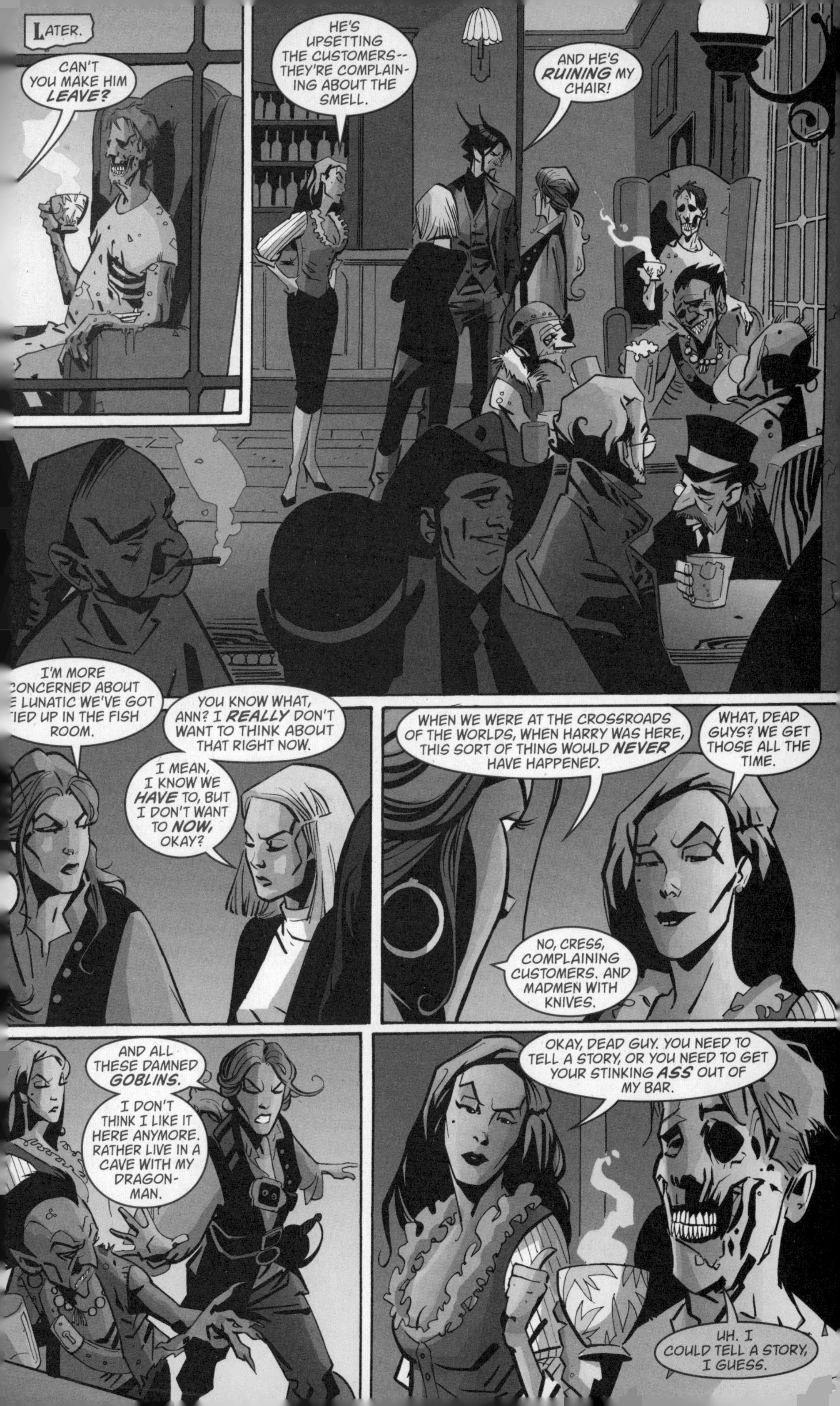
LATER.
CAN'T YOU MAKE HIM LEAVE?
HE'S UPSETTING THE CUSTOMERS-- THEY'RE COMPLAINING ABOUT THE SMELL.
AND HE'S RUINING MY CHAIR!
I'M MORE CONCERNED ABOUT E LUNATIC WE'VE GOT TIED UP IN THE FISH ROOM.
YOU KNOW WHAT, ANN? I REALLY DON'T WANT TO THINK ABOUT THAT RIGHT NOW.
I MEAN, I KNOW WE HAVE TO, BUT I DON'T WANT TO NOW, OKAY?
WHEN WE WERE AT THE CROSSROADS OF THE WORLDS, WHEN HARRY WAS HERE, THIS SORT OF THING WOULD NEVER HAVE HAPPENED.
WHAT, DEAD GUYS? WE GET THOSE ALL THE TIME.
NO, CRESS, COMPLAINING CUSTOMERS. AND MADMEN WITH KNIVES.
AND ALL THESE DAMNED GOBLINS.
I DON'T THINK I LIKE IT HERE ANYMORE. RATHER LIVE IN A CAVE WITH MY DRAGON-MAN.
OKAY, DEAD GUY. YOU NEED TO TELL A STORY, OR YOU NEED TO GET YOUR STINKING ASS OUT OF MY BAR.
UH. I COULD TELL A STORY, I GUESS.

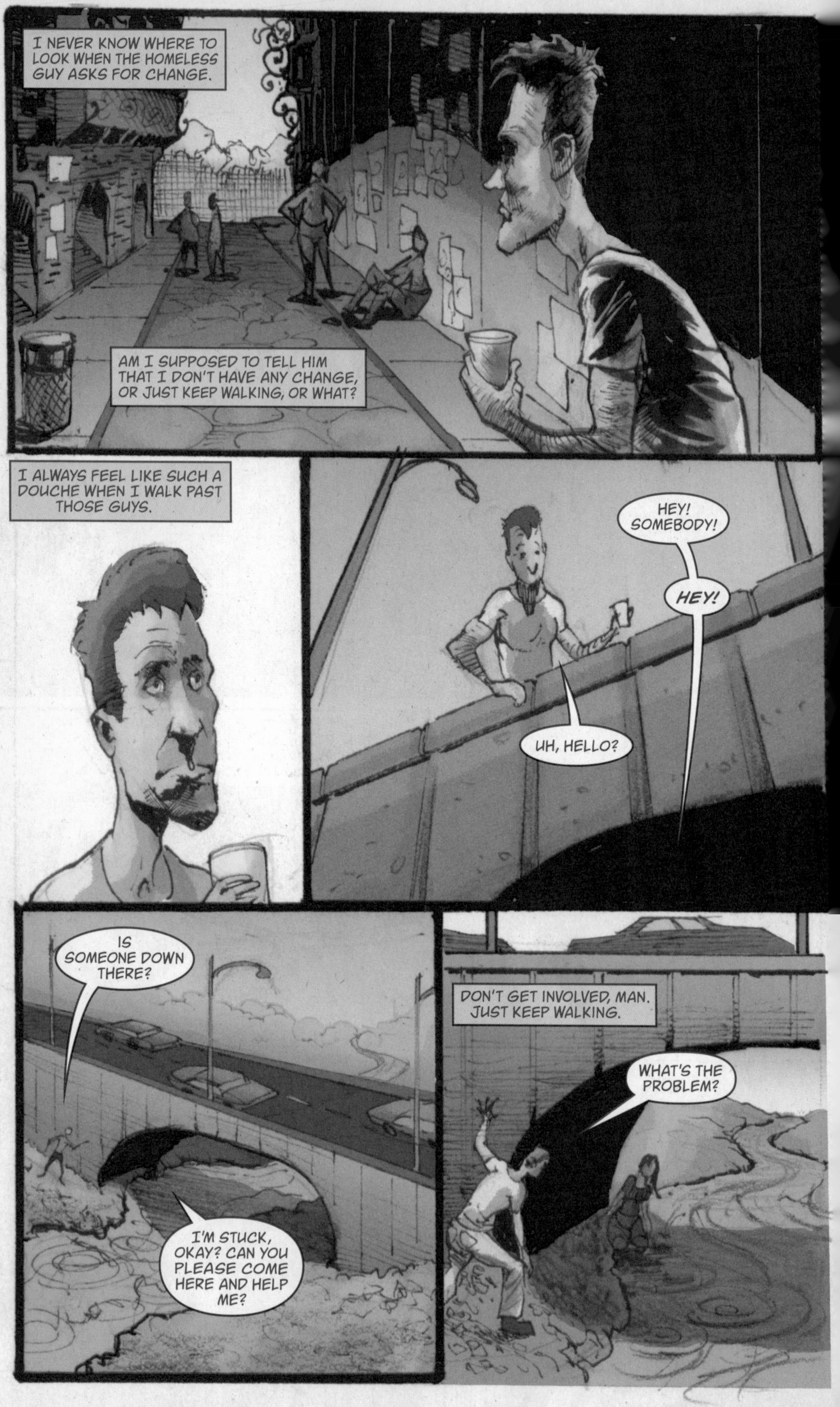
I NEVER KNOW WHERE TO LOOK WHEN THE HOMELESS GUY ASKS FOR CHANGE.
AM I SUPPOSED TO TELL HIM THAT I DON'T HAVE ANY CHANGE, OR JUST KEEP WALKING, OR WHAT?
I ALWAYS FEEL LIKE SUCH A DOUCHE WHEN I WALK PAST THOSE GUYS.
HEY! SOMEBODY!
HEY!
UH, HELLO?
IS SOMEONE DOWN THERE?
I'M STUCK, OKAY? CAN YOU PLEASE COME HERE AND HELP ME?
DON'T GET INVOLVED, MAN. JUST KEEP WALKING.
WHAT'S THE PROBLEM?

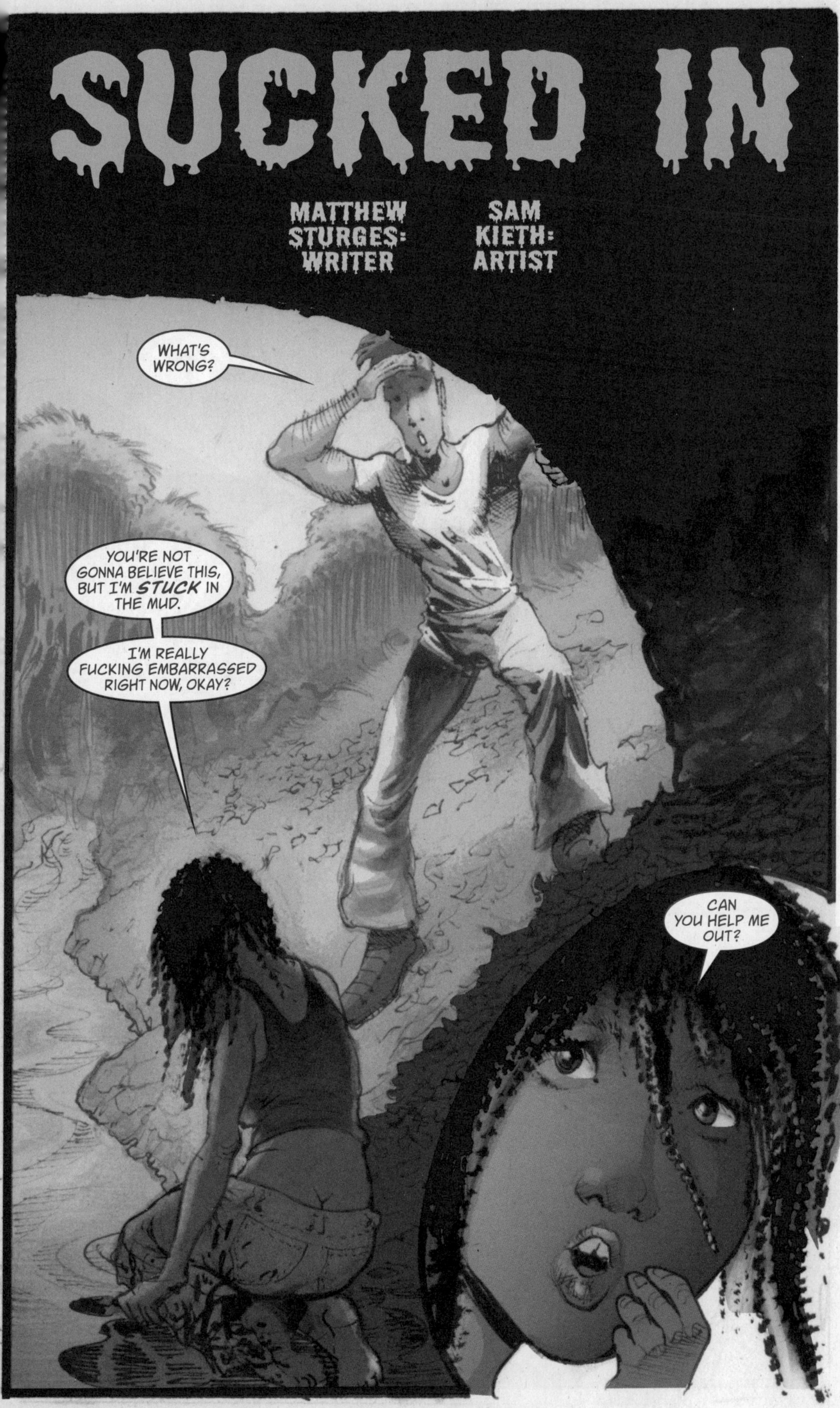
SUCKED IN
MATTHEW STURGES: WRITER
SAM KIETH: ARTIST
WHAT'S WRONG?
YOU'RE NOT GONNA BELIEVE THIS, BUT I'M STUCK IN THE MUD.
I'M REALLY FUCKING EMBARRASSED RIGHT NOW, OKAY?
CAN YOU HELP ME OUT?

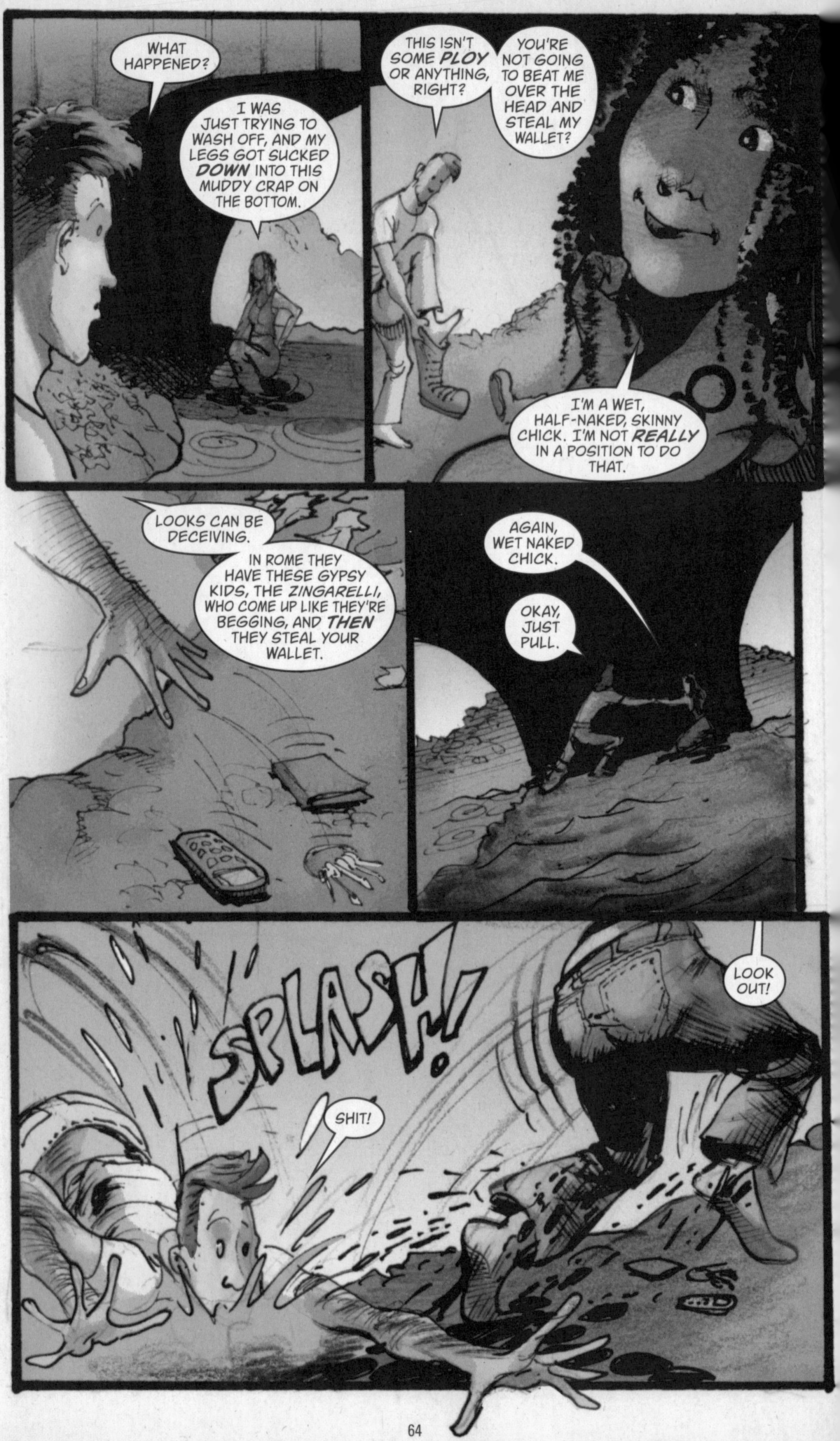
WHAT HAPPENED?
I WAS JUST TRYING TO WASH OFF, AND MY LEGS GOT SUCKED DOWN INTO THIS MUDDY CRAP ON THE BOTTOM.
THIS ISN'T SOME PLOY OR ANYTHING, RIGHT?
YOU'RE NOT GOING TO BEAT ME OVER THE HEAD AND STEAL MY WALLET?
I'M A WET, HALF-NAKED, SKINNY CHICK. I'M NOT REALLY IN A POSITION TO DO THAT.
LOOKS CAN BE DECEIVING.
IN ROME THEY HAVE THESE GYPSY KIDS, THE ZINGARELLI, WHO COME UP LIKE THEY'RE BEGGING, AND THEN THEY STEAL YOUR WALLET.
AGAIN, WET NAKED CHICK.
OKAY, JUST PULL.
LOOK OUT!
SPLASH!
SHIT!

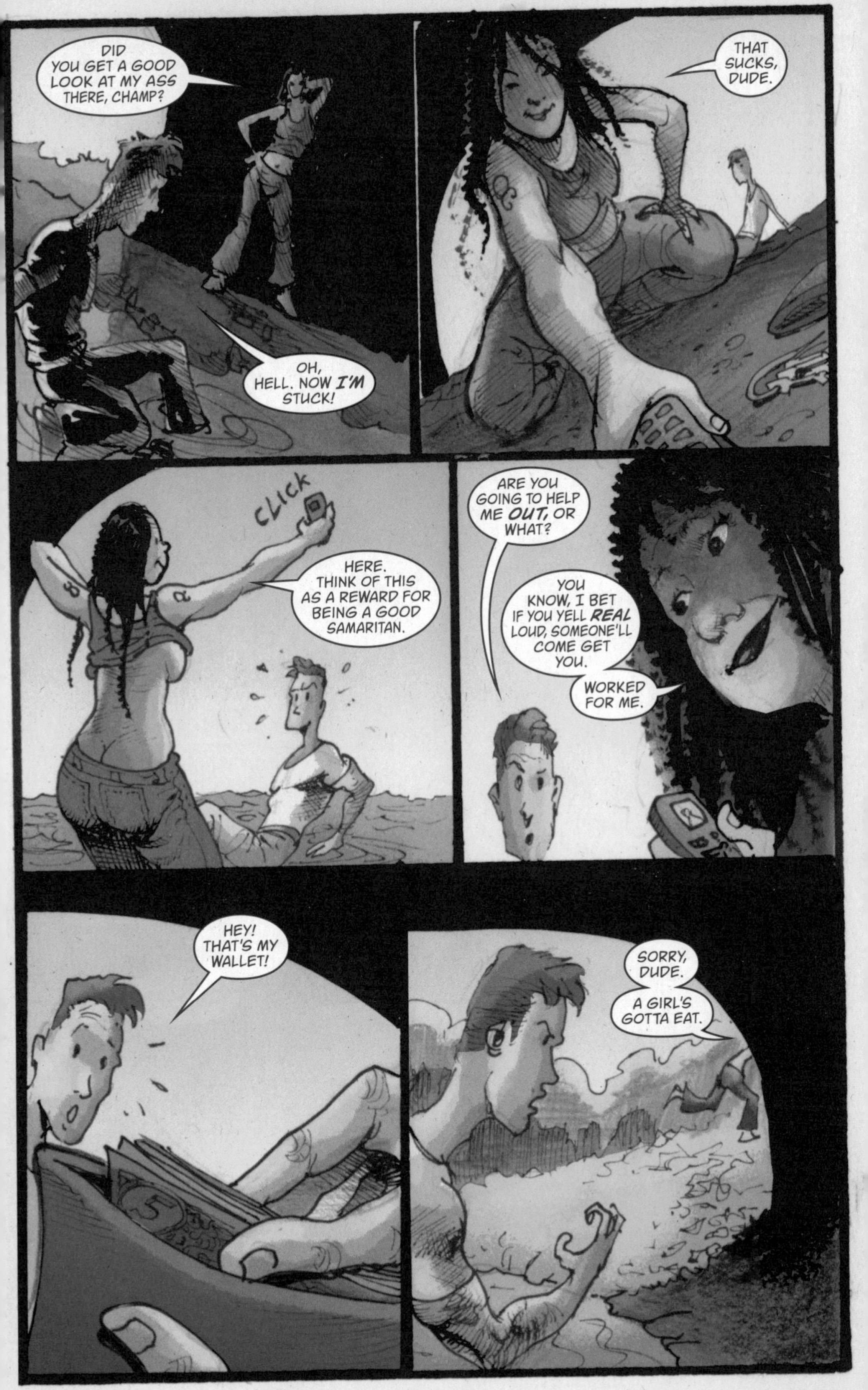
DID YOU GET A GOOD LOOK AT MY ASS THERE, CHAMP?
OH, HELL. NOW I'M STUCK!
THAT SUCKS, DUDE.
CLICK
HERE. THINK OF THIS AS A REWARD FOR BEING A GOOD SAMARITAN.
ARE YOU GOING TO HELP ME OUT, OR WHAT?
YOU KNOW, I BET IF YOU YELL REAL LOUD, SOMEONE'LL COME GET YOU.
WORKED FOR ME.
HEY! THAT'S MY WALLET!
SORRY, DUDE.
A GIRL'S GOTTA EAT.

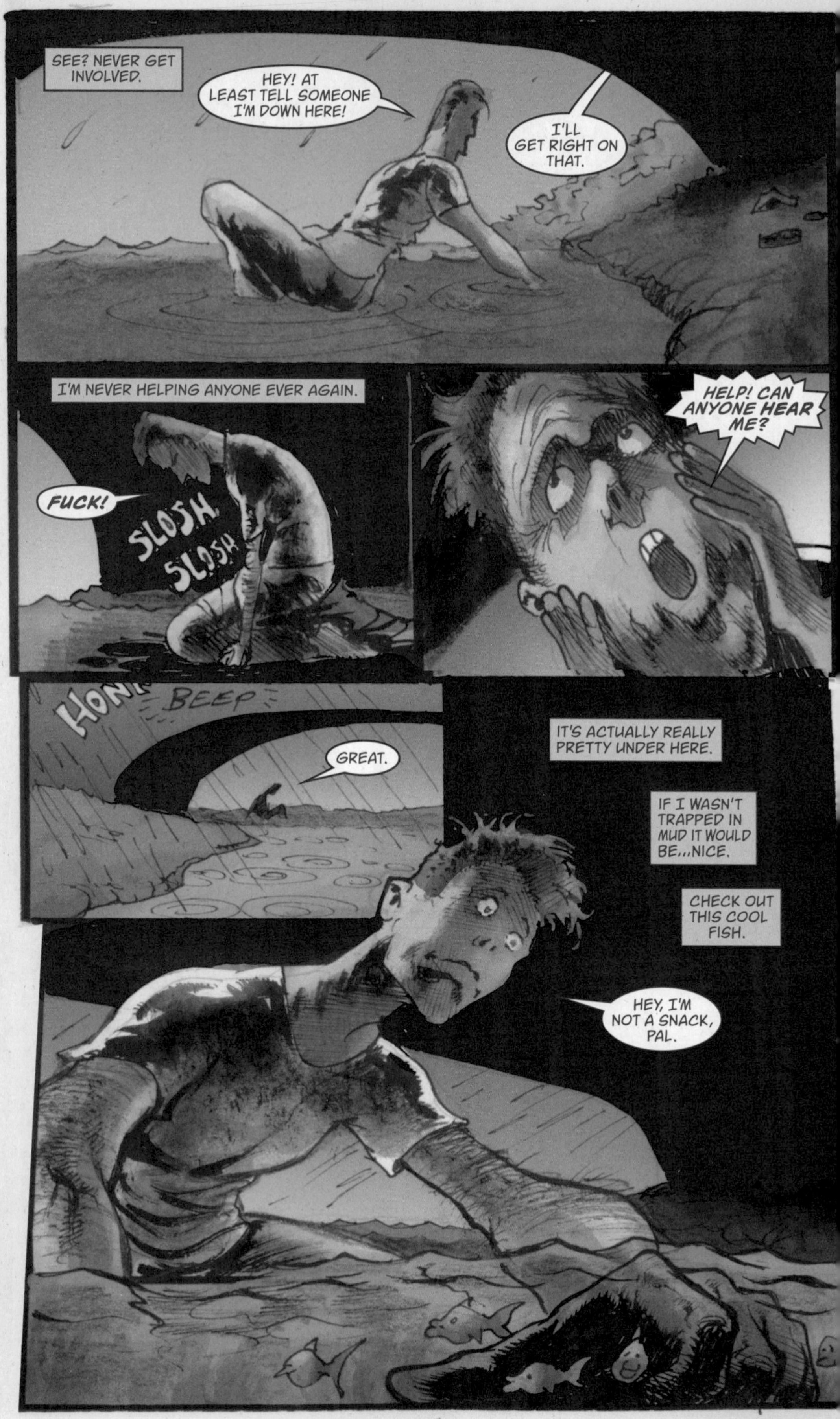
SEE? NEVER GET INVOLVED.
HEY! AT LEAST TELL SOMEONE I'M DOWN HERE!
I'LL GET RIGHT ON THAT.
I'M NEVER HELPING ANYONE EVER AGAIN.
FUCK!
SLOSH, SLOSH
HELP! CAN ANYONE HEAR ME?
BEEP
GREAT.
IT'S ACTUALLY REALLY PRETTY UNDER HERE.
IF I WASN'T TRAPPED IN MUD IT WOULD BE...NICE.
CHECK OUT THIS COOL FISH.
HEY, I'M NOT A SNACK, PAL.

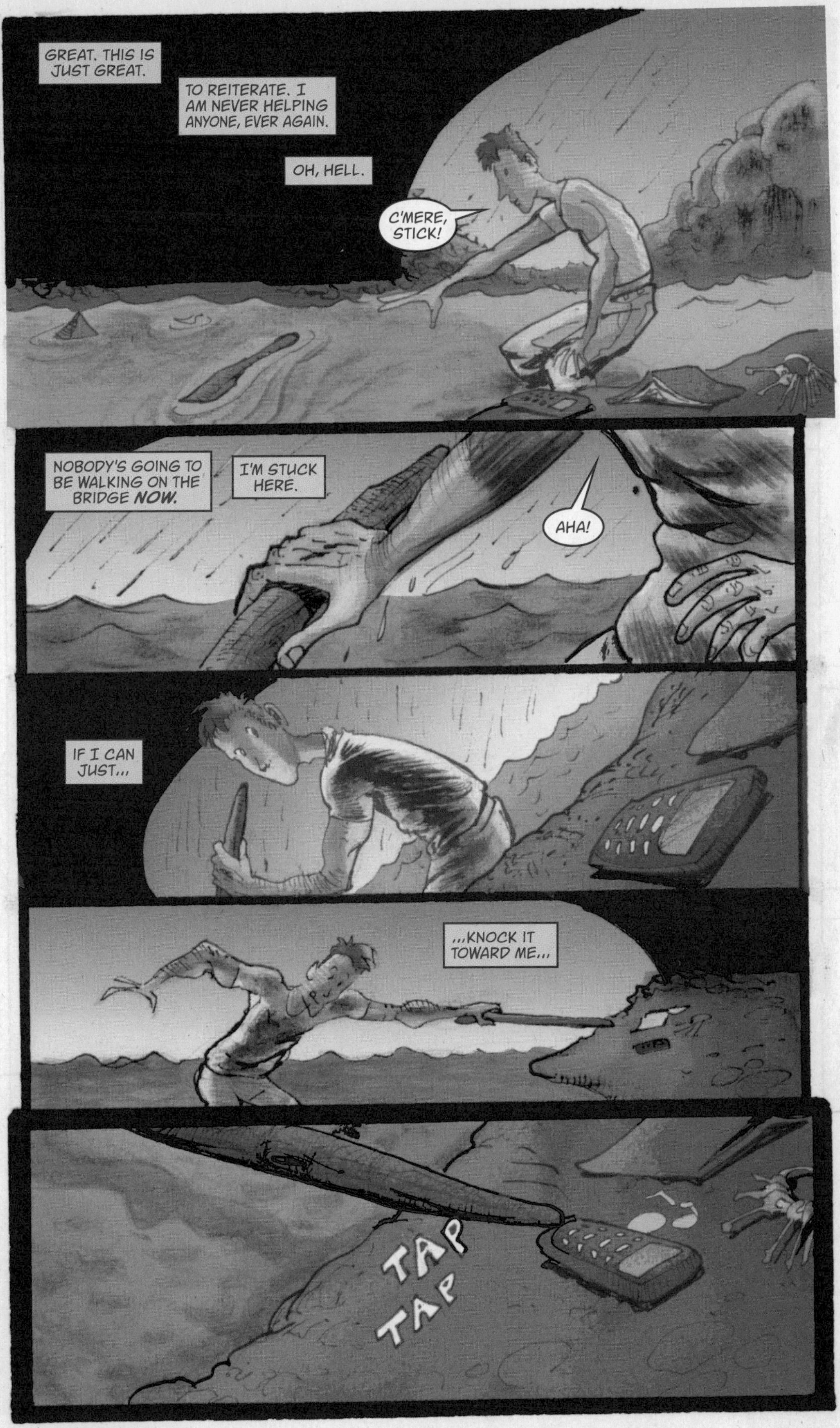
GREAT. THIS IS JUST GREAT.
TO REITERATE. I AM NEVER HELPING ANYONE, EVER AGAIN.
OH, HELL.
C'MERE, STICK!
NOBODY'S GOING TO BE WALKING ON THE BRIDGE *NOW.*
I'M STUCK HERE.
AHA!
IF I CAN JUST...
...KNOCK IT TOWARD ME...
TAP
TAP

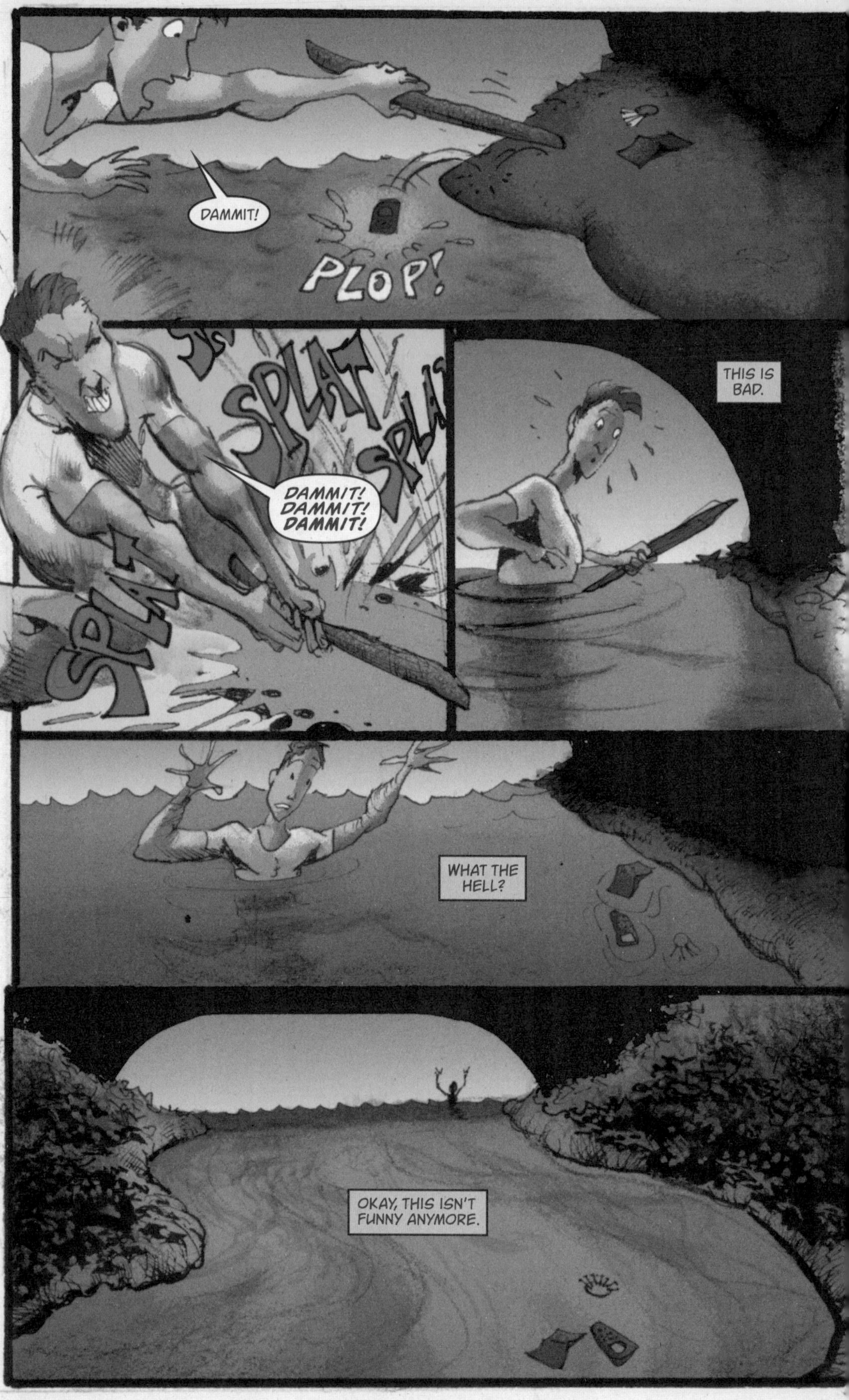
DAMMIT!
PLOP!
SPLAT
SPLAT
DAMMIT! DAMMIT! DAMMIT!
SPLAT
THIS IS BAD.
WHAT THE HELL?
OKAY, THIS ISN'T FUNNY ANYMORE.

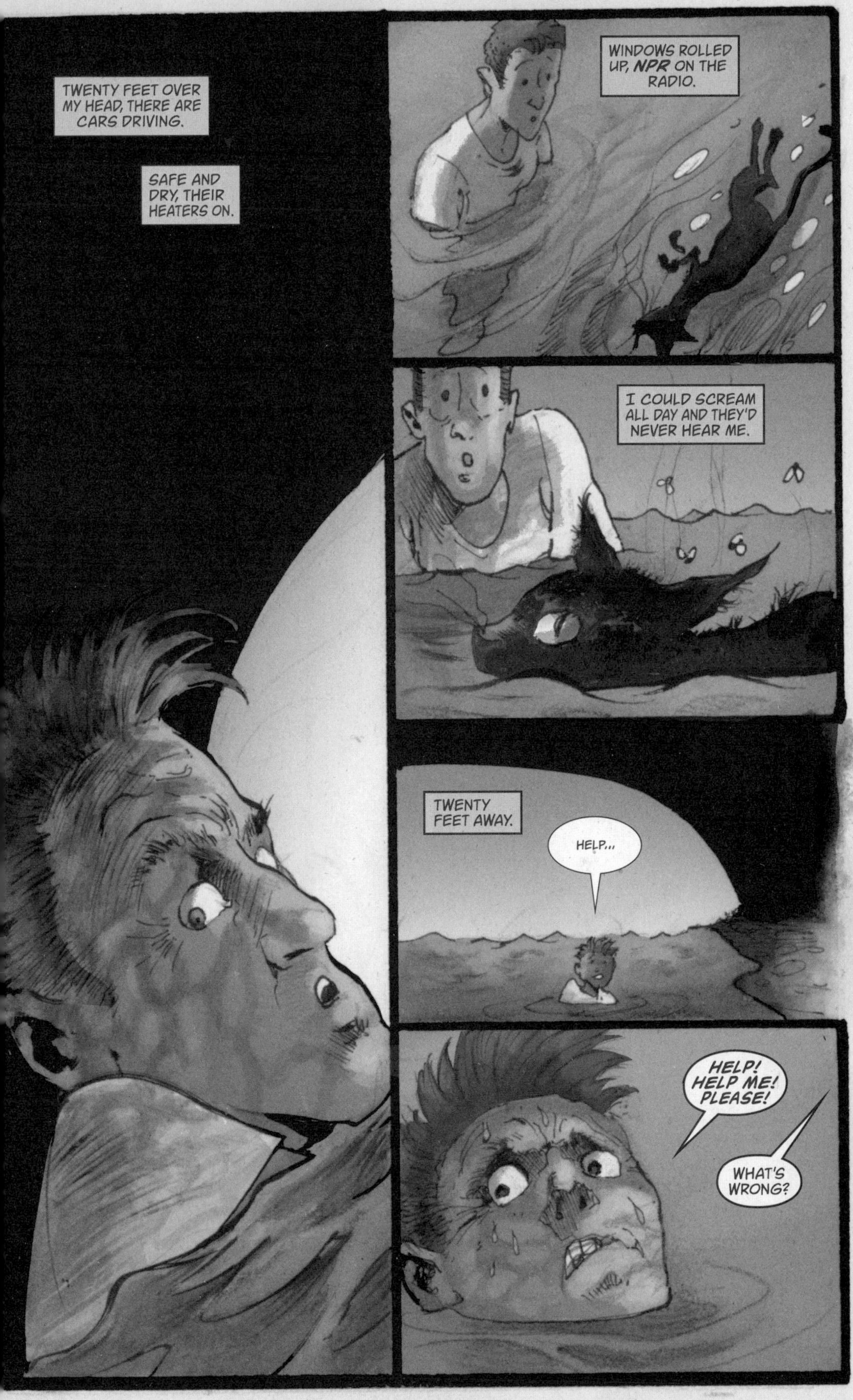
TWENTY FEET OVER MY HEAD, THERE ARE CARS DRIVING.
SAFE AND DRY, THEIR HEATERS ON.
WINDOWS ROLLED UP, NPR ON THE RADIO.
I COULD SCREAM ALL DAY AND THEY'D NEVER HEAR ME.
TWENTY FEET AWAY.
HELP...
HELP! HELP ME! PLEASE!
WHAT'S WRONG?

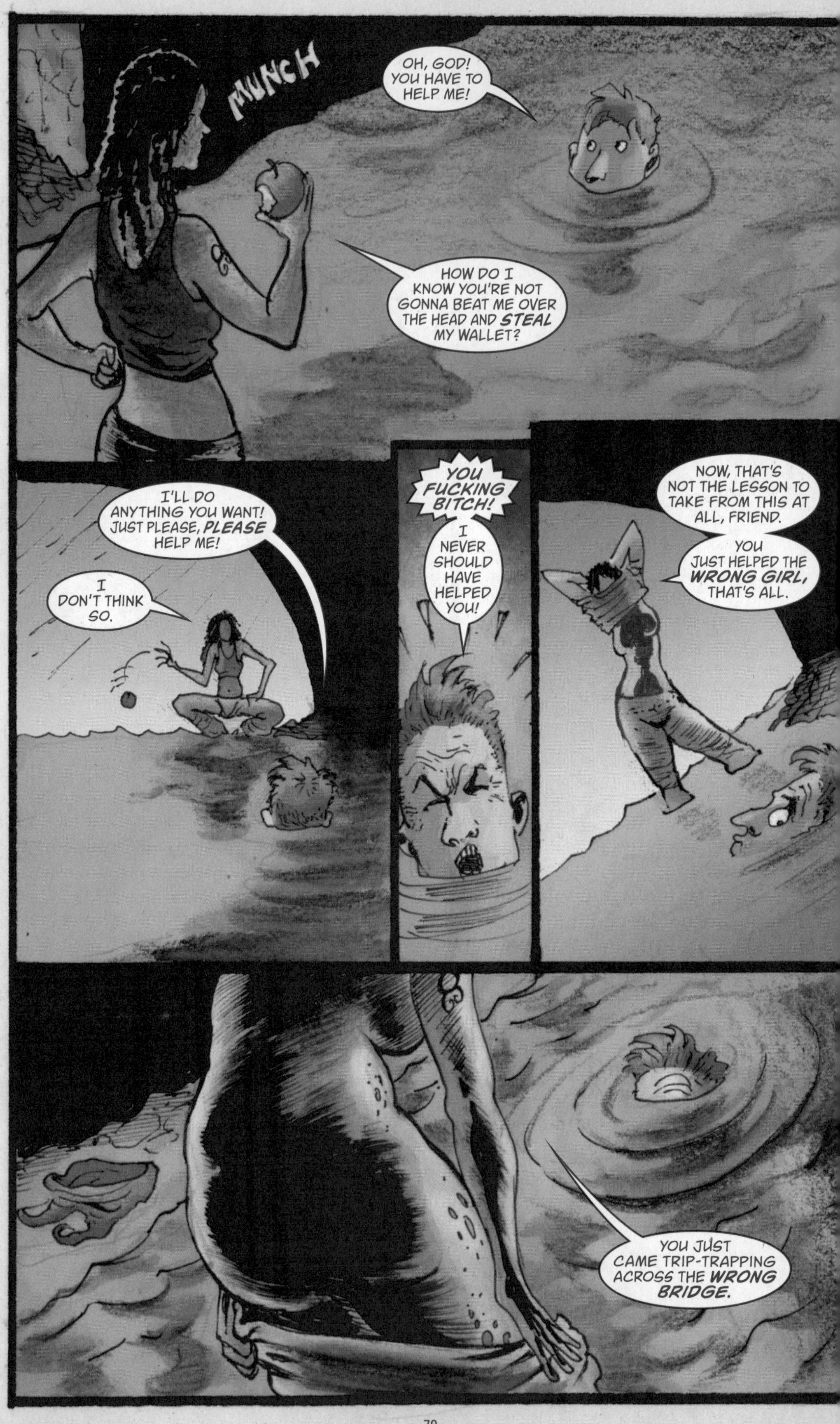
MUNCH
OH, GOD! YOU HAVE TO HELP ME!
HOW DO I KNOW YOU'RE NOT GONNA BEAT ME OVER THE HEAD AND STEAL MY WALLET?
I'LL DO ANYTHING YOU WANT! JUST PLEASE, PLEASE HELP ME!
I DON'T THINK SO.
YOU FUCKING BITCH!
I NEVER SHOULD HAVE HELPED YOU!
NOW, THAT'S NOT THE LESSON TO TAKE FROM THIS AT ALL, FRIEND.
YOU JUST HELPED THE WRONG GIRL, THAT'S ALL.
YOU JUST CAME TRIP-TRAPPING ACROSS THE WRONG BRIDGE.

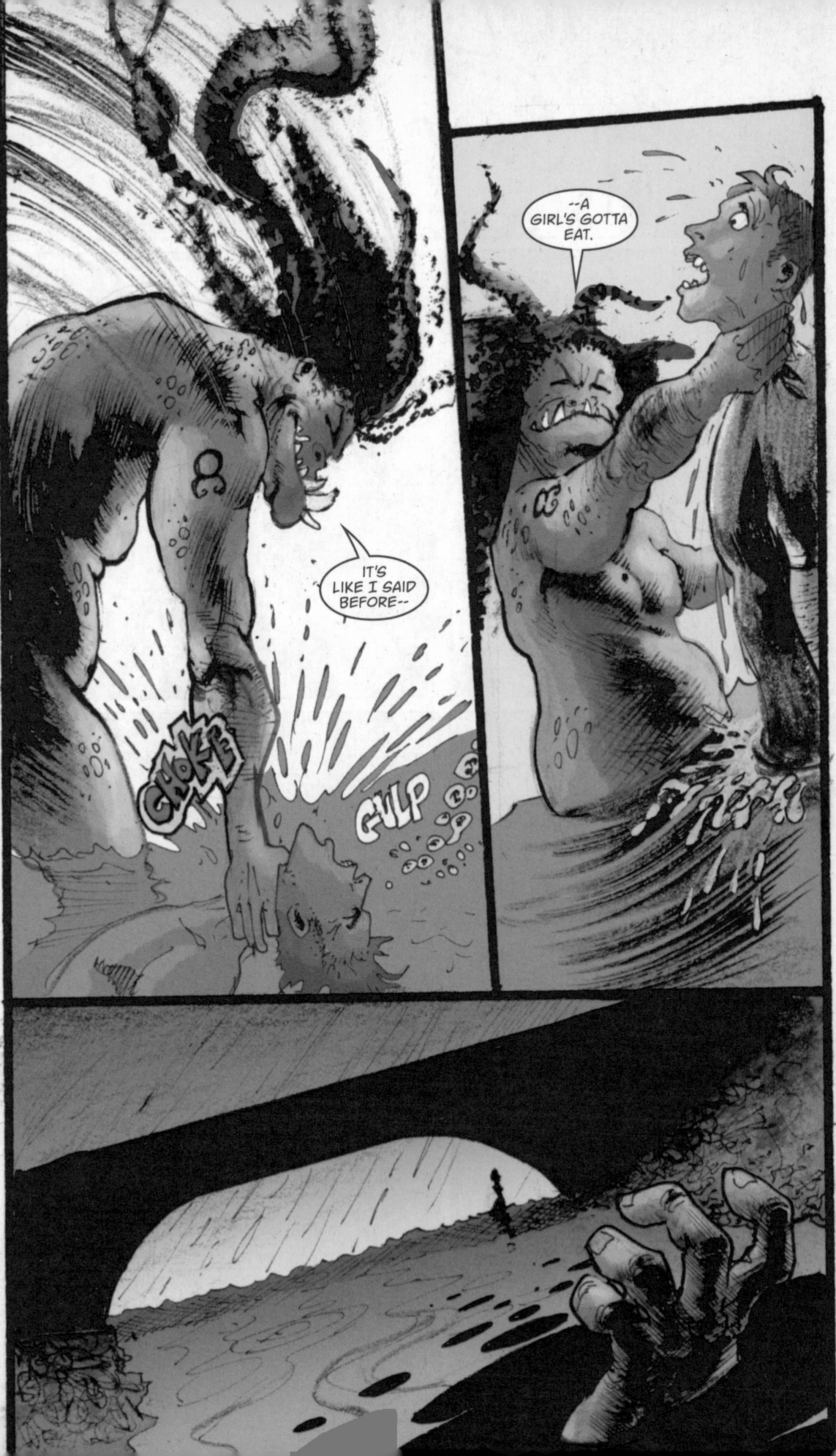

IT'S LIKE I SAID BEFORE--
CHOKE
GULP
--A GIRL'S GOTTA EAT.

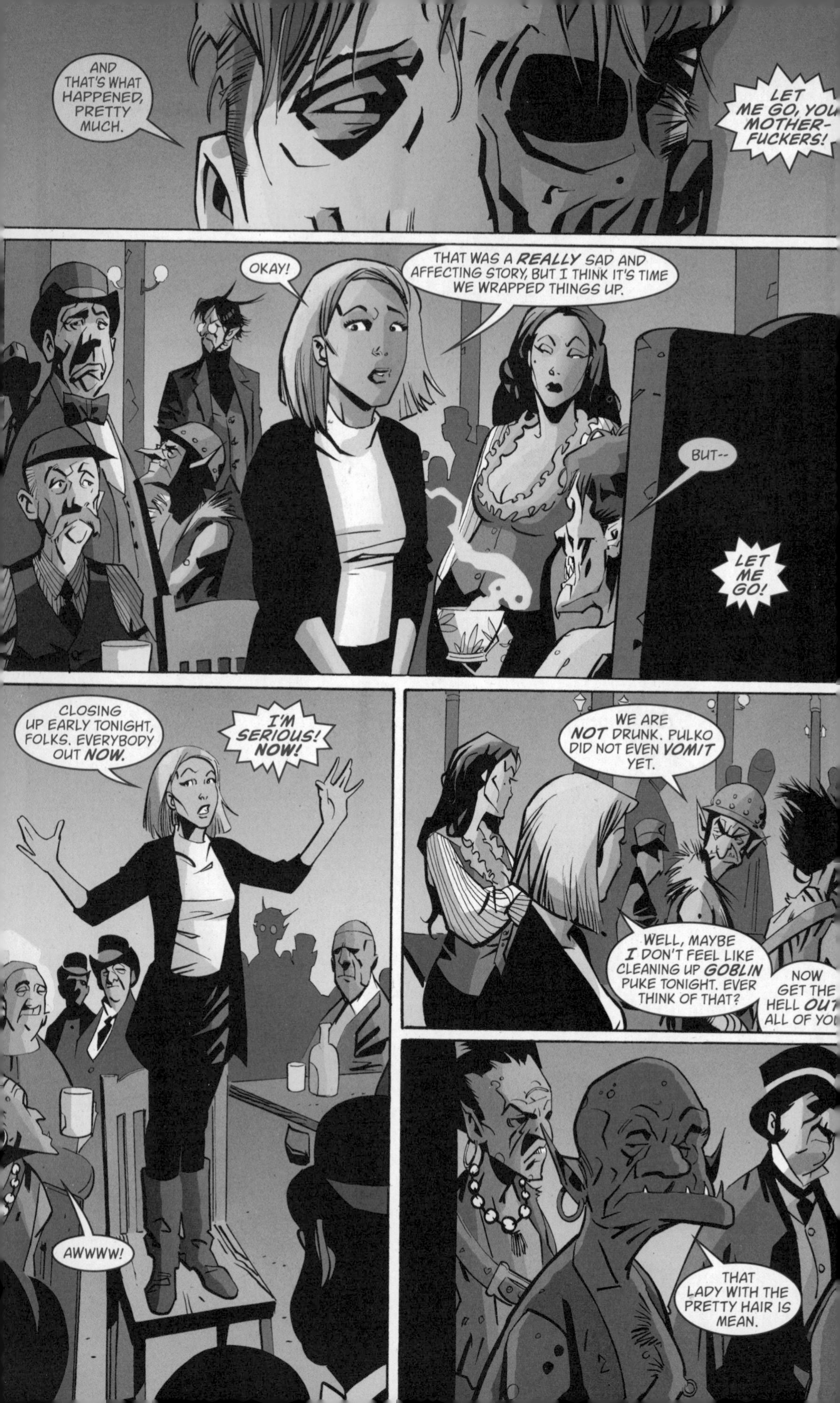
AND THAT'S WHAT HAPPENED, PRETTY MUCH.
LET ME GO, YOU MOTHER-FUCKERS!
OKAY!
THAT WAS A REALLY SAD AND AFFECTING STORY, BUT I THINK IT'S TIME WE WRAPPED THINGS UP.
BUT--
LET ME GO!
CLOSING UP EARLY TONIGHT, FOLKS. EVERYBODY OUT NOW.
I'M SERIOUS! NOW!
AWWWW!
WE ARE NOT DRUNK. PULKO DID NOT EVEN VOMIT YET.
WELL, MAYBE I DON'T FEEL LIKE CLEANING UP GOBLIN PUKE TONIGHT. EVER THINK OF THAT?
NOW GET THE HELL OUT ALL OF YO
THAT LADY WITH THE PRETTY HAIR IS MEAN.

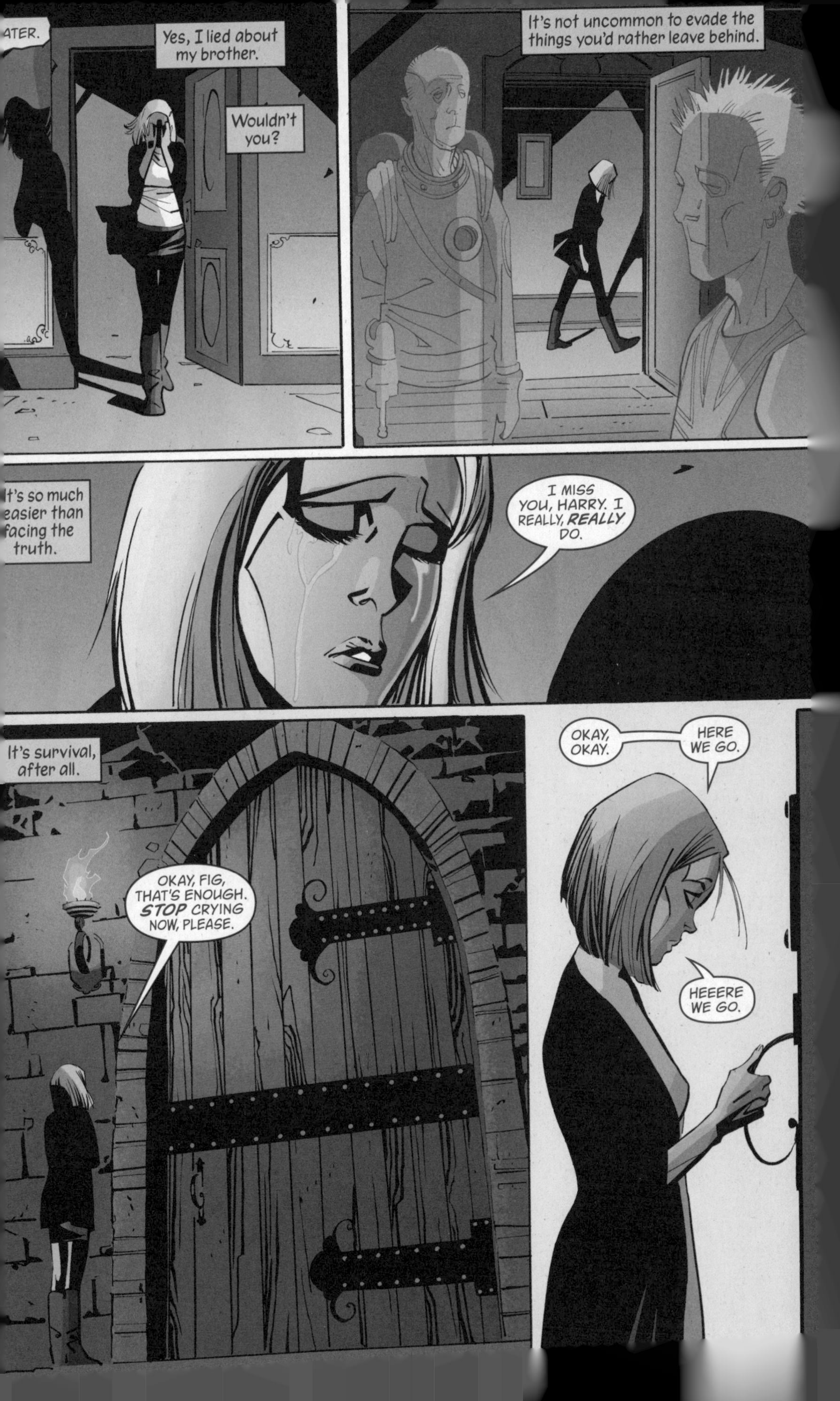
ATER.
Yes, I lied about my brother.
Wouldn't you?
It's not uncommon to evade the things you'd rather leave behind.
It's so much easier than facing the truth.
I MISS YOU, HARRY. I REALLY, REALLY DO.
It's survival, after all.
OKAY, FIG, THAT'S ENOUGH. STOP CRYING NOW, PLEASE.
OKAY, OKAY.
HERE WE GO.
HEEERE WE GO.

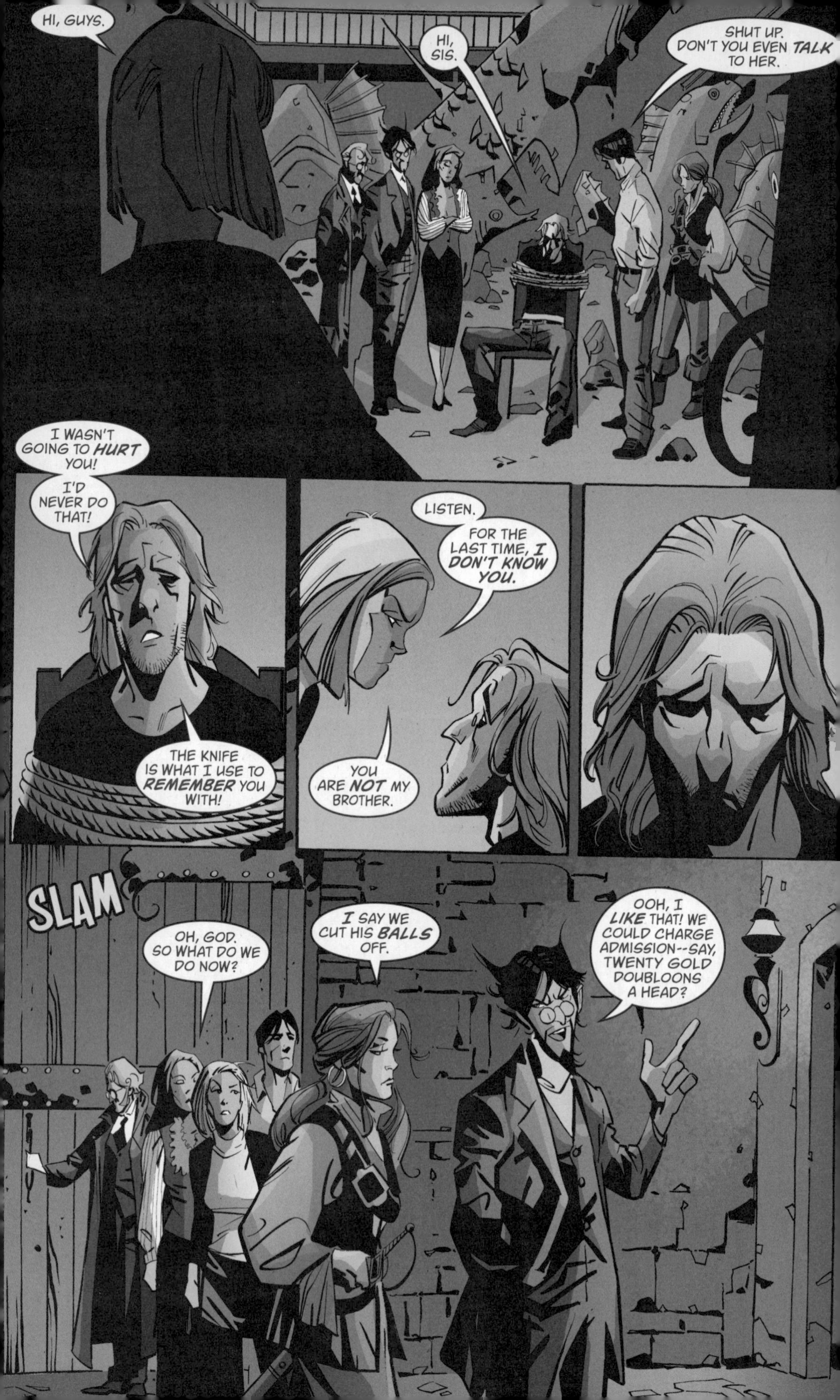
HI, GUYS.
HI, SIS.
SHUT UP. DON'T YOU EVEN TALK TO HER.
I WASN'T GOING TO HURT YOU!
I'D NEVER DO THAT!
THE KNIFE IS WHAT I USE TO REMEMBER YOU WITH!
LISTEN.
FOR THE LAST TIME, I DON'T KNOW YOU.
YOU ARE NOT MY BROTHER.
SLAM
OH, GOD. SO WHAT DO WE DO NOW?
I SAY WE CUT HIS BALLS OFF.
OOH, I LIKE THAT! WE COULD CHARGE ADMISSION--SAY, TWENTY GOLD DOUBLOONS A HEAD?

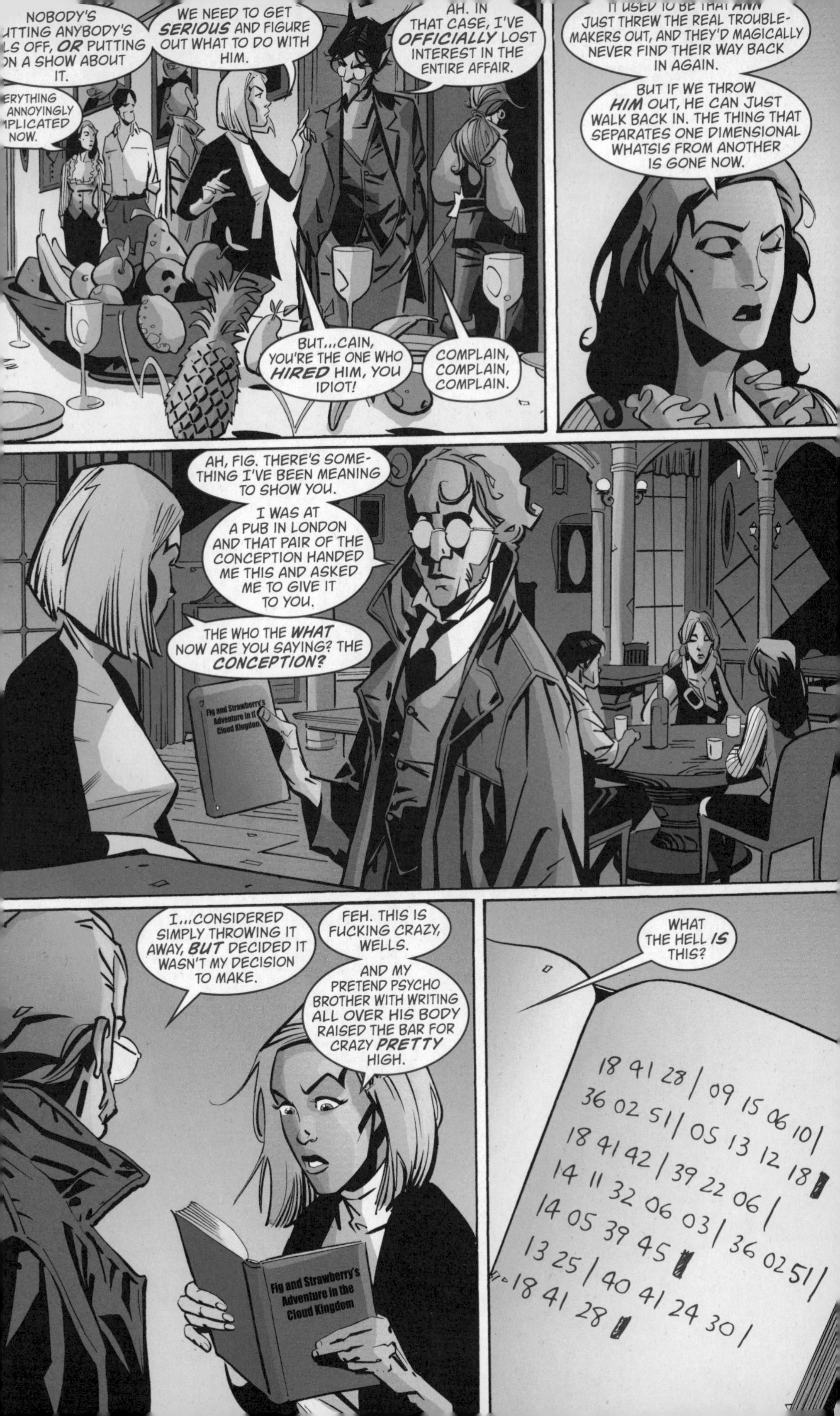
NOBODY'S UTTING ANYBODY'S LS OFF, OR PUTTING ON A SHOW ABOUT IT.
ERYTHING ANNOYINGLY MPLICATED NOW.
WE NEED TO GET SERIOUS AND FIGURE OUT WHAT TO DO WITH HIM.
AH. IN THAT CASE, I'VE OFFICIALLY LOST INTEREST IN THE ENTIRE AFFAIR.
BUT...CAIN, YOU'RE THE ONE WHO HIRED HIM, YOU IDIOT!
COMPLAIN, COMPLAIN, COMPLAIN.
IT USED TO BE THAT ANN JUST THREW THE REAL TROUBLE-MAKERS OUT, AND THEY'D MAGICALLY NEVER FIND THEIR WAY BACK IN AGAIN.
BUT IF WE THROW HIM OUT, HE CAN JUST WALK BACK IN. THE THING THAT SEPARATES ONE DIMENSIONAL WHATSIS FROM ANOTHER IS GONE NOW.
AH, FIG. THERE'S SOMETHING I'VE BEEN MEANING TO SHOW YOU.
I WAS AT A PUB IN LONDON AND THAT PAIR OF THE CONCEPTION HANDED ME THIS AND ASKED ME TO GIVE IT TO YOU.
THE WHO THE WHAT NOW ARE YOU SAYING? THE CONCEPTION?
Fig and Strawberry's Adventure in the Cloud Kingdom
I...CONSIDERED SIMPLY THROWING IT AWAY, BUT DECIDED IT WASN'T MY DECISION TO MAKE.
FEH. THIS IS FUCKING CRAZY, WELLS.
AND MY PRETEND PSYCHO BROTHER WITH WRITING ALL OVER HIS BODY RAISED THE BAR FOR CRAZY PRETTY HIGH.
Fig and Strawberry's Adventure in the Cloud Kingdom
WHAT THE HELL IS THIS?
18 41 28 / 09 15 06 10 /
36 02 51 / 05 13 12 18
18 41 42 / 39 22 06 /
14 11 32 06 03 / 36 02 51 /
14 05 39 45
13 25 / 40 41 24 30 /
18 41 28

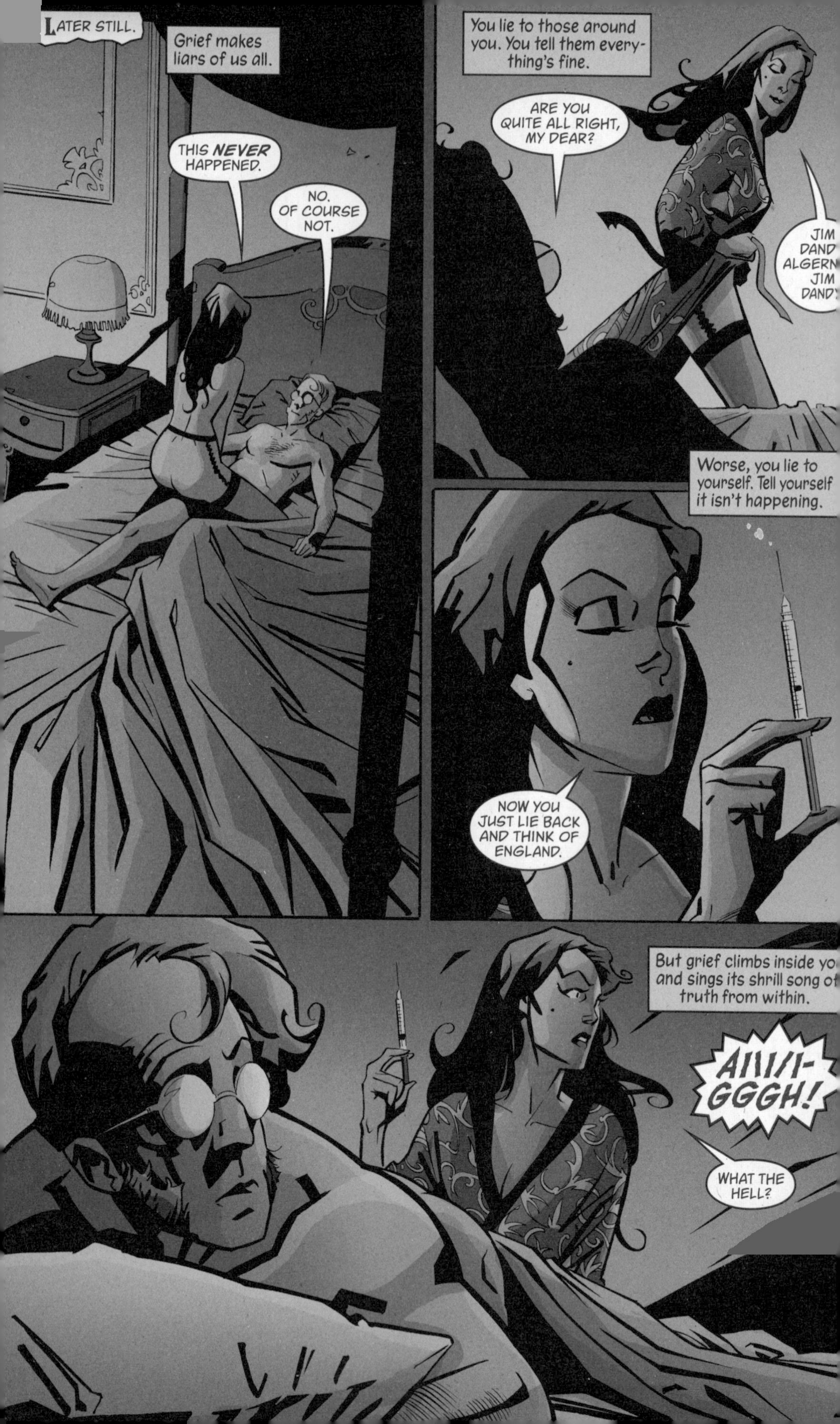

LATER STILL.
Grief makes liars of us all.
THIS NEVER HAPPENED.
NO. OF COURSE NOT.
You lie to those around you. You tell them everything's fine.
ARE YOU QUITE ALL RIGHT, MY DEAR?
JIM DAND ALGERN JIM DAND
Worse, you lie to yourself. Tell yourself it isn't happening.
NOW YOU JUST LIE BACK AND THINK OF ENGLAND.
But grief climbs inside yo and sings its shrill song o truth from within.
AIIIII-GGGH!
WHAT THE HELL?

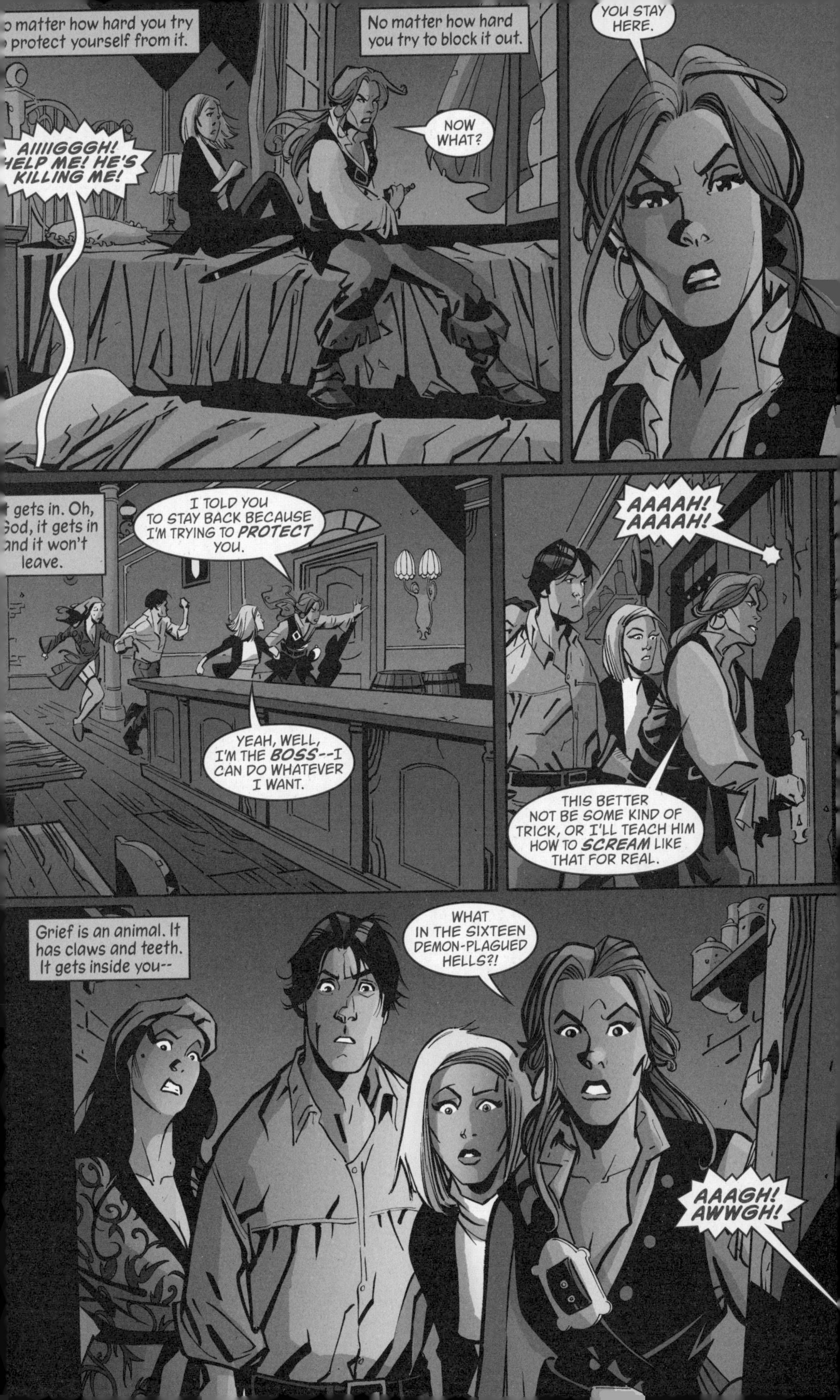

o matter how hard you try
protect yourself from it.
AIIIIGGGH! HELP ME! HE'S KILLING ME!
No matter how hard you try to block it out.
NOW WHAT?
YOU STAY HERE.
t gets in. Oh, God, it gets in and it won't leave.
I TOLD YOU TO STAY BACK BECAUSE I'M TRYING TO PROTECT YOU.
YEAH, WELL, I'M THE BOSS--I CAN DO WHATEVER I WANT.
AAAAH! AAAAH!
THIS BETTER NOT BE SOME KIND OF TRICK, OR I'LL TEACH HIM HOW TO SCREAM LIKE THAT FOR REAL.
Grief is an animal. It has claws and teeth. It gets inside you--
WHAT IN THE SIXTEEN DEMON-PLAGUED HELLS?!
AAAGH! AWWGH!

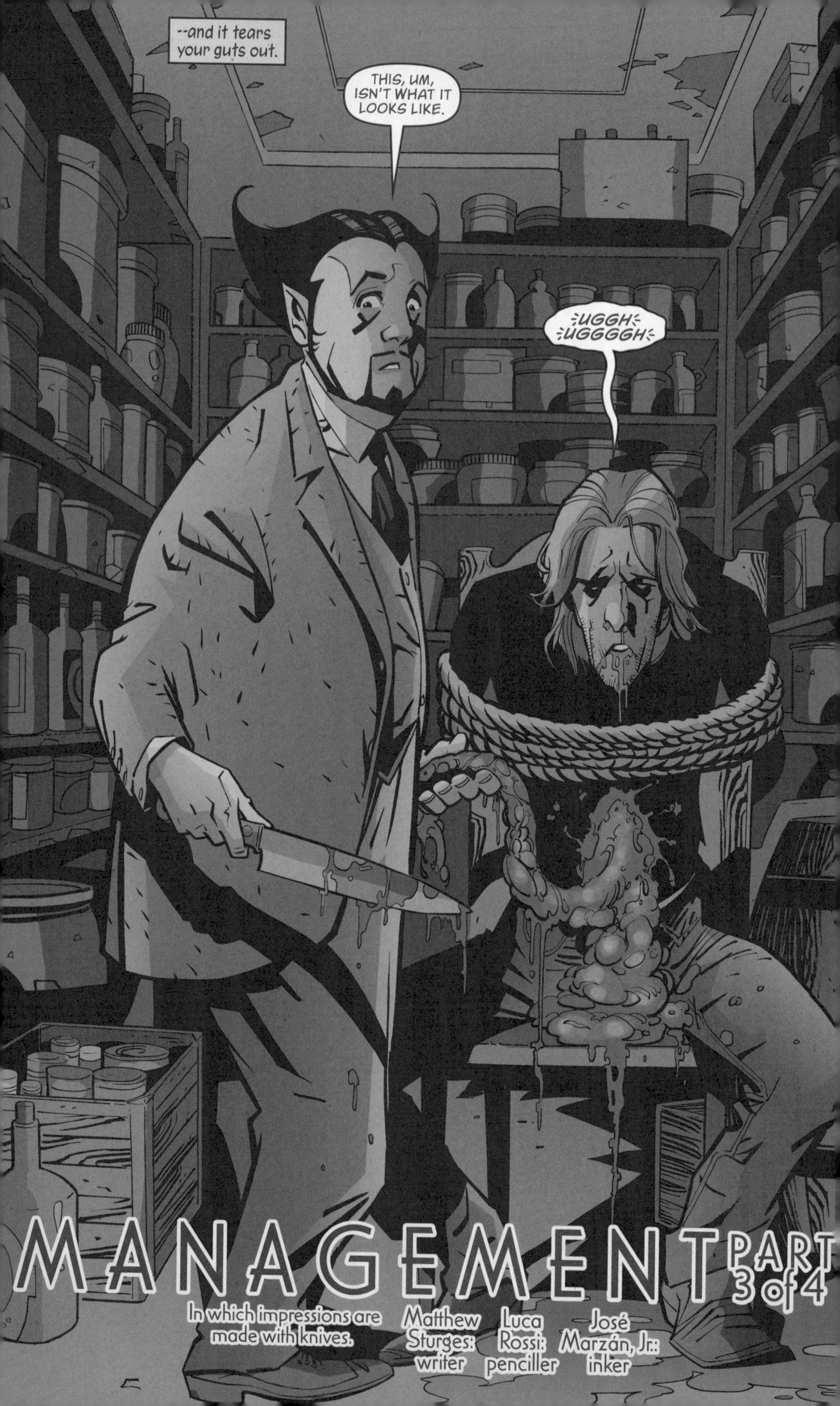

--and it tears your guts out.
THIS, UM, ISN'T WHAT IT LOOKS LIKE.
UGGH UGGGGH
MANAGEMENT PART 3 of 4
In which impressions are made with knives.
Matthew Sturges: writer
Luca Rossi: penciller
José Marzán, Jr.: inker

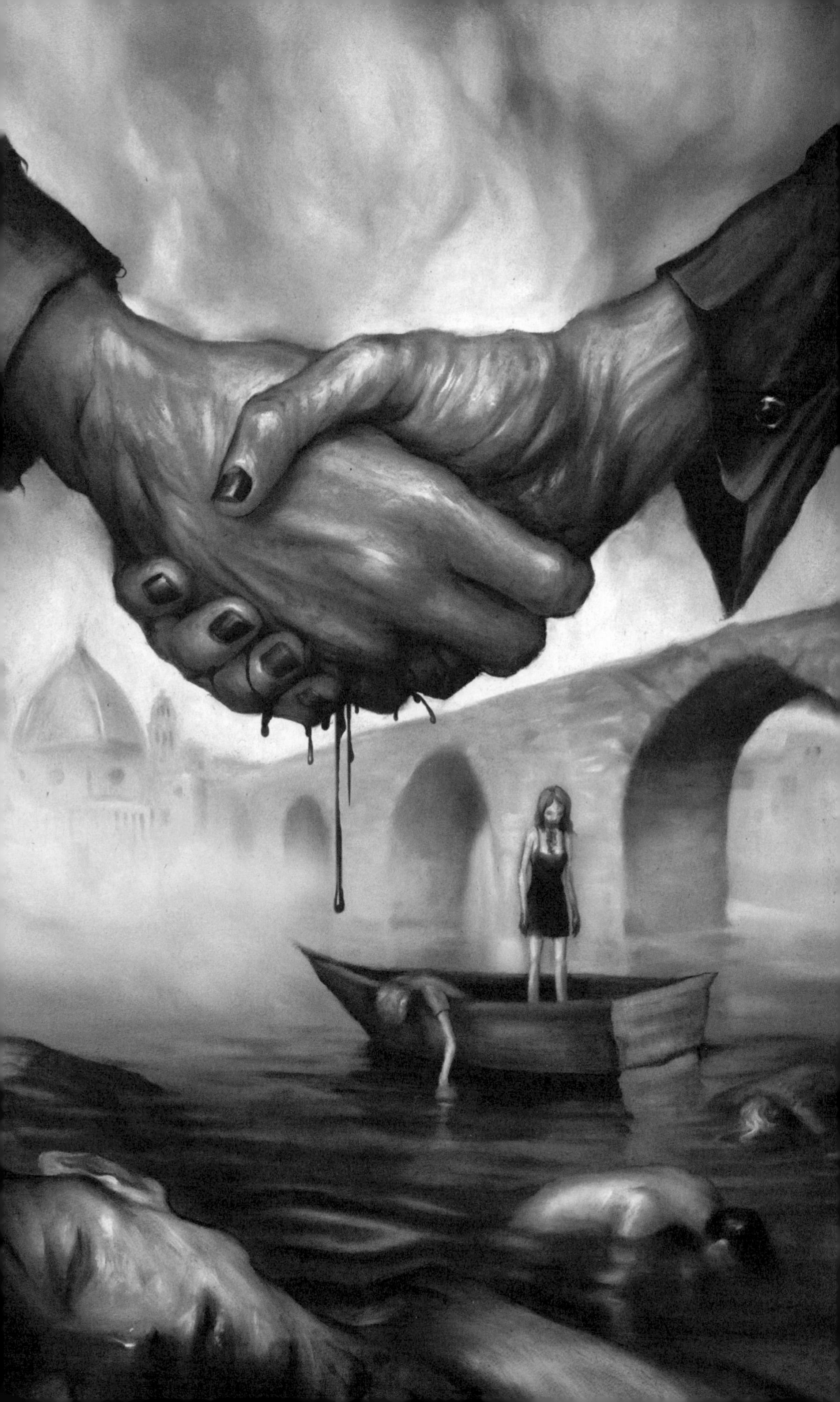

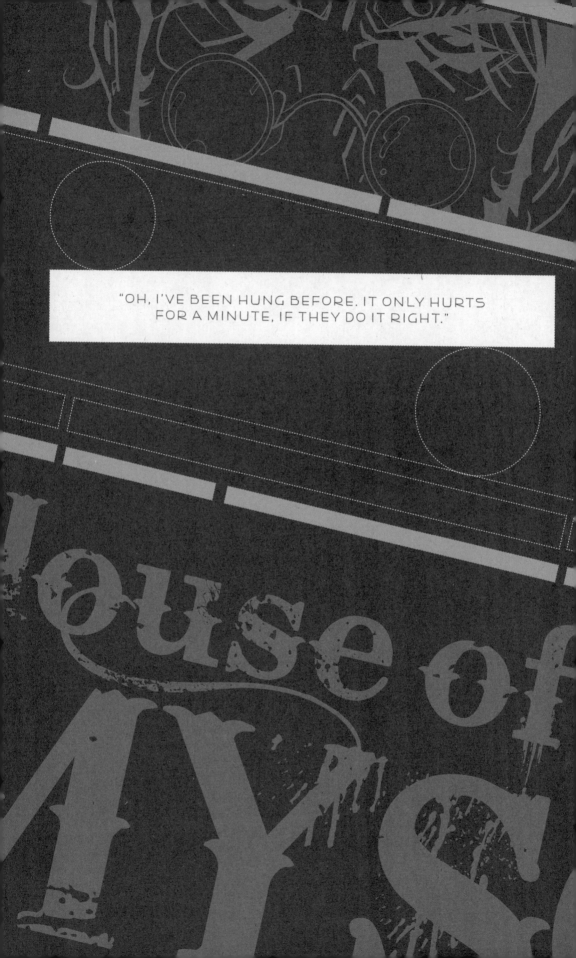

"OH, I'VE BEEN HUNG BEFORE. IT ONLY HURTS FOR A MINUTE, IF THEY DO IT RIGHT."

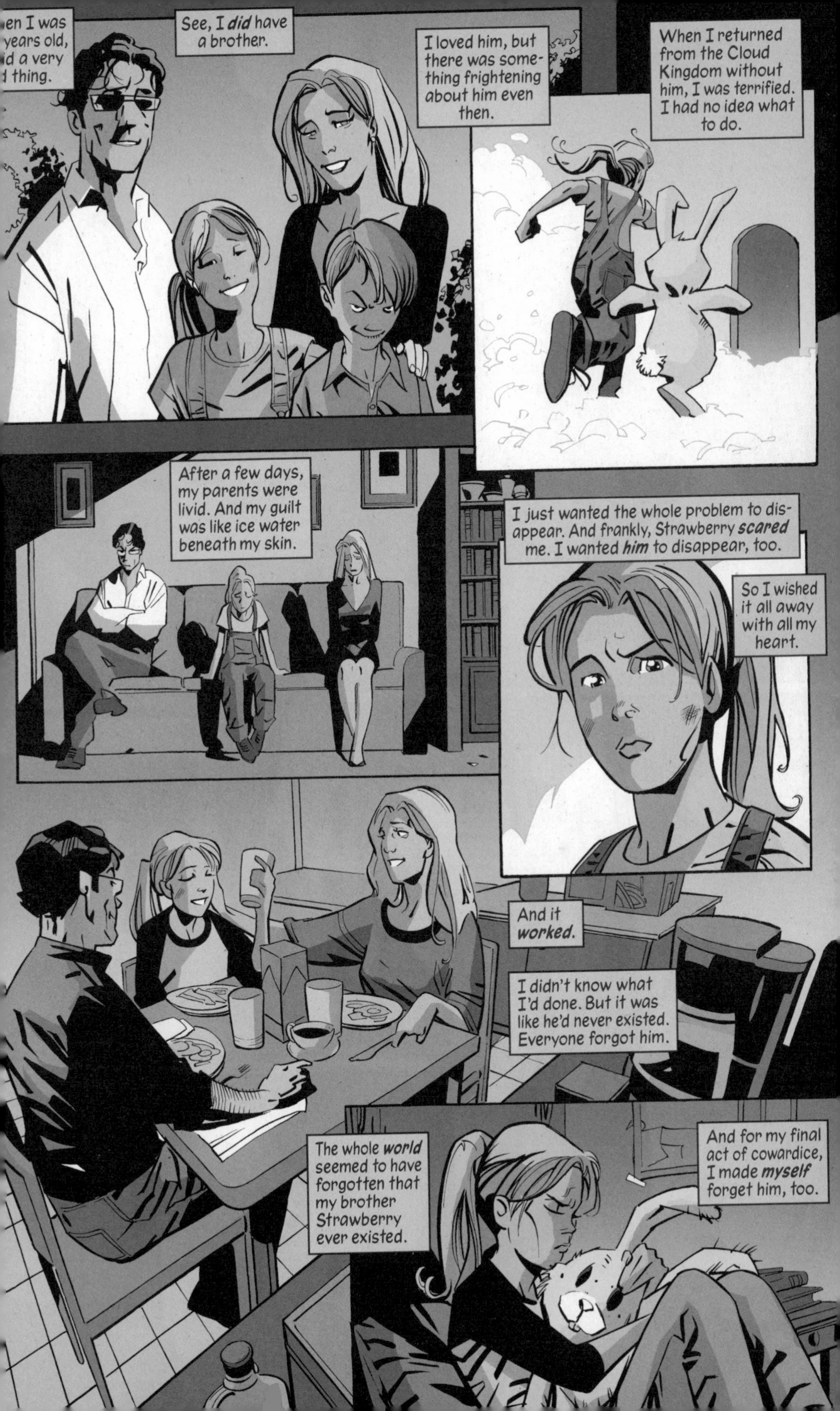

en I was
years old,
d a very
l thing.
See, I *did* have a brother.
I loved him, but there was something frightening about him even then.
When I returned from the Cloud Kingdom without him, I was terrified. I had no idea what to do.
After a few days, my parents were livid. And my guilt was like ice water beneath my skin.
I just wanted the whole problem to disappear. And frankly, Strawberry *scared* me. I wanted *him* to disappear, too.
So I wished it all away with all my heart.
And it *worked*.
I didn't know what I'd done. But it was like he'd never existed. Everyone forgot him.
The whole *world* seemed to have forgotten that my brother Strawberry ever existed.
And for my final act of cowardice, I made *myself* forget him, too.

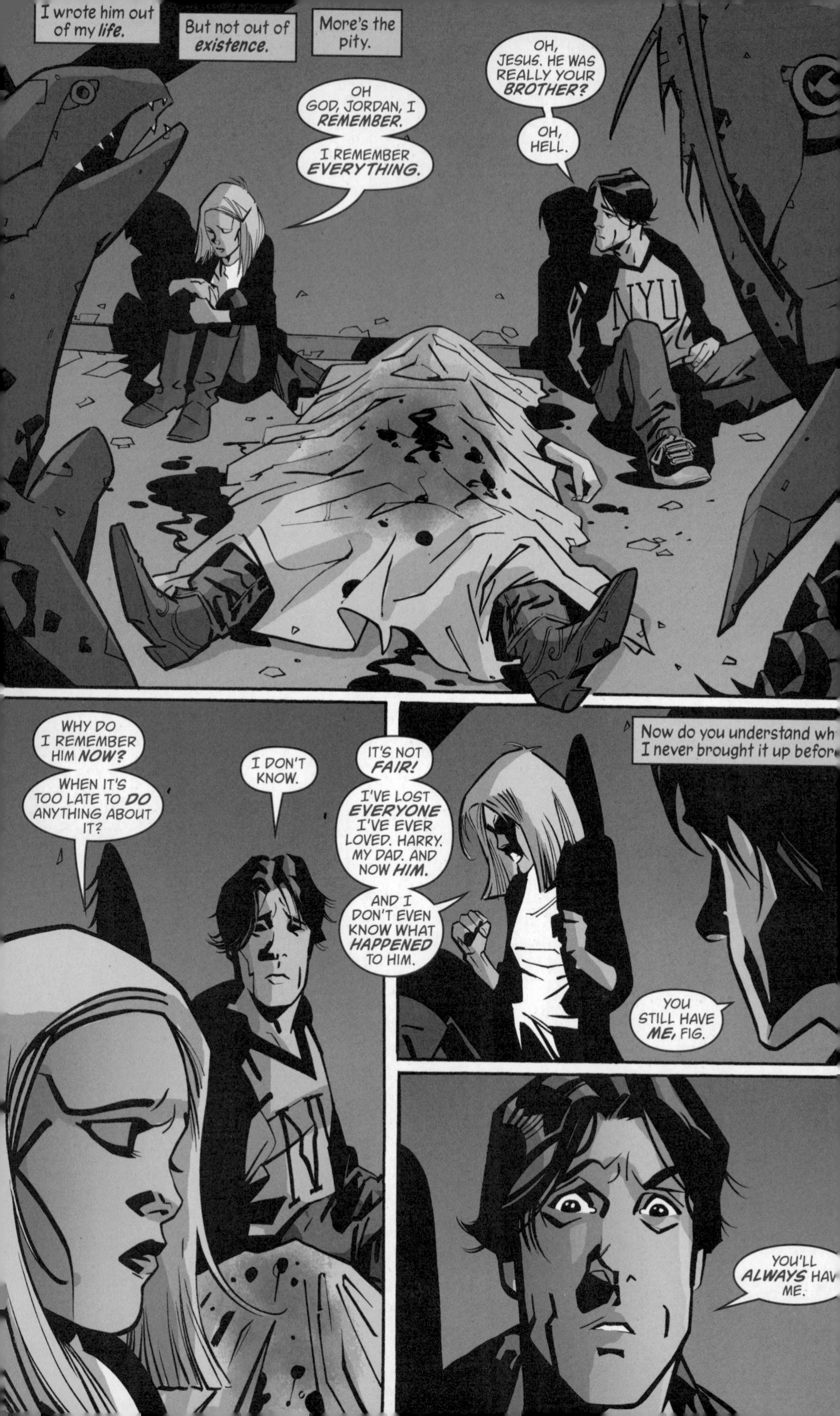

I wrote him out of my *life.*
But not out of *existence.*
More's the pity.
OH GOD, JORDAN, I *REMEMBER.*
I REMEMBER *EVERYTHING.*
OH, JESUS. HE WAS REALLY YOUR *BROTHER?*
OH, HELL.
WHY DO I REMEMBER HIM *NOW?*
WHEN IT'S TOO LATE TO *DO* ANYTHING ABOUT IT?
I DON'T KNOW.
IT'S NOT *FAIR!*
I'VE LOST *EVERYONE* I'VE EVER LOVED. HARRY. MY DAD. AND NOW *HIM.*
AND I DON'T EVEN KNOW WHAT *HAPPENED* TO HIM.
Now do you understand wh
I never brought it up befor
YOU STILL HAVE *ME,* FIG.
YOU'LL *ALWAYS* HAV
ME.

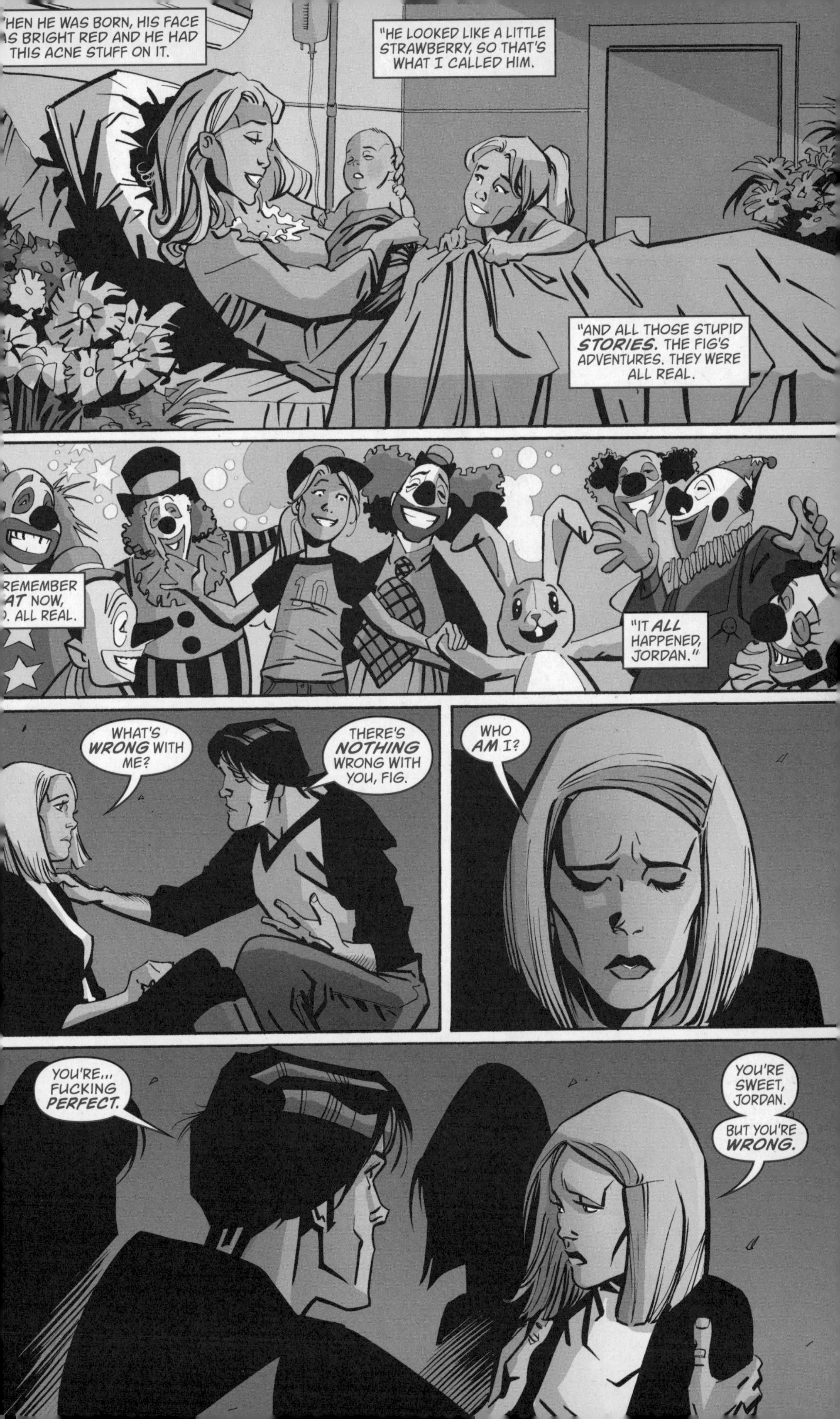
"WHEN HE WAS BORN, HIS FACE WAS BRIGHT RED AND HE HAD THIS ACNE STUFF ON IT.
"HE LOOKED LIKE A LITTLE STRAWBERRY, SO THAT'S WHAT I CALLED HIM.
"AND ALL THOSE STUPID STORIES. THE FIG'S ADVENTURES. THEY WERE ALL REAL.
REMEMBER AT NOW, . ALL REAL.
"IT ALL HAPPENED, JORDAN."
WHAT'S WRONG WITH ME?
THERE'S NOTHING WRONG WITH YOU, FIG.
WHO AM I?
YOU'RE... FUCKING PERFECT.
YOU'RE SWEET, JORDAN.
BUT YOU'RE WRONG.

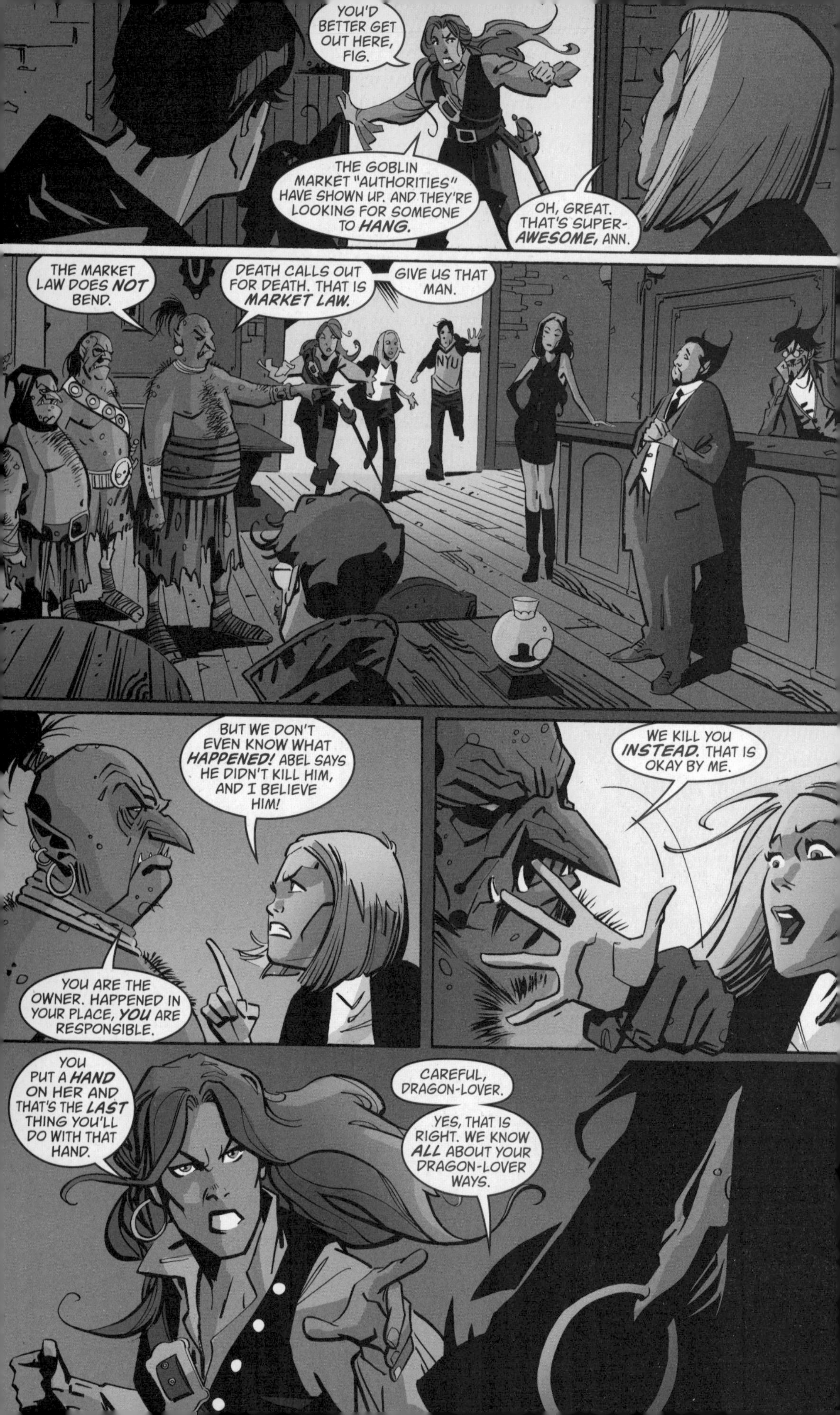
YOU'D BETTER GET OUT HERE, FIG.
THE GOBLIN MARKET "AUTHORITIES" HAVE SHOWN UP. AND THEY'RE LOOKING FOR SOMEONE TO HANG.
OH, GREAT. THAT'S SUPER-AWESOME, ANN.
THE MARKET LAW DOES NOT BEND.
DEATH CALLS OUT FOR DEATH. THAT IS MARKET LAW.
GIVE US THAT MAN.
NYU
BUT WE DON'T EVEN KNOW WHAT HAPPENED! ABEL SAYS HE DIDN'T KILL HIM, AND I BELIEVE HIM!
YOU ARE THE OWNER. HAPPENED IN YOUR PLACE, YOU ARE RESPONSIBLE.
WE KILL YOU INSTEAD. THAT IS OKAY BY ME.
YOU PUT A HAND ON HER AND THAT'S THE LAST THING YOU'LL DO WITH THAT HAND.
CAREFUL, DRAGON-LOVER.
YES, THAT IS RIGHT. WE KNOW ALL ABOUT YOUR DRAGON-LOVER WAYS.

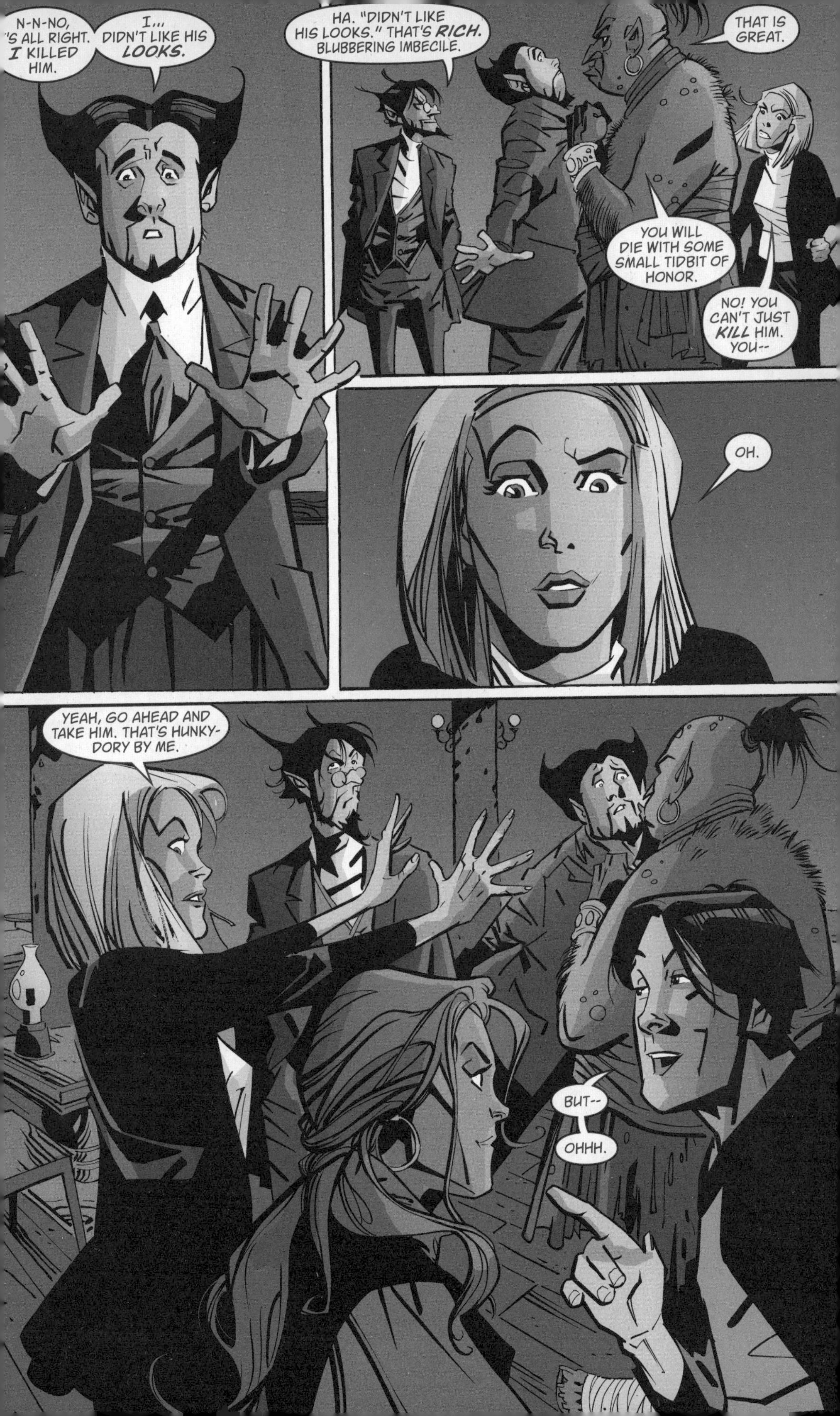

N-N-NO, 'S ALL RIGHT. I KILLED HIM.
I... DIDN'T LIKE HIS LOOKS.
HA. "DIDN'T LIKE HIS LOOKS." THAT'S RICH. BLUBBERING IMBECILE.
THAT IS GREAT.
YOU WILL DIE WITH SOME SMALL TIDBIT OF HONOR.
NO! YOU CAN'T JUST KILL HIM. YOU--
OH.
YEAH, GO AHEAD AND TAKE HIM. THAT'S HUNKY-DORY BY ME.
BUT--
OHHH.

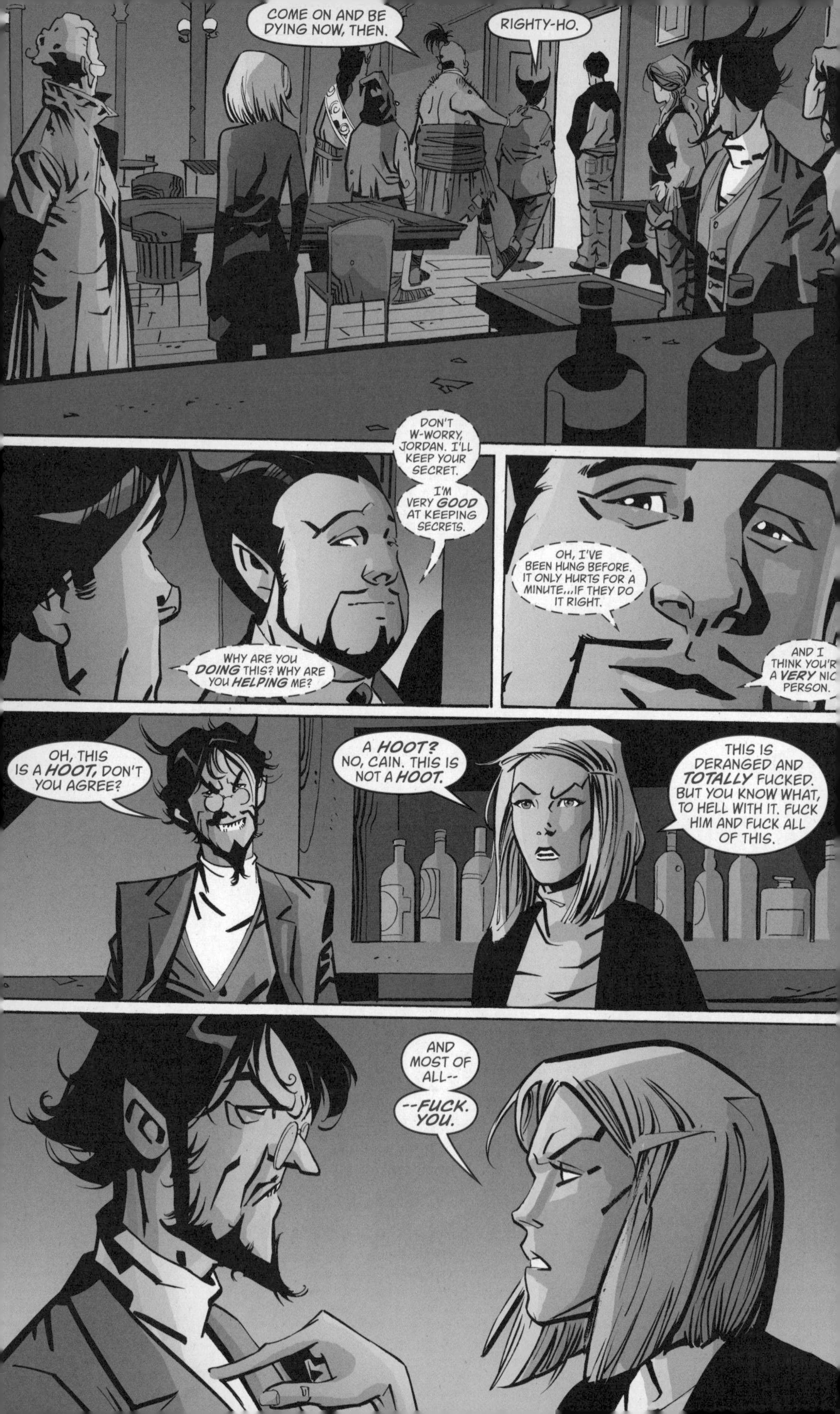
COME ON AND BE DYING NOW, THEN.
RIGHTY-HO.
DON'T W-WORRY, JORDAN. I'LL KEEP YOUR SECRET.
I'M VERY GOOD AT KEEPING SECRETS.
WHY ARE YOU DOING THIS? WHY ARE YOU HELPING ME?
OH, I'VE BEEN HUNG BEFORE. IT ONLY HURTS FOR A MINUTE...IF THEY DO IT RIGHT.
AND I THINK YOU'R A VERY NIC PERSON.
OH, THIS IS A HOOT, DON'T YOU AGREE?
A HOOT? NO, CAIN. THIS IS NOT A HOOT.
THIS IS DERANGED AND TOTALLY FUCKED. BUT YOU KNOW WHAT, TO HELL WITH IT. FUCK HIM AND FUCK ALL OF THIS.
AND MOST OF ALL--
--FUCK. YOU.

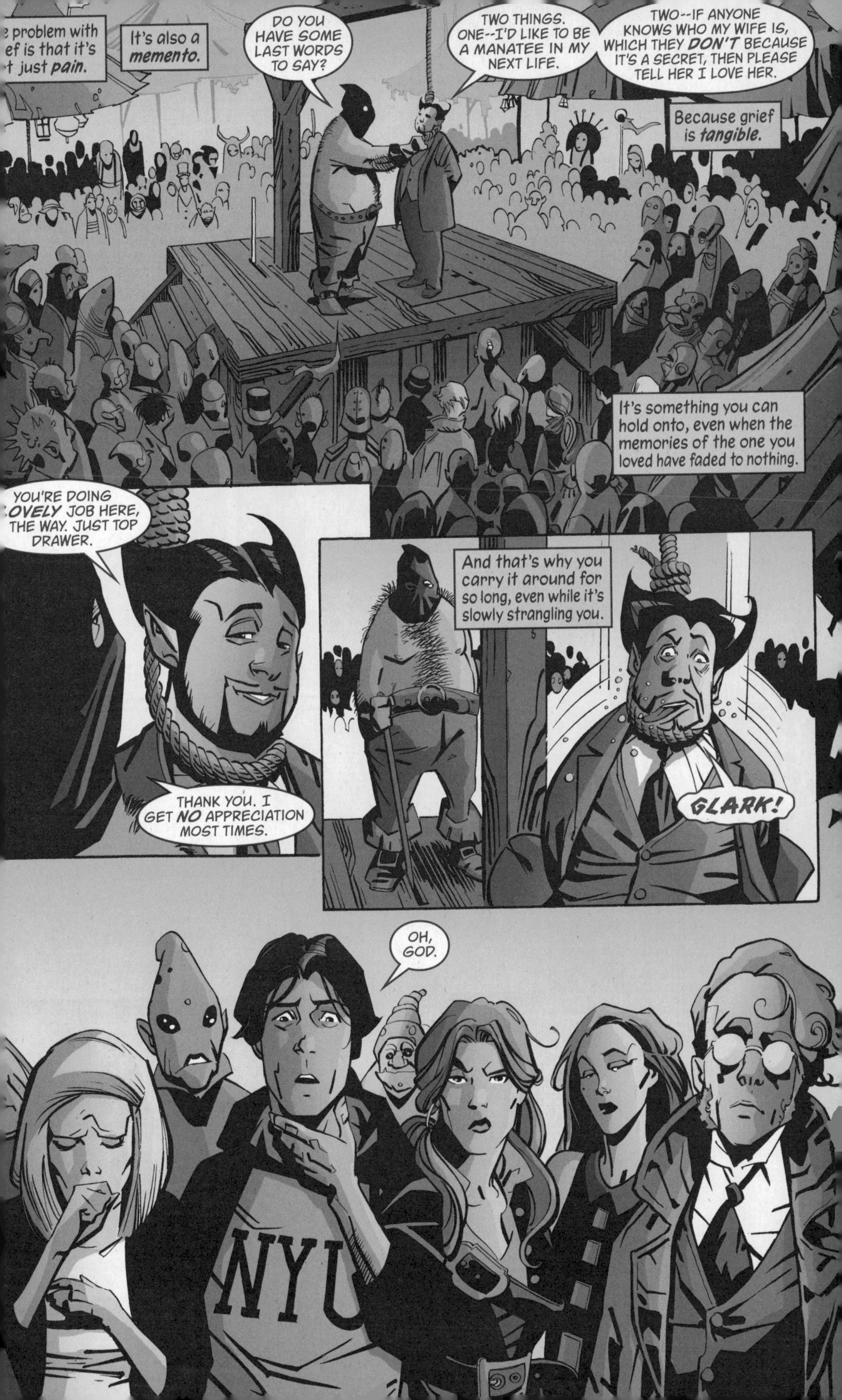

e problem with
ef is that it's
t just *pain*.
It's also a *memento*.
DO YOU HAVE SOME LAST WORDS TO SAY?
TWO THINGS. ONE--I'D LIKE TO BE A MANATEE IN MY NEXT LIFE.
TWO--IF ANYONE KNOWS WHO MY WIFE IS, WHICH THEY *DON'T* BECAUSE IT'S A SECRET, THEN PLEASE TELL HER I LOVE HER.
Because grief is *tangible*.
It's something you can hold onto, even when the memories of the one you loved have faded to nothing.
YOU'RE DOING OVELY JOB HERE, THE WAY. JUST TOP DRAWER.
THANK YOU. I GET *NO* APPRECIATION MOST TIMES.
And that's why you carry it around for so long, even while it's slowly strangling you.
GLARK!
OH, GOD.
NYU

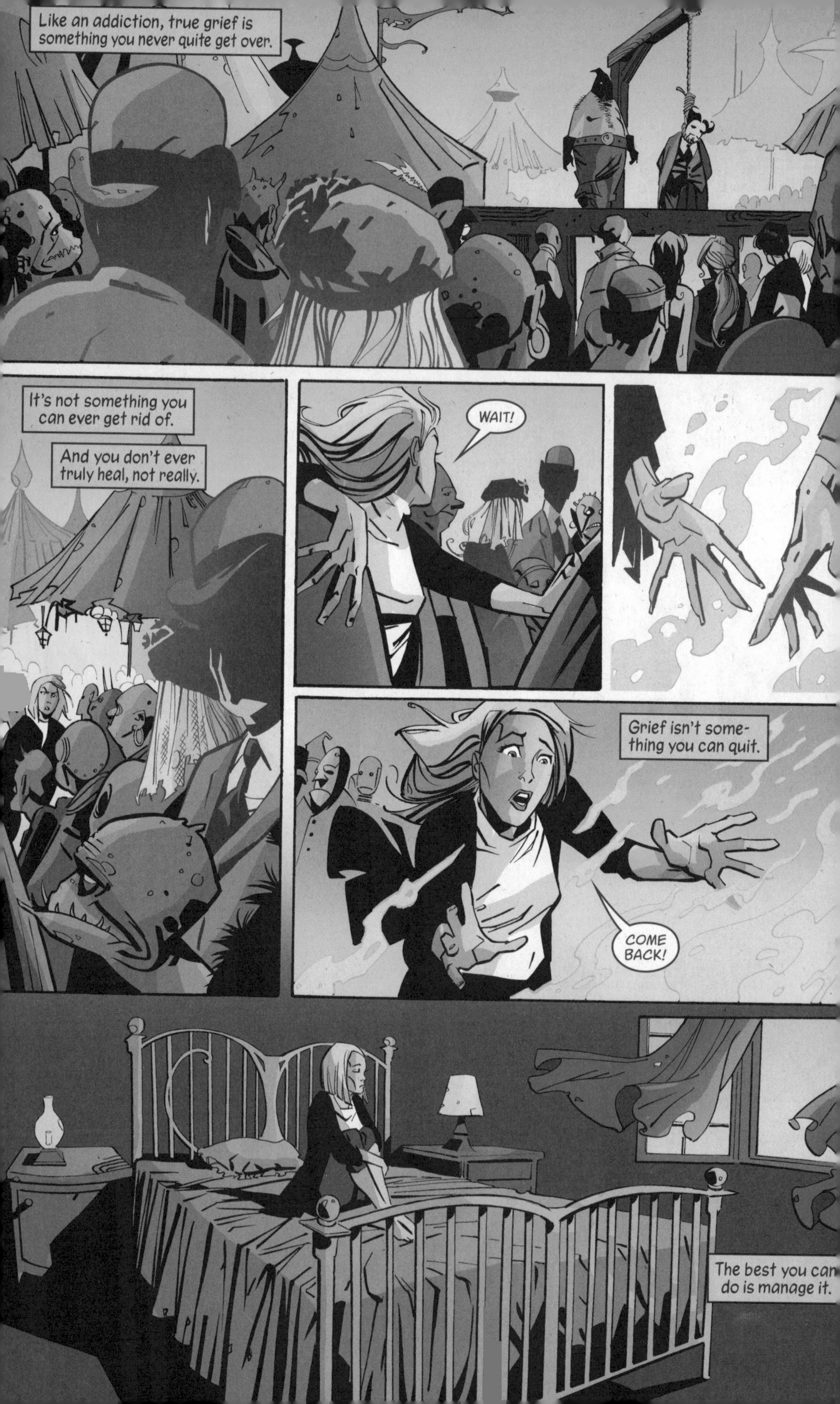

Like an addiction, true grief is something you never quite get over.
It's not something you can ever get rid of.
And you don't ever truly heal, not really.
WAIT!
Grief isn't some-thing you can quit.
COME BACK!
The best you can do is manage it.

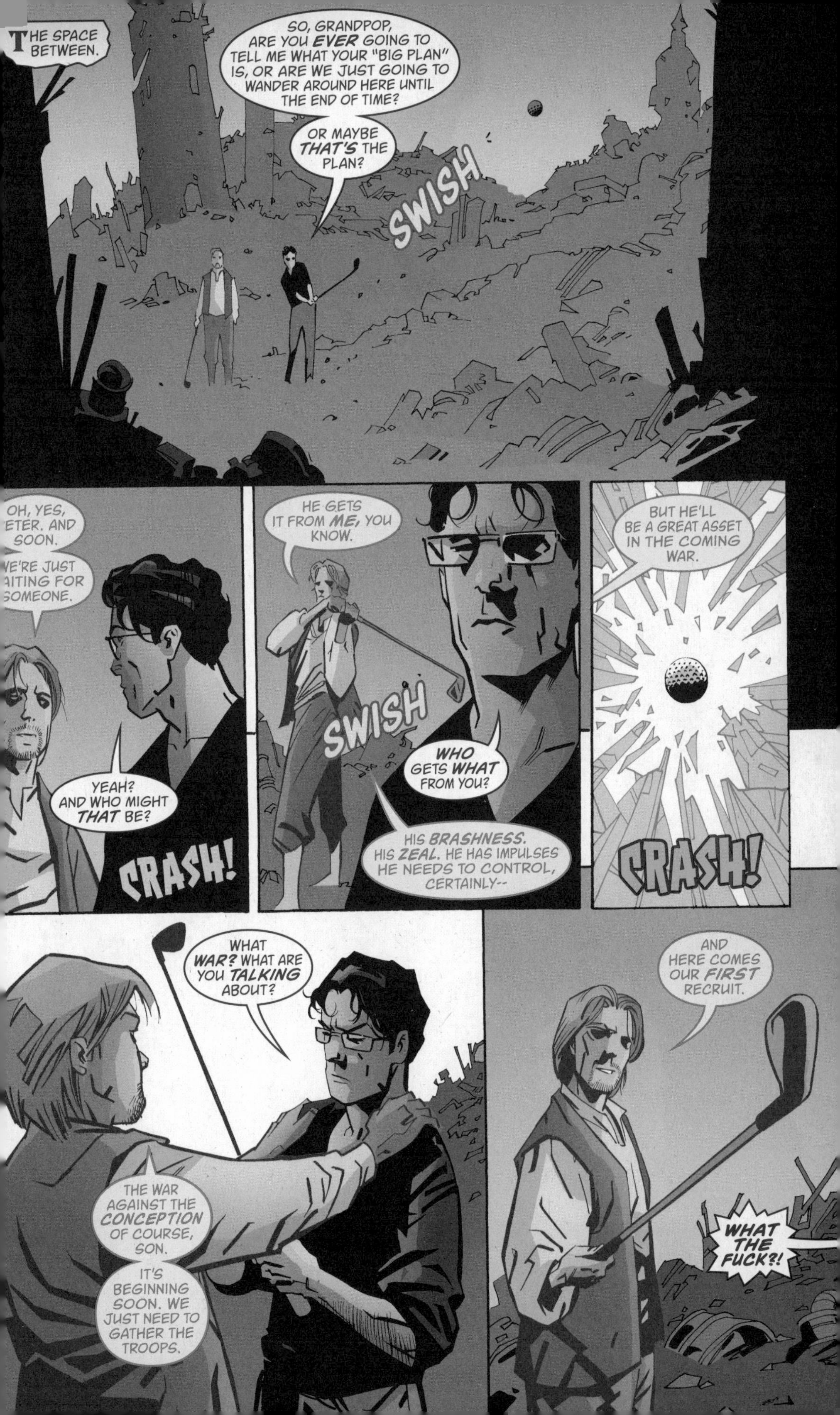
THE SPACE BETWEEN.
SO, GRANDPOP, ARE YOU EVER GOING TO TELL ME WHAT YOUR "BIG PLAN" IS, OR ARE WE JUST GOING TO WANDER AROUND HERE UNTIL THE END OF TIME?
OR MAYBE THAT'S THE PLAN?
SWISH
OH, YES, ETER. AND SOON.
E'RE JUST AITING FOR SOMEONE.
YEAH? AND WHO MIGHT THAT BE?
CRASH!
HE GETS IT FROM ME, YOU KNOW.
SWISH
WHO GETS WHAT FROM YOU?
HIS BRASHNESS. HIS ZEAL. HE HAS IMPULSES HE NEEDS TO CONTROL, CERTAINLY--
BUT HE'LL BE A GREAT ASSET IN THE COMING WAR.
CRASH!
WHAT WAR? WHAT ARE YOU TALKING ABOUT?
THE WAR AGAINST THE CONCEPTION OF COURSE, SON.
IT'S BEGINNING SOON. WE JUST NEED TO GATHER THE TROOPS.
AND HERE COMES OUR FIRST RECRUIT.
WHAT THE FUCK?!

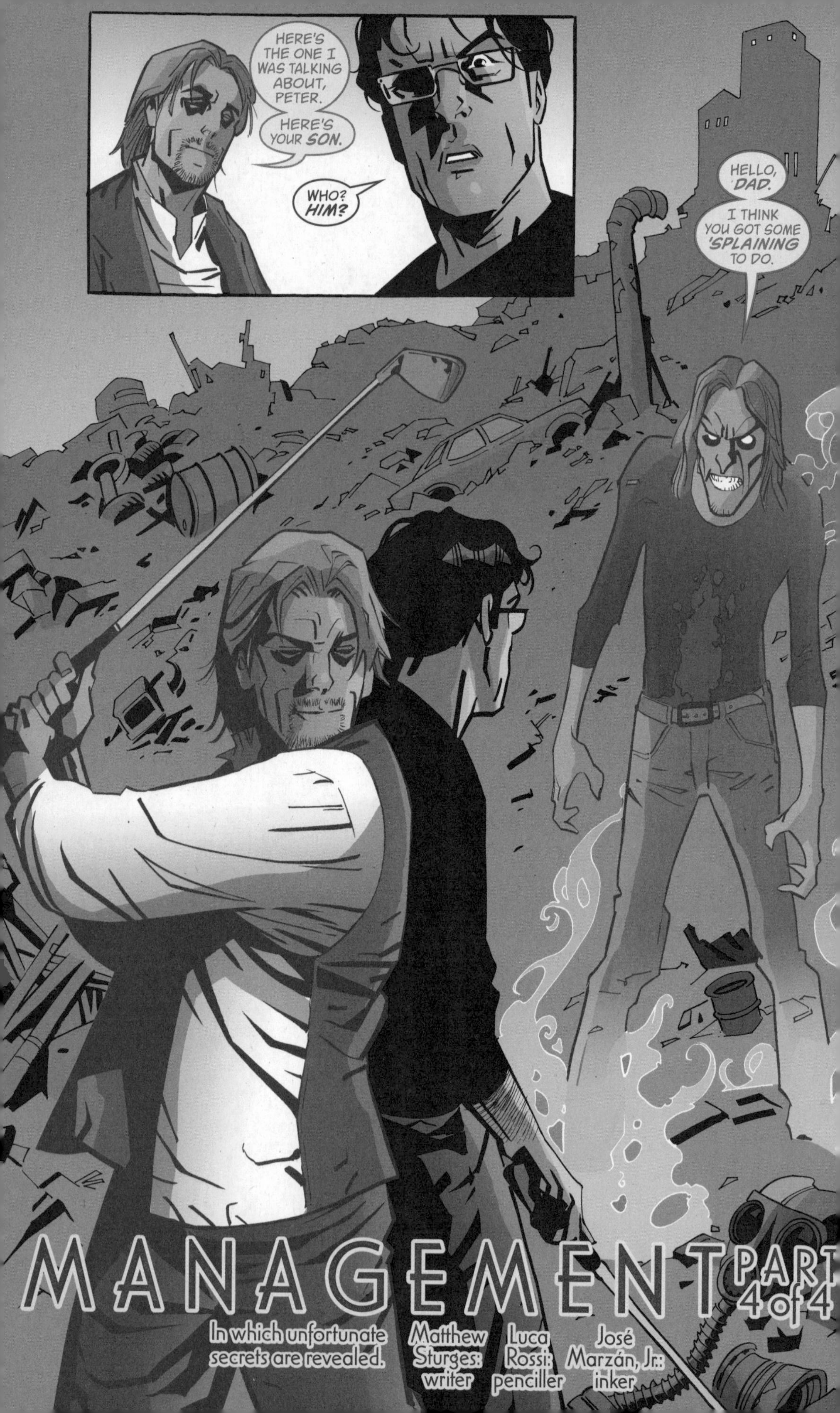
HERE'S THE ONE I WAS TALKING ABOUT, PETER.
HERE'S YOUR SON.
WHO? HIM?
HELLO, DAD.
I THINK YOU GOT SOME 'SPLAINING TO DO.
MANAGEMENT PART 4 of 4
In which unfortunate secrets are revealed.
Matthew Sturges: writer
Luca Rossi: penciller
José Marzán, Jr.: inker

OPEN ON A STREET SCENE IN FLORENCE, ITALY. IT'S MORNING.

CUE MUSIC: SOMETHING FUNKY WITH A BEAT TO IT. ENGLISH LYRICS SO WE KNOW THIS ISN'T ONE OF THOSE FOREIGN FILMS WHERE YOU HAVE TO READ.

MY WHOLE LIFE IS THE OPENING SEQUENCE OF A ROMANTIC COMEDY.

PENSIONE ZANNE

YES, MOM, I'M *GOING* TO BE AT THE WEDDING.

PUSH IN ON MY ROOM AT THE PENSIONE. I'VE COME TO FLORENCE FOR MY SISTER'S WEDDING.

IT GOES WITHOUT SAYING THAT I'M DUE FOR A ROMANTIC ENCOUNTER, BUT SO FAR NO SUCH LUCK.

YES, MOTHER, OF *COURSE* I HAVE A DATE.

TURNS OUT I *DON'T* HAVE A DATE TO MY SISTER'S WEDDING.

WE'VE ALL BEEN THERE. RIGHT, LADIES?

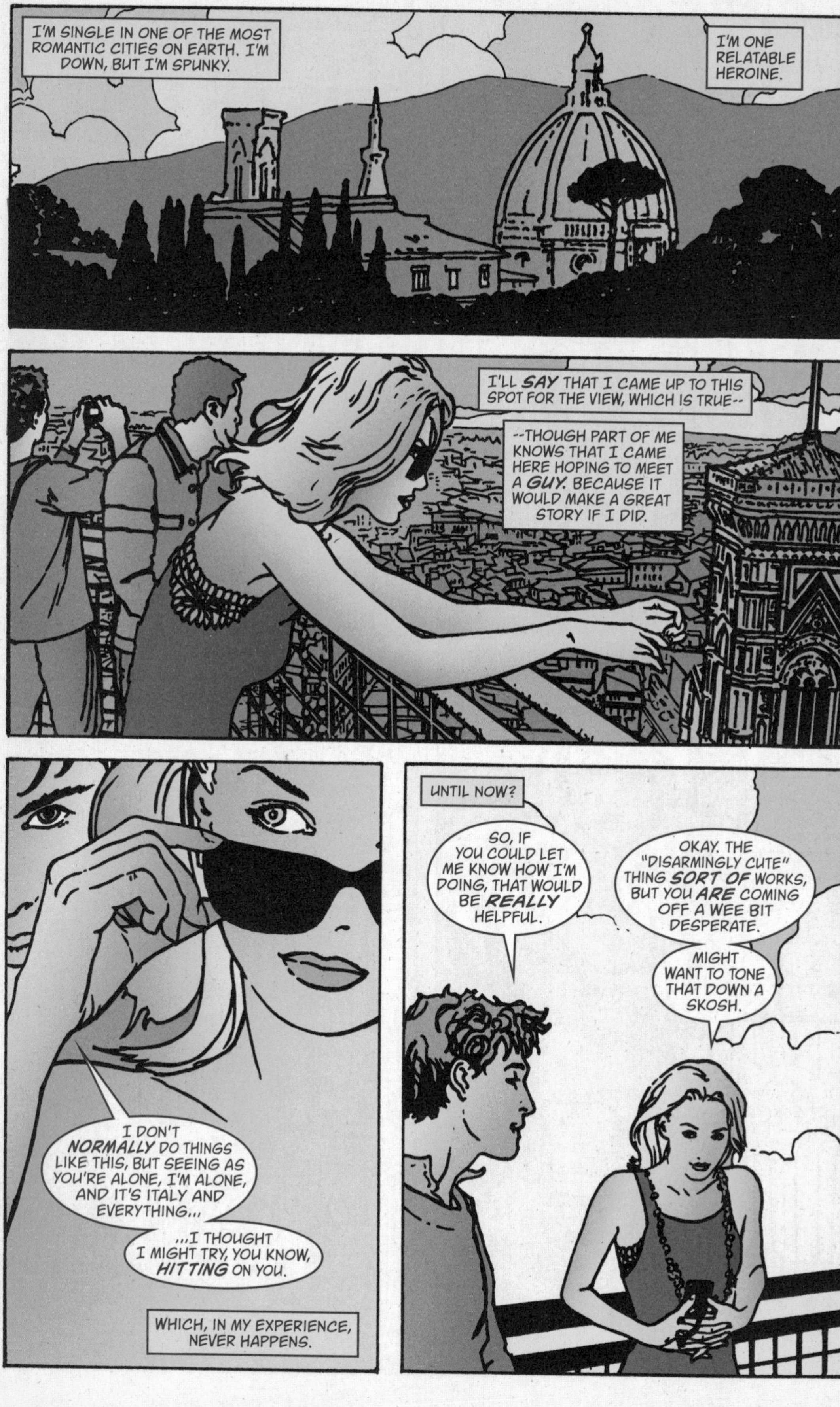
I'M SINGLE IN ONE OF THE MOST ROMANTIC CITIES ON EARTH. I'M DOWN, BUT I'M SPUNKY.
I'M ONE RELATABLE HEROINE.
I'LL SAY THAT I CAME UP TO THIS SPOT FOR THE VIEW, WHICH IS TRUE--
--THOUGH PART OF ME KNOWS THAT I CAME HERE HOPING TO MEET A GUY. BECAUSE IT WOULD MAKE A GREAT STORY IF I DID.
I DON'T NORMALLY DO THINGS LIKE THIS, BUT SEEING AS YOU'RE ALONE, I'M ALONE, AND IT'S ITALY AND EVERYTHING...
...I THOUGHT I MIGHT TRY, YOU KNOW, HITTING ON YOU.
WHICH, IN MY EXPERIENCE, NEVER HAPPENS.
UNTIL NOW?
SO, IF YOU COULD LET ME KNOW HOW I'M DOING, THAT WOULD BE REALLY HELPFUL.
OKAY. THE "DISARMINGLY CUTE" THING SORT OF WORKS, BUT YOU ARE COMING OFF A WEE BIT DESPERATE.
MIGHT WANT TO TONE THAT DOWN A SKOSH.

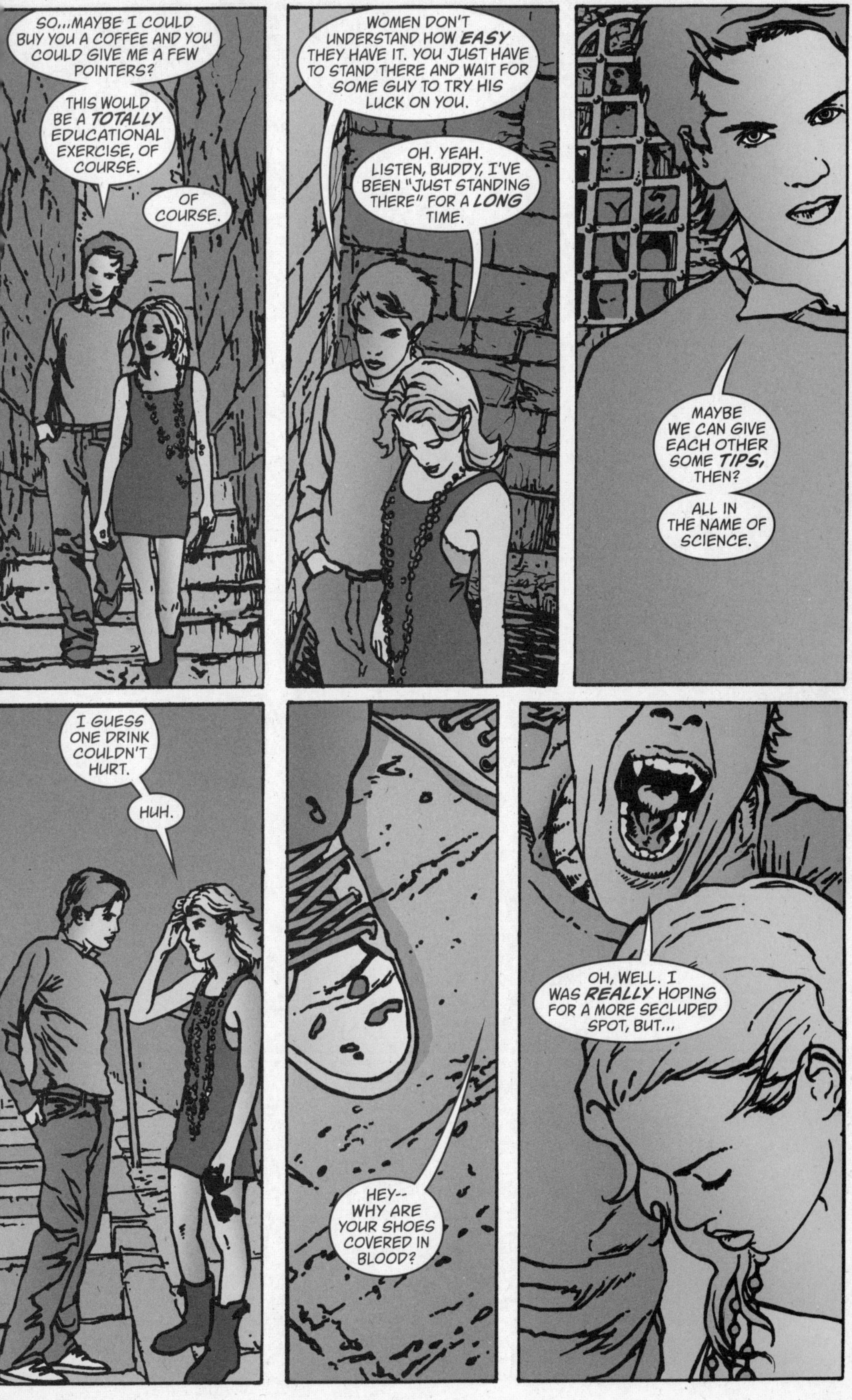
SO...MAYBE I COULD BUY YOU A COFFEE AND YOU COULD GIVE ME A FEW POINTERS?
THIS WOULD BE A TOTALLY EDUCATIONAL EXERCISE, OF COURSE.
OF COURSE.
WOMEN DON'T UNDERSTAND HOW EASY THEY HAVE IT. YOU JUST HAVE TO STAND THERE AND WAIT FOR SOME GUY TO TRY HIS LUCK ON YOU.
OH. YEAH. LISTEN, BUDDY, I'VE BEEN "JUST STANDING THERE" FOR A LONG TIME.
MAYBE WE CAN GIVE EACH OTHER SOME TIPS, THEN?
ALL IN THE NAME OF SCIENCE.
I GUESS ONE DRINK COULDN'T HURT.
HUH.
HEY-- WHY ARE YOUR SHOES COVERED IN BLOOD?
OH, WELL. I WAS REALLY HOPING FOR A MORE SECLUDED SPOT, BUT...

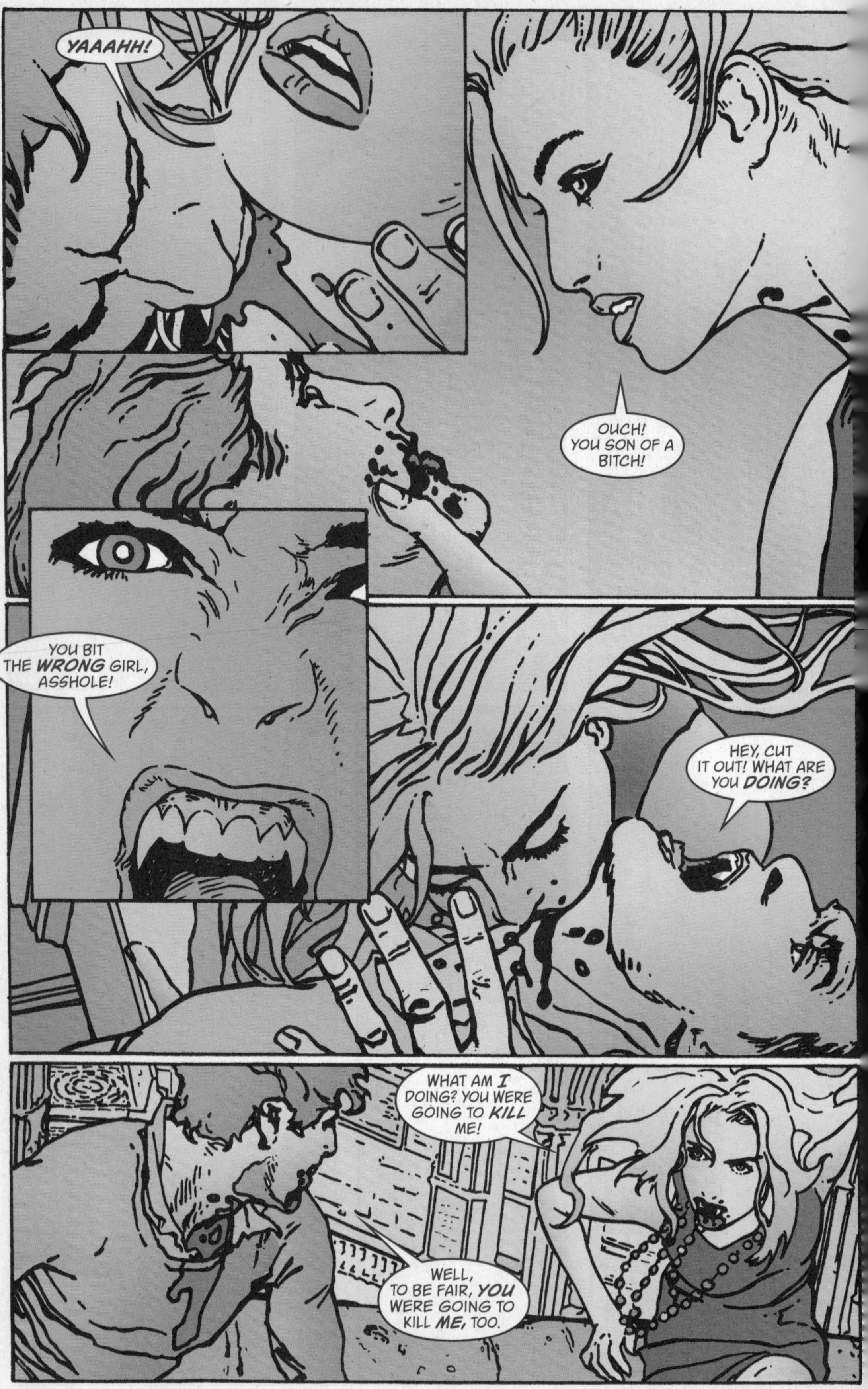
YAAAHH!
OUCH! YOU SON OF A BITCH!
YOU BIT THE WRONG GIRL, ASSHOLE!
HEY, CUT IT OUT! WHAT ARE YOU DOING?
WHAT AM I DOING? YOU WERE GOING TO KILL ME!
WELL, TO BE FAIR, YOU WERE GOING TO KILL ME, TOO.

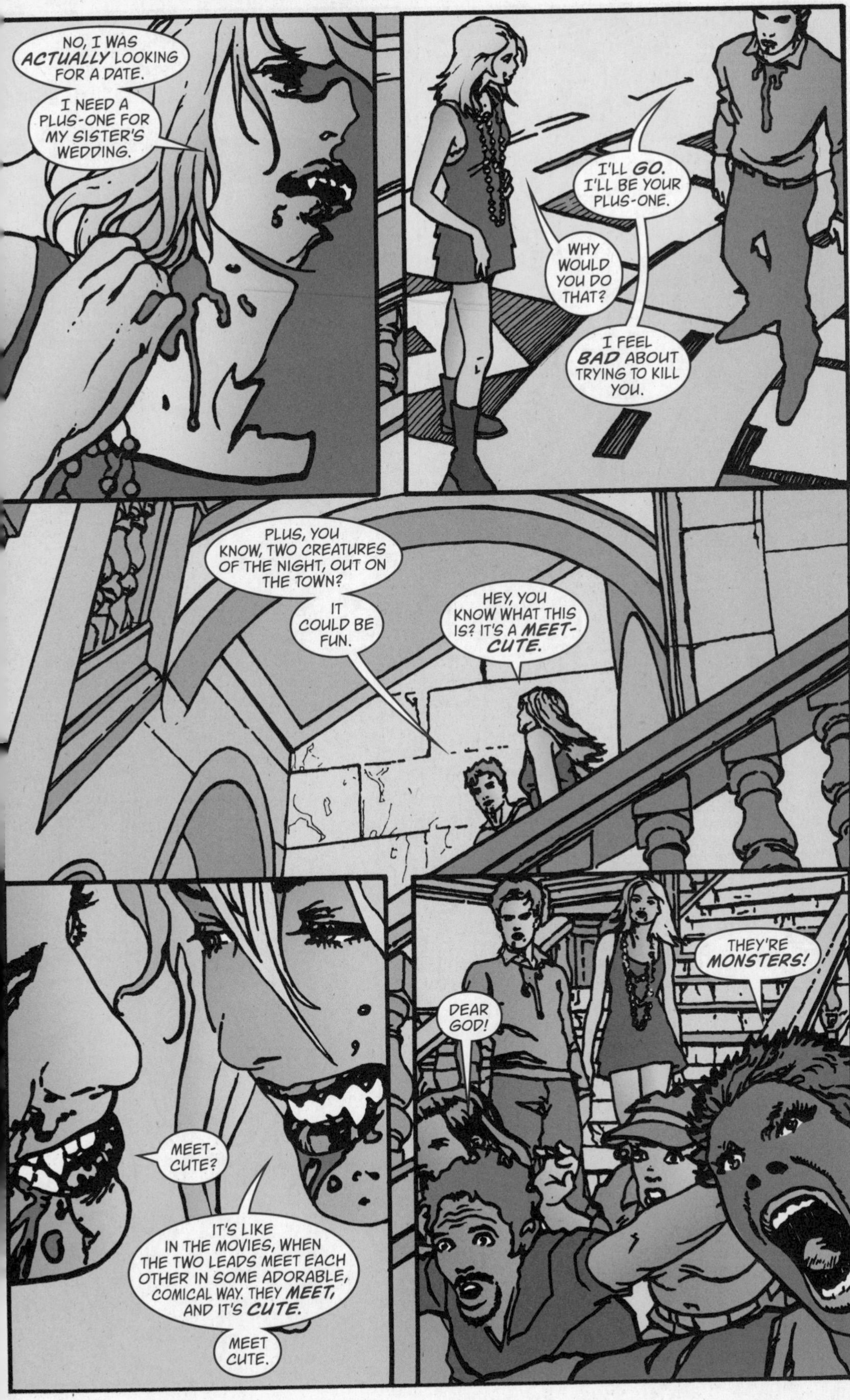
NO, I WAS *ACTUALLY* LOOKING FOR A DATE.
I NEED A PLUS-ONE FOR MY SISTER'S WEDDING.
I'LL *GO.* I'LL BE YOUR PLUS-ONE.
WHY WOULD YOU DO THAT?
I FEEL *BAD* ABOUT TRYING TO KILL YOU.
PLUS, YOU KNOW, TWO CREATURES OF THE NIGHT, OUT ON THE TOWN?
IT COULD BE FUN.
HEY, YOU KNOW WHAT THIS IS? IT'S A *MEET-CUTE.*
MEET-CUTE?
IT'S LIKE IN THE MOVIES, WHEN THE TWO LEADS MEET EACH OTHER IN SOME ADORABLE, COMICAL WAY. THEY *MEET,* AND IT'S *CUTE.*
MEET CUTE.
THEY'RE *MONSTERS!*
DEAR GOD!

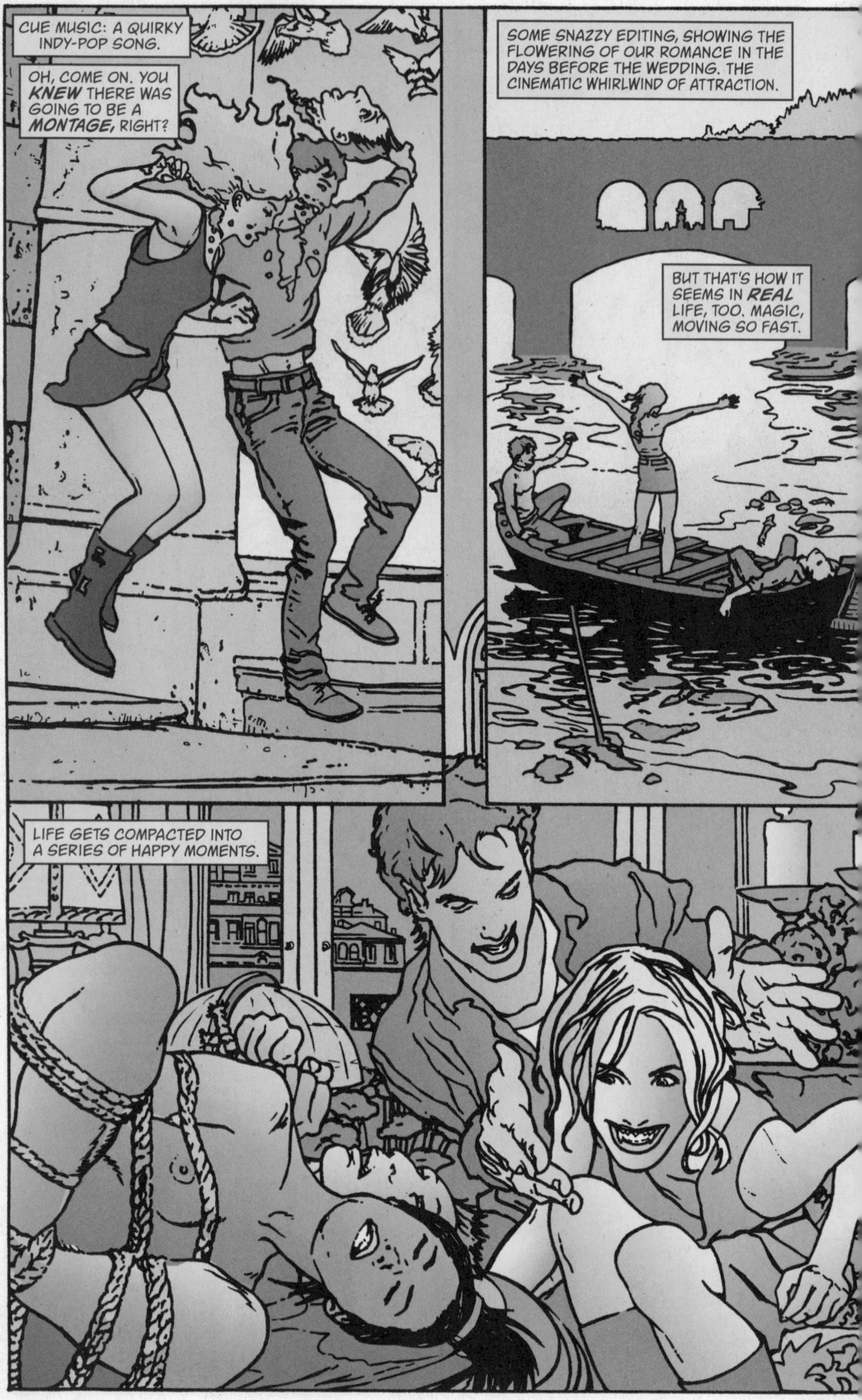
CUE MUSIC: A QUIRKY INDY-POP SONG.
OH, COME ON. YOU *KNEW* THERE WAS GOING TO BE A *MONTAGE,* RIGHT?
SOME SNAZZY EDITING, SHOWING THE FLOWERING OF OUR ROMANCE IN THE DAYS BEFORE THE WEDDING. THE CINEMATIC WHIRLWIND OF ATTRACTION.
BUT THAT'S HOW IT SEEMS IN *REAL* LIFE, TOO. MAGIC, MOVING SO FAST.
LIFE GETS COMPACTED INTO A SERIES OF HAPPY MOMENTS.

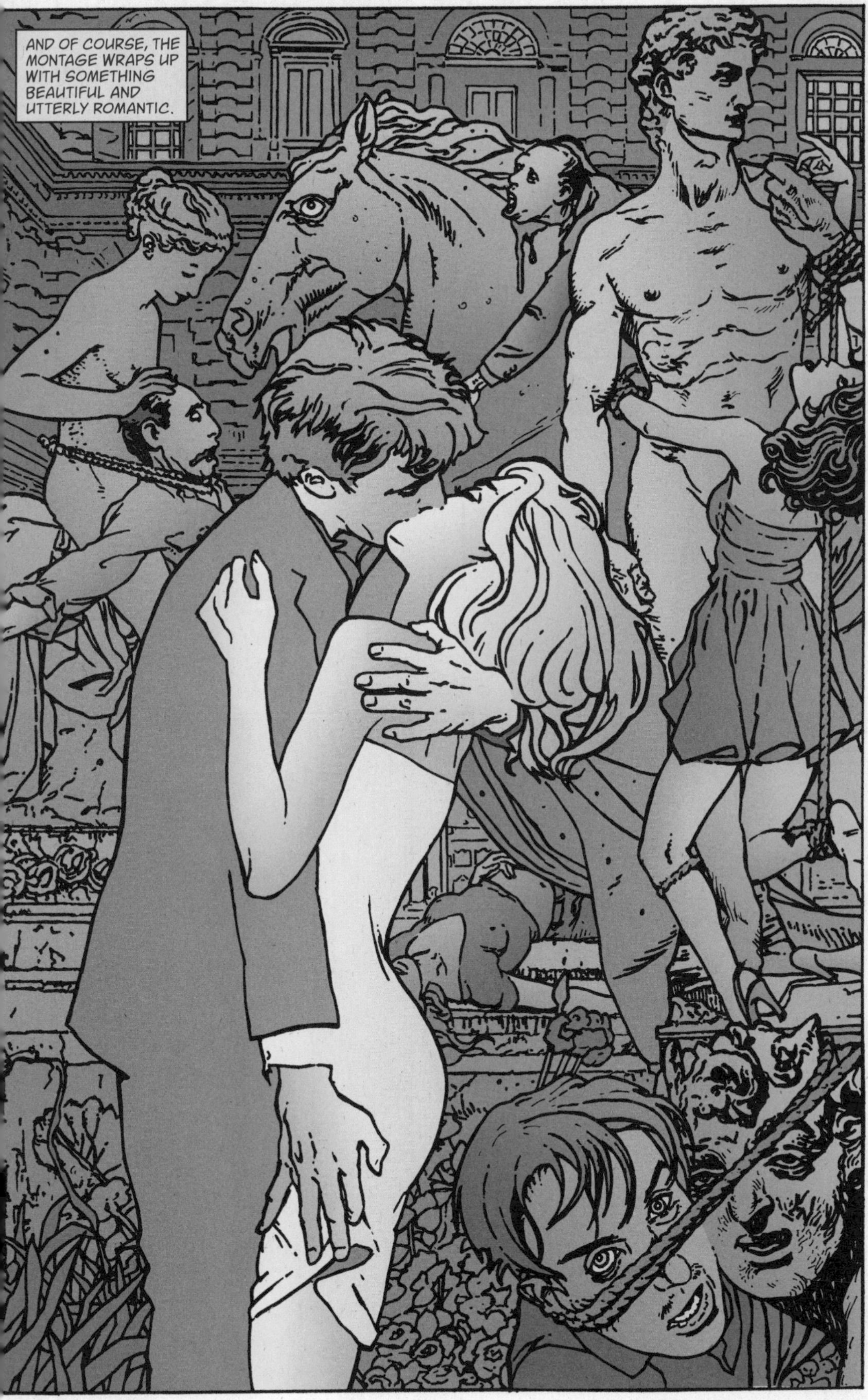
AND OF COURSE, THE MONTAGE WRAPS UP WITH SOMETHING BEAUTIFUL AND UTTERLY ROMANTIC.

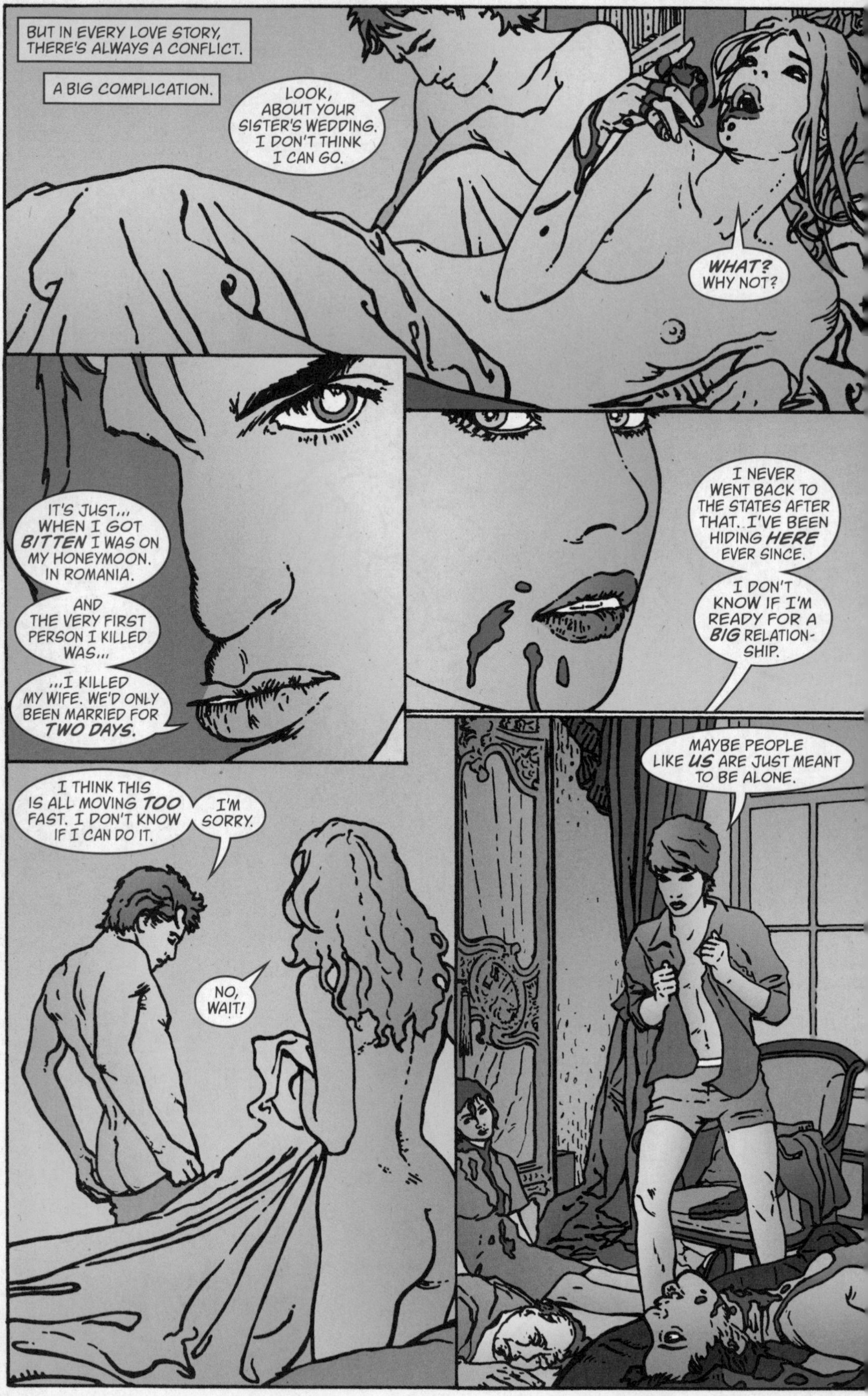
BUT IN EVERY LOVE STORY, THERE'S ALWAYS A CONFLICT.
A BIG COMPLICATION.
LOOK, ABOUT YOUR SISTER'S WEDDING. I DON'T THINK I CAN GO.
WHAT? WHY NOT?
IT'S JUST... WHEN I GOT BITTEN I WAS ON MY HONEYMOON. IN ROMANIA.
AND THE VERY FIRST PERSON I KILLED WAS...
...I KILLED MY WIFE. WE'D ONLY BEEN MARRIED FOR TWO DAYS.
I NEVER WENT BACK TO THE STATES AFTER THAT. I'VE BEEN HIDING HERE EVER SINCE.
I DON'T KNOW IF I'M READY FOR A BIG RELATIONSHIP.
I THINK THIS IS ALL MOVING TOO FAST. I DON'T KNOW IF I CAN DO IT.
I'M SORRY.
NO, WAIT!
MAYBE PEOPLE LIKE US ARE JUST MEANT TO BE ALONE.

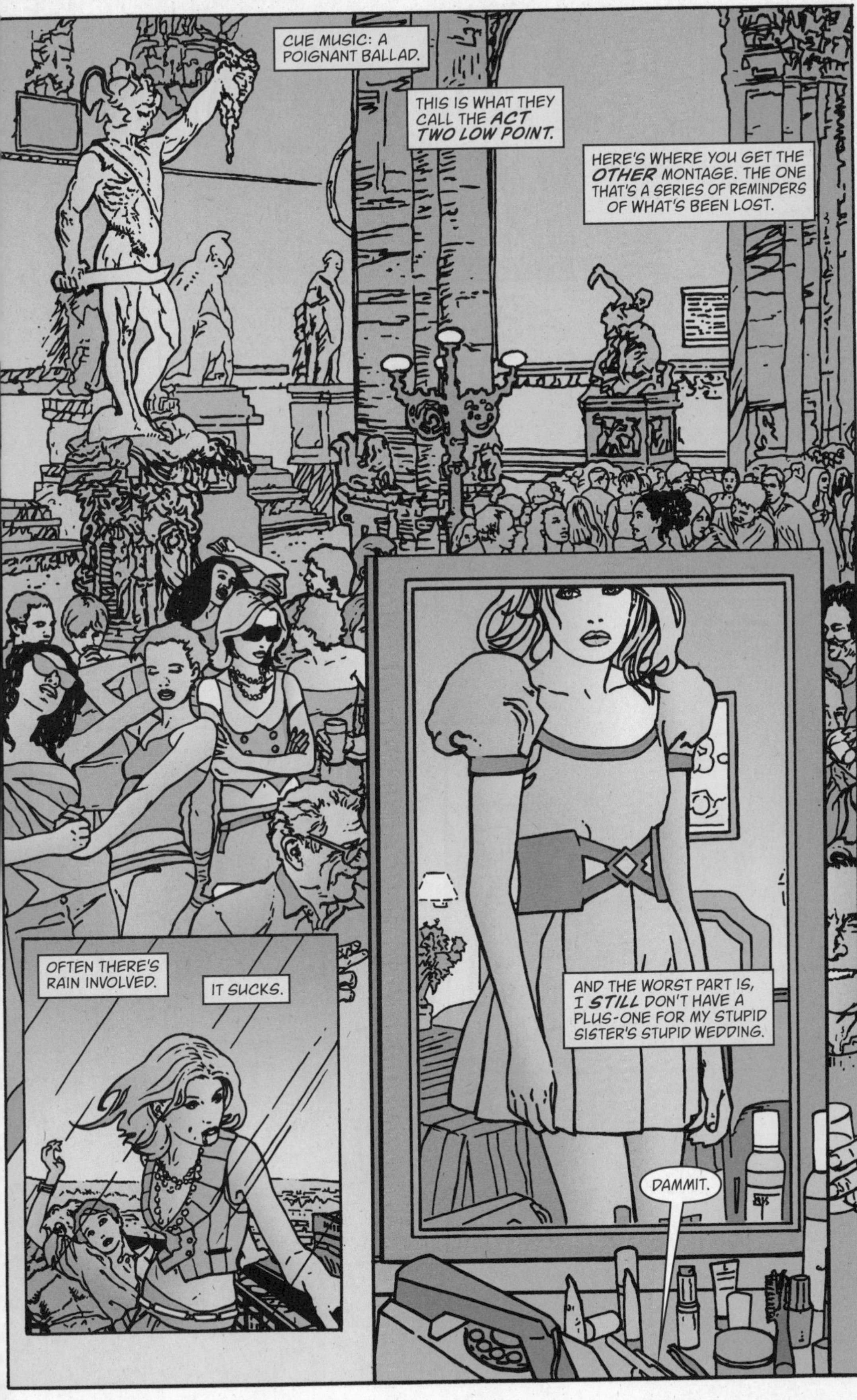
CUE MUSIC: A POIGNANT BALLAD.
THIS IS WHAT THEY CALL THE ACT TWO LOW POINT.
HERE'S WHERE YOU GET THE OTHER MONTAGE. THE ONE THAT'S A SERIES OF REMINDERS OF WHAT'S BEEN LOST.
OFTEN THERE'S RAIN INVOLVED.
IT SUCKS.
AND THE WORST PART IS, I STILL DON'T HAVE A PLUS-ONE FOR MY STUPID SISTER'S STUPID WEDDING.
DAMMIT.

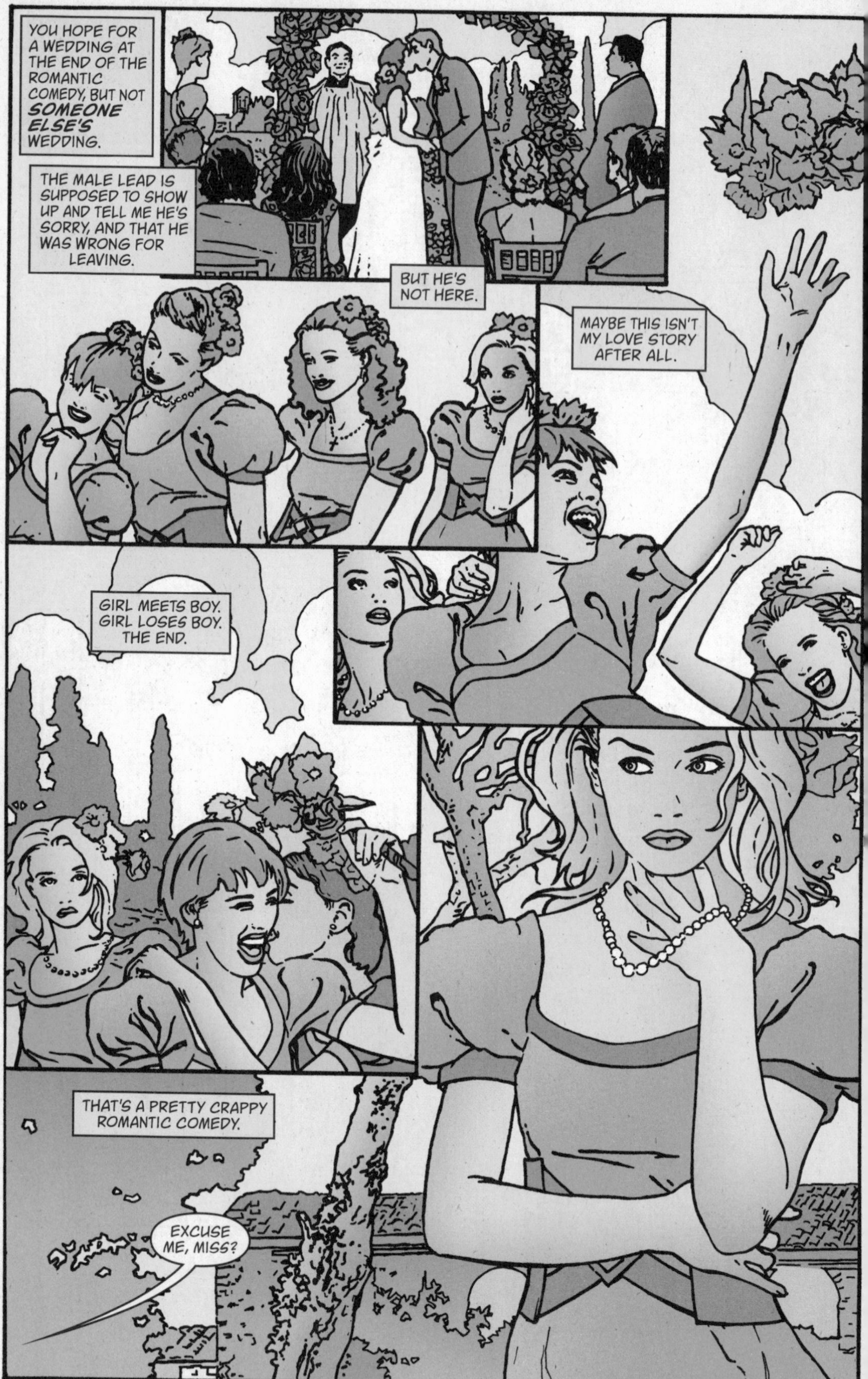
YOU HOPE FOR A WEDDING AT THE END OF THE ROMANTIC COMEDY, BUT NOT **SOMEONE ELSE'S** WEDDING.
THE MALE LEAD IS SUPPOSED TO SHOW UP AND TELL ME HE'S SORRY, AND THAT HE WAS WRONG FOR LEAVING.
BUT HE'S NOT HERE.
MAYBE THIS ISN'T MY LOVE STORY AFTER ALL.
GIRL MEETS BOY. GIRL LOSES BOY. THE END.
THAT'S A PRETTY CRAPPY ROMANTIC COMEDY.
EXCUSE ME, MISS?

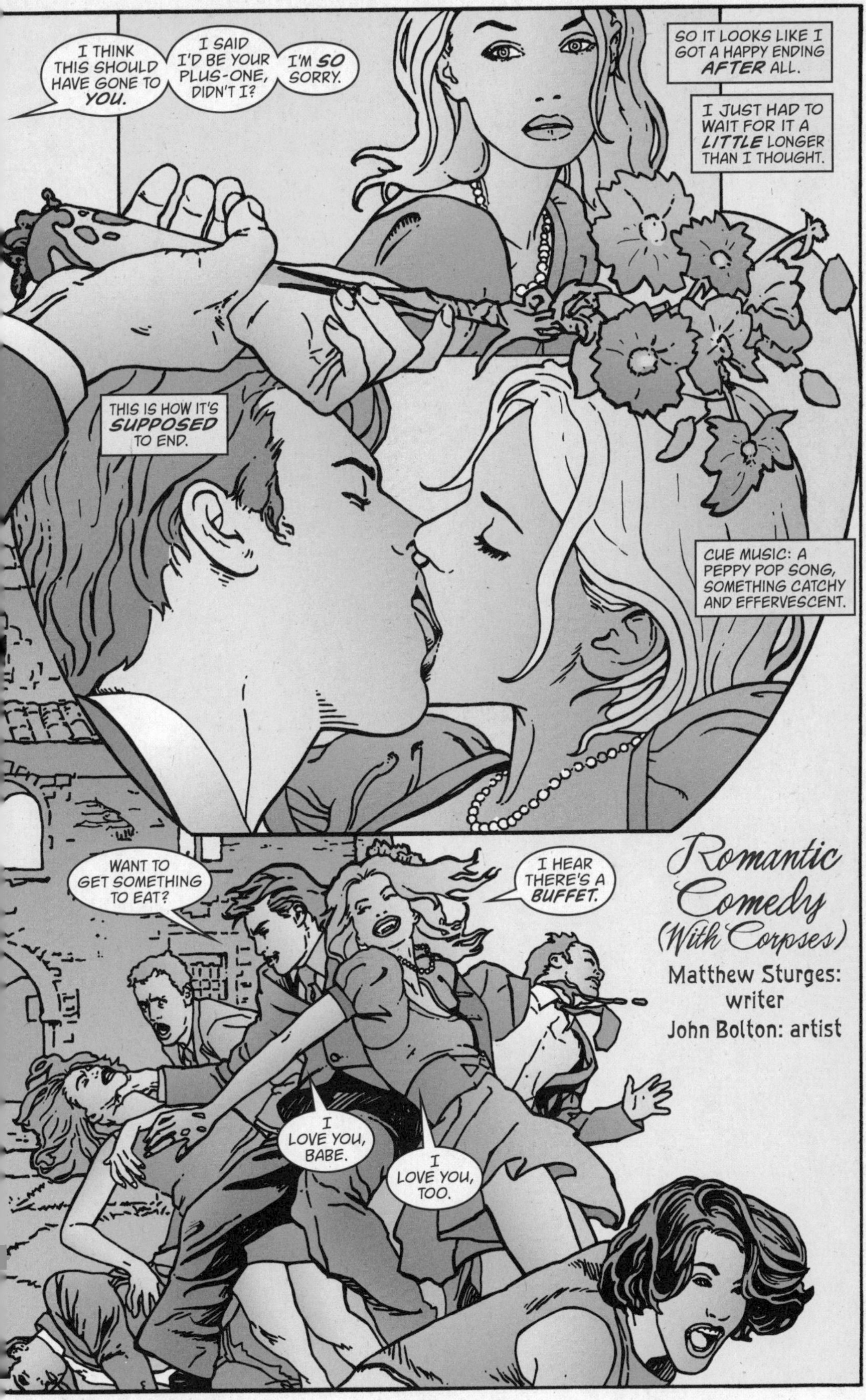
I THINK THIS SHOULD HAVE GONE TO YOU.
I SAID I'D BE YOUR PLUS-ONE, DIDN'T I?
I'M SO SORRY.
SO IT LOOKS LIKE I GOT A HAPPY ENDING AFTER ALL.
I JUST HAD TO WAIT FOR IT A LITTLE LONGER THAN I THOUGHT.
THIS IS HOW IT'S SUPPOSED TO END.
CUE MUSIC: A PEPPY POP SONG, SOMETHING CATCHY AND EFFERVESCENT.
WANT TO GET SOMETHING TO EAT?
I HEAR THERE'S A BUFFET.
Romantic Comedy (With Corpses)
Matthew Sturges: writer
John Bolton: artist
I LOVE YOU, BABE.
I LOVE YOU, TOO.

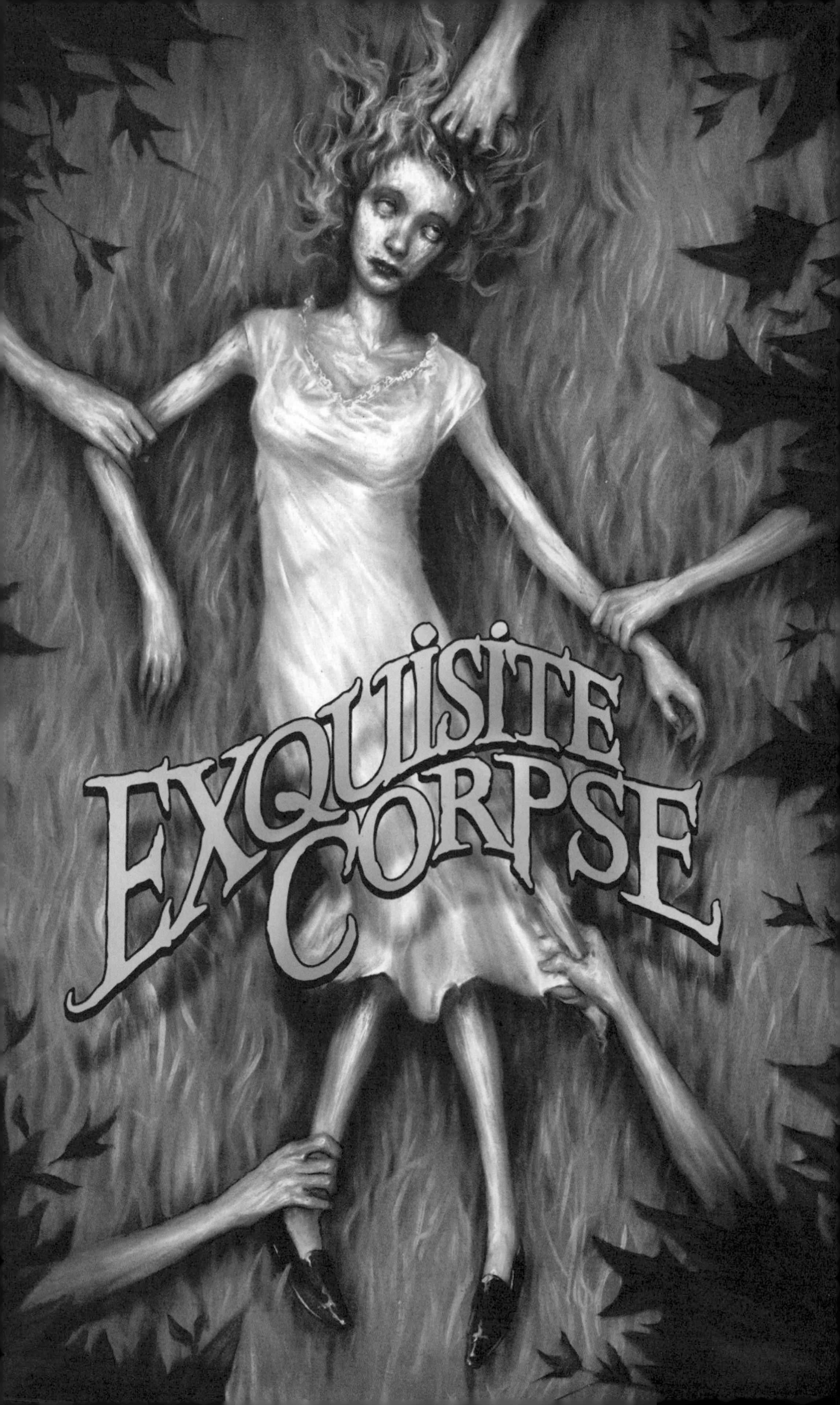
EXQUISITE
CORPSE

"YOU PEOPLE WITH YOUR QUESTS
ANNOY THE PANTS OFF ME."

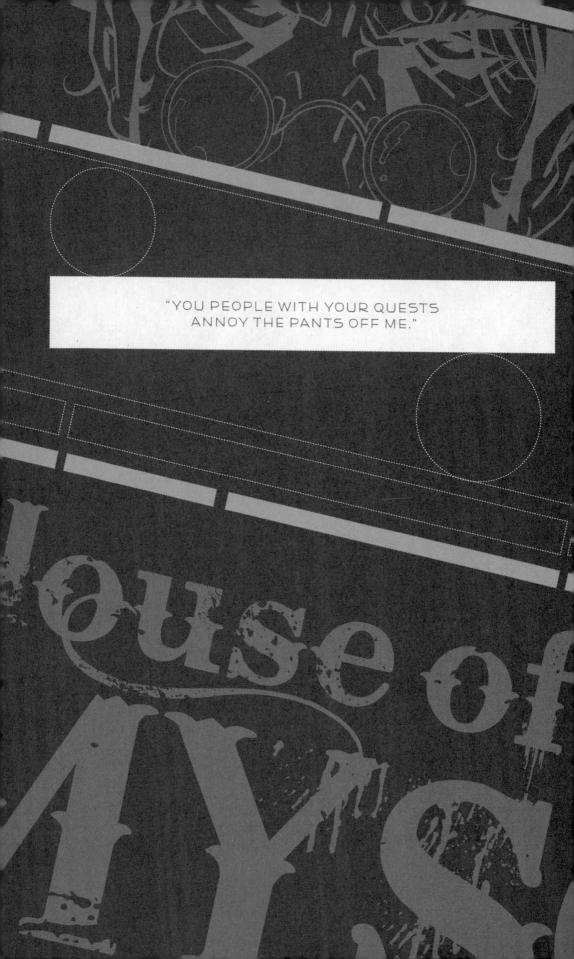

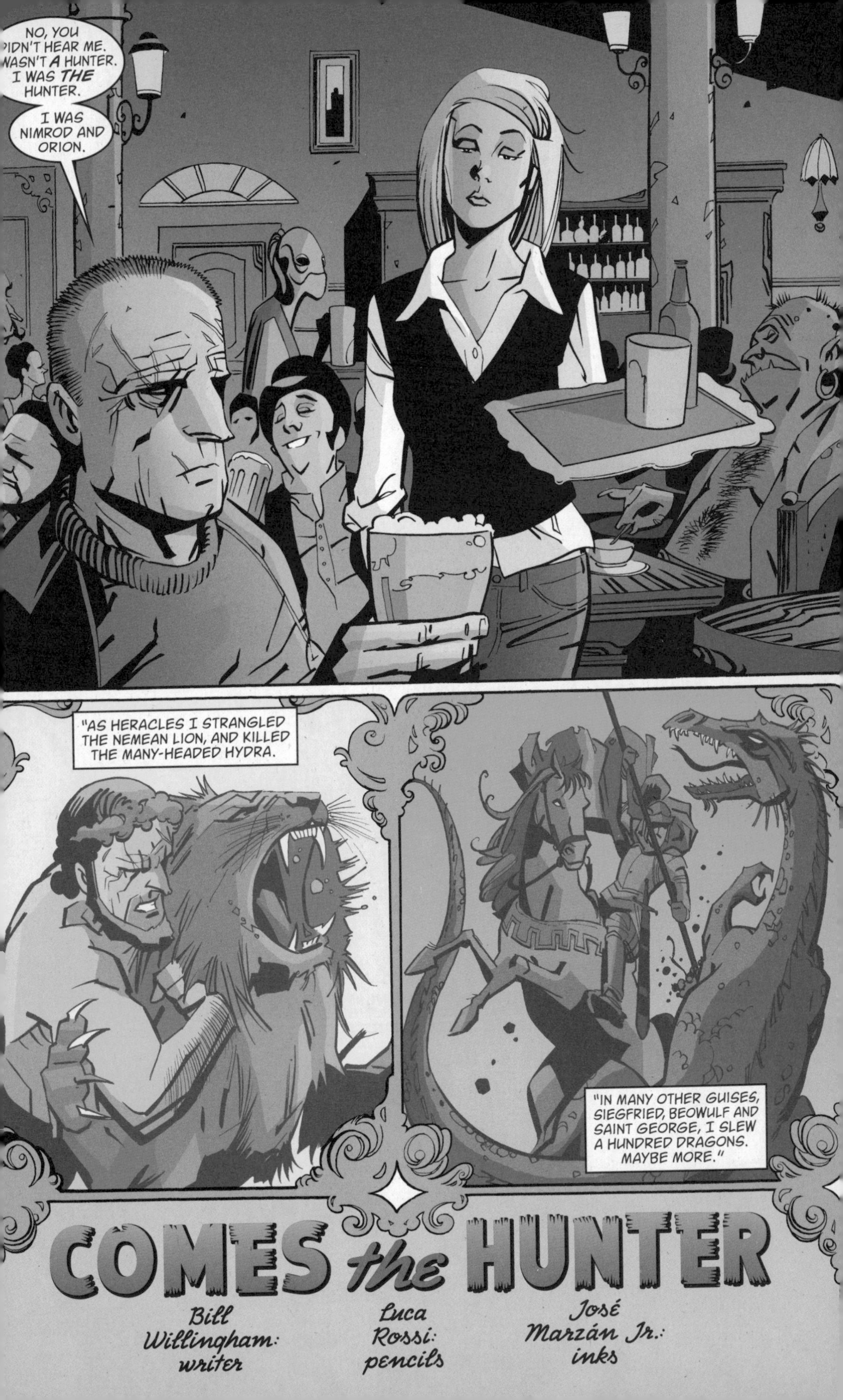

NO, YOU DIDN'T HEAR ME. I WASN'T A HUNTER. I WAS THE HUNTER.
I WAS NIMROD AND ORION.
"AS HERACLES I STRANGLED THE NEMEAN LION, AND KILLED THE MANY-HEADED HYDRA.
"IN MANY OTHER GUISES, SIEGFRIED, BEOWULF AND SAINT GEORGE, I SLEW A HUNDRED DRAGONS. MAYBE MORE."
COMES the HUNTER
Bill Willingham: writer
Luca Rossi: pencils
José Marzán Jr.: inks

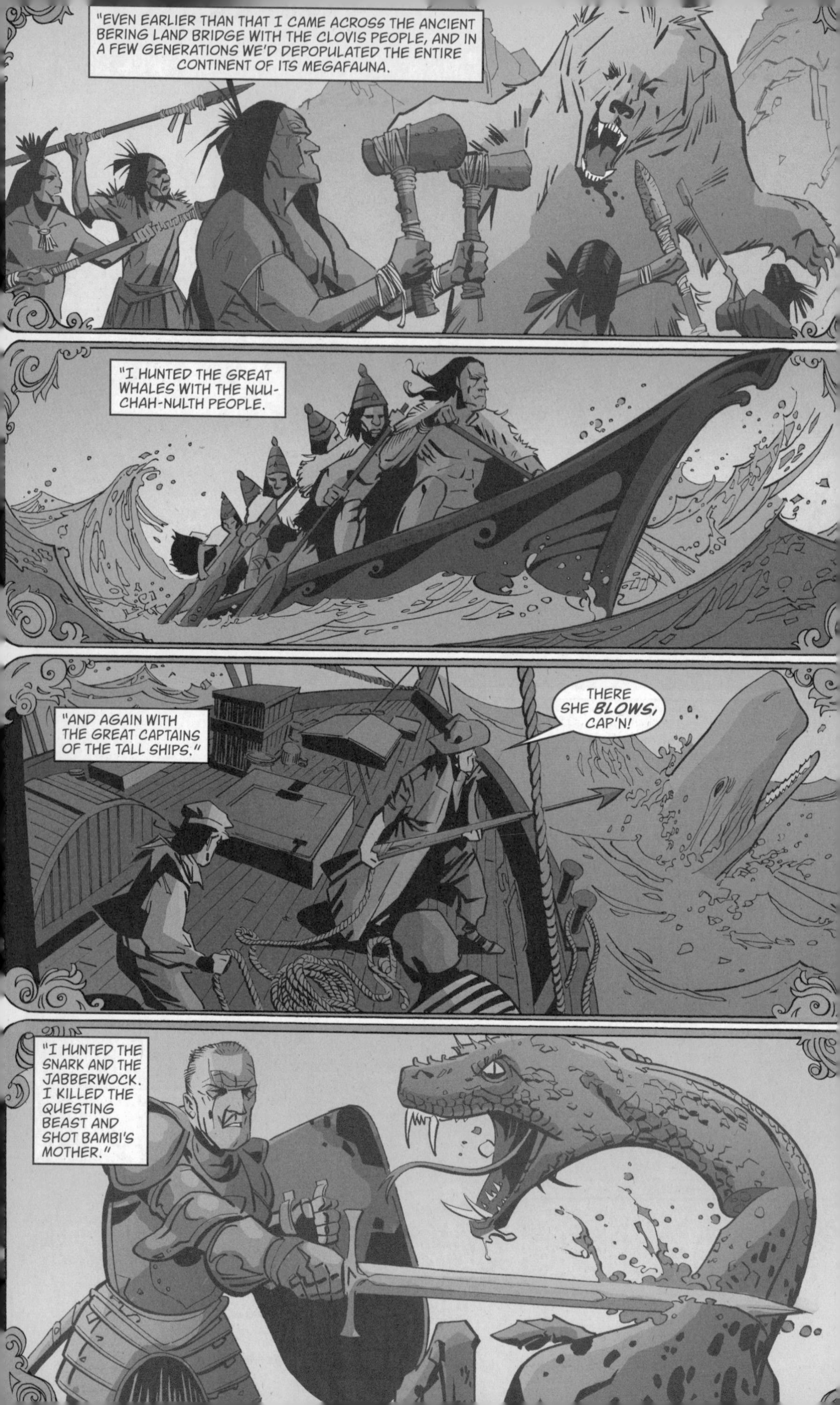
"EVEN EARLIER THAN THAT I CAME ACROSS THE ANCIENT BERING LAND BRIDGE WITH THE CLOVIS PEOPLE, AND IN A FEW GENERATIONS WE'D DEPOPULATED THE ENTIRE CONTINENT OF ITS MEGAFAUNA.
"I HUNTED THE GREAT WHALES WITH THE NUU-CHAH-NULTH PEOPLE.
"AND AGAIN WITH THE GREAT CAPTAINS OF THE TALL SHIPS."
THERE SHE BLOWS, CAP'N!
"I HUNTED THE SNARK AND THE JABBERWOCK. I KILLED THE QUESTING BEAST AND SHOT BAMBI'S MOTHER."

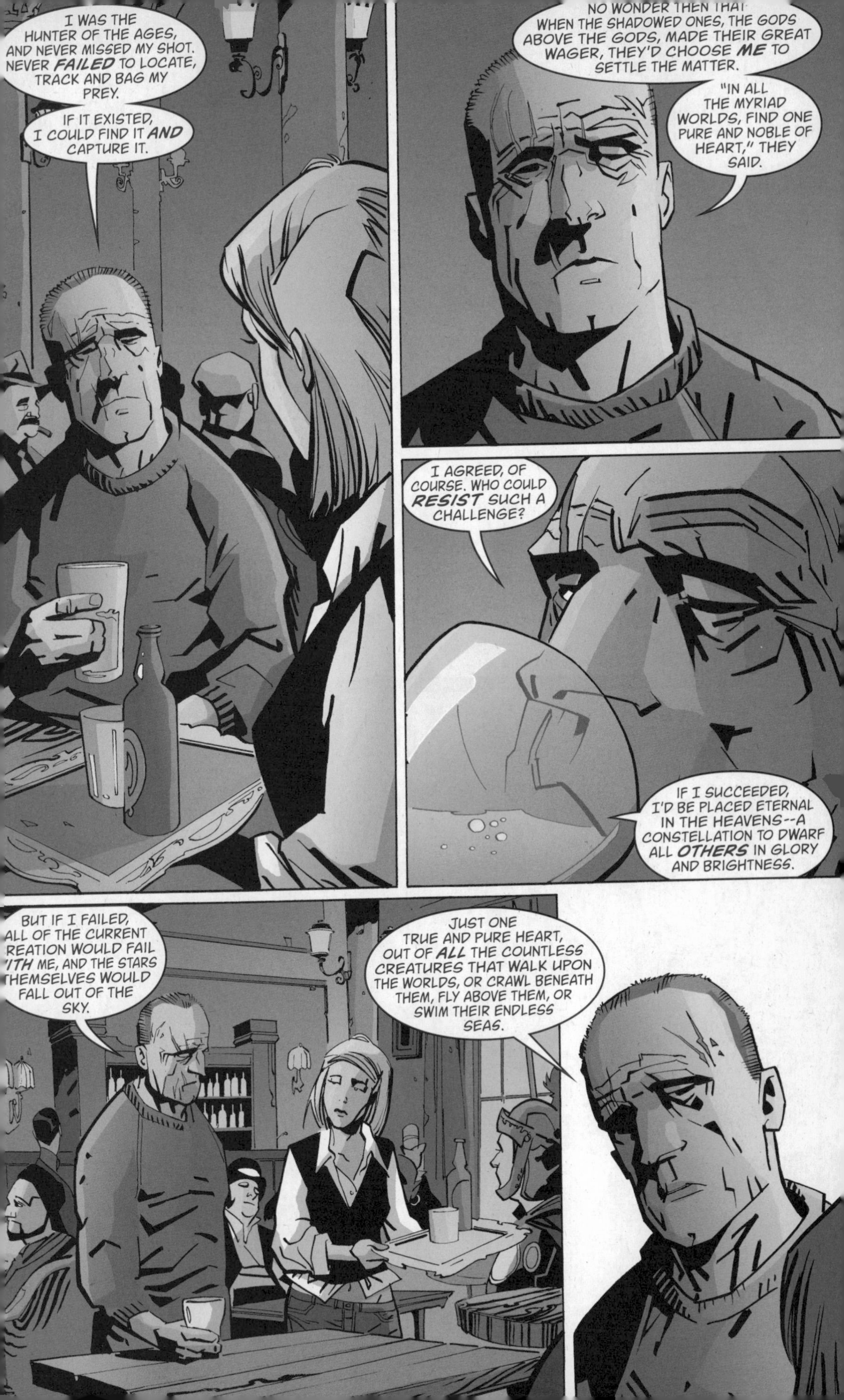
I WAS THE HUNTER OF THE AGES, AND NEVER MISSED MY SHOT. NEVER FAILED TO LOCATE, TRACK AND BAG MY PREY.
IF IT EXISTED, I COULD FIND IT AND CAPTURE IT.
NO WONDER THEN THAT WHEN THE SHADOWED ONES, THE GODS ABOVE THE GODS, MADE THEIR GREAT WAGER, THEY'D CHOOSE ME TO SETTLE THE MATTER.
"IN ALL THE MYRIAD WORLDS, FIND ONE PURE AND NOBLE OF HEART," THEY SAID.
I AGREED, OF COURSE. WHO COULD RESIST SUCH A CHALLENGE?
IF I SUCCEEDED, I'D BE PLACED ETERNAL IN THE HEAVENS--A CONSTELLATION TO DWARF ALL OTHERS IN GLORY AND BRIGHTNESS.
BUT IF I FAILED, ALL OF THE CURRENT REATION WOULD FAIL ITH ME, AND THE STARS THEMSELVES WOULD FALL OUT OF THE SKY.
JUST ONE TRUE AND PURE HEART, OUT OF ALL THE COUNTLESS CREATURES THAT WALK UPON THE WORLDS, OR CRAWL BENEATH THEM, FLY ABOVE THEM, OR SWIM THEIR ENDLESS SEAS.

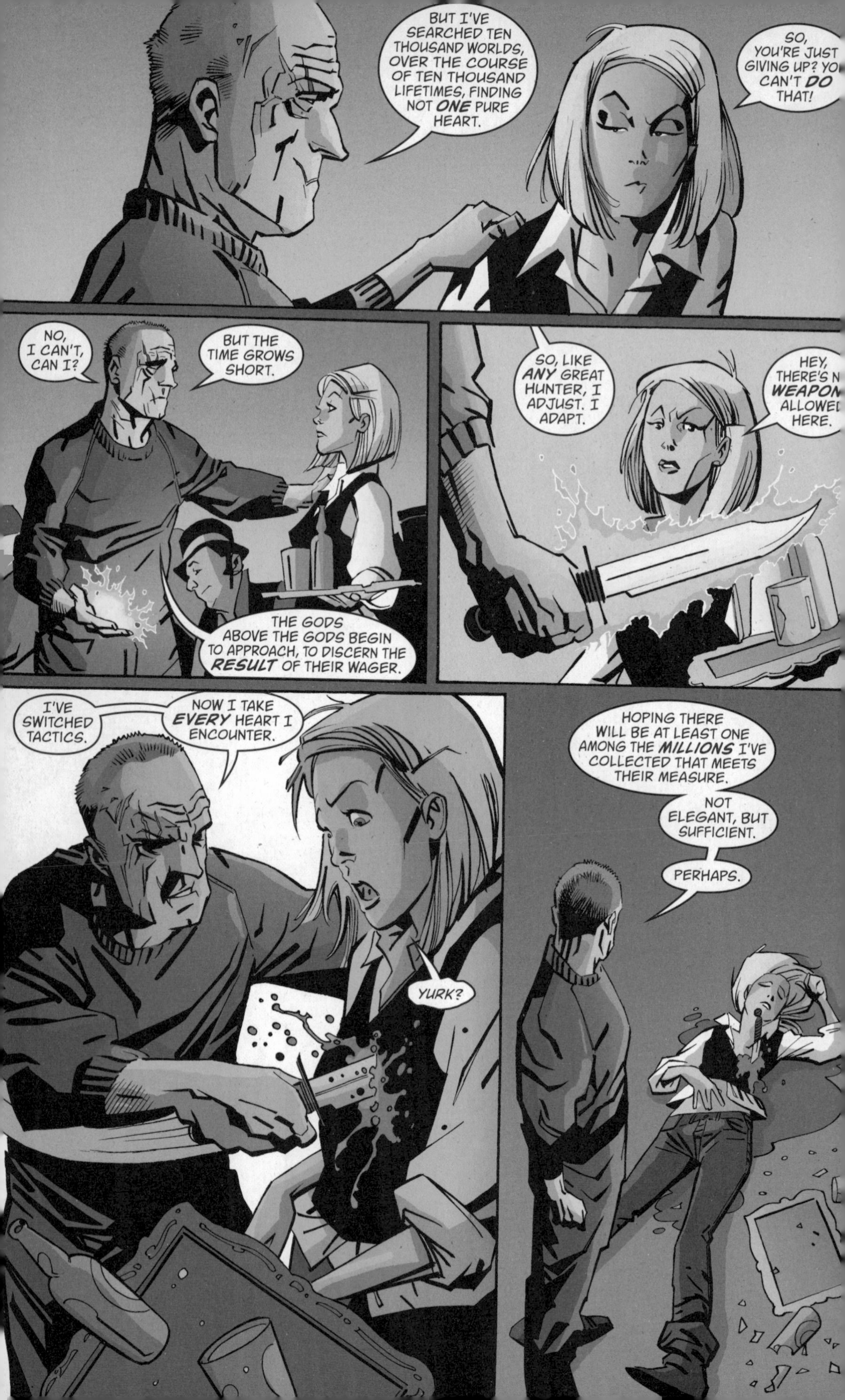
BUT I'VE SEARCHED TEN THOUSAND WORLDS, OVER THE COURSE OF TEN THOUSAND LIFETIMES, FINDING NOT ONE PURE HEART.
SO, YOU'RE JUST GIVING UP? YOU CAN'T DO THAT!
NO, I CAN'T, CAN I?
BUT THE TIME GROWS SHORT.
THE GODS ABOVE THE GODS BEGIN TO APPROACH, TO DISCERN THE RESULT OF THEIR WAGER.
SO, LIKE ANY GREAT HUNTER, I ADJUST. I ADAPT.
HEY, THERE'S NO WEAPONS ALLOWED HERE.
I'VE SWITCHED TACTICS.
NOW I TAKE EVERY HEART I ENCOUNTER.
YURK?
HOPING THERE WILL BE AT LEAST ONE AMONG THE MILLIONS I'VE COLLECTED THAT MEETS THEIR MEASURE.
NOT ELEGANT, BUT SUFFICIENT.
PERHAPS.

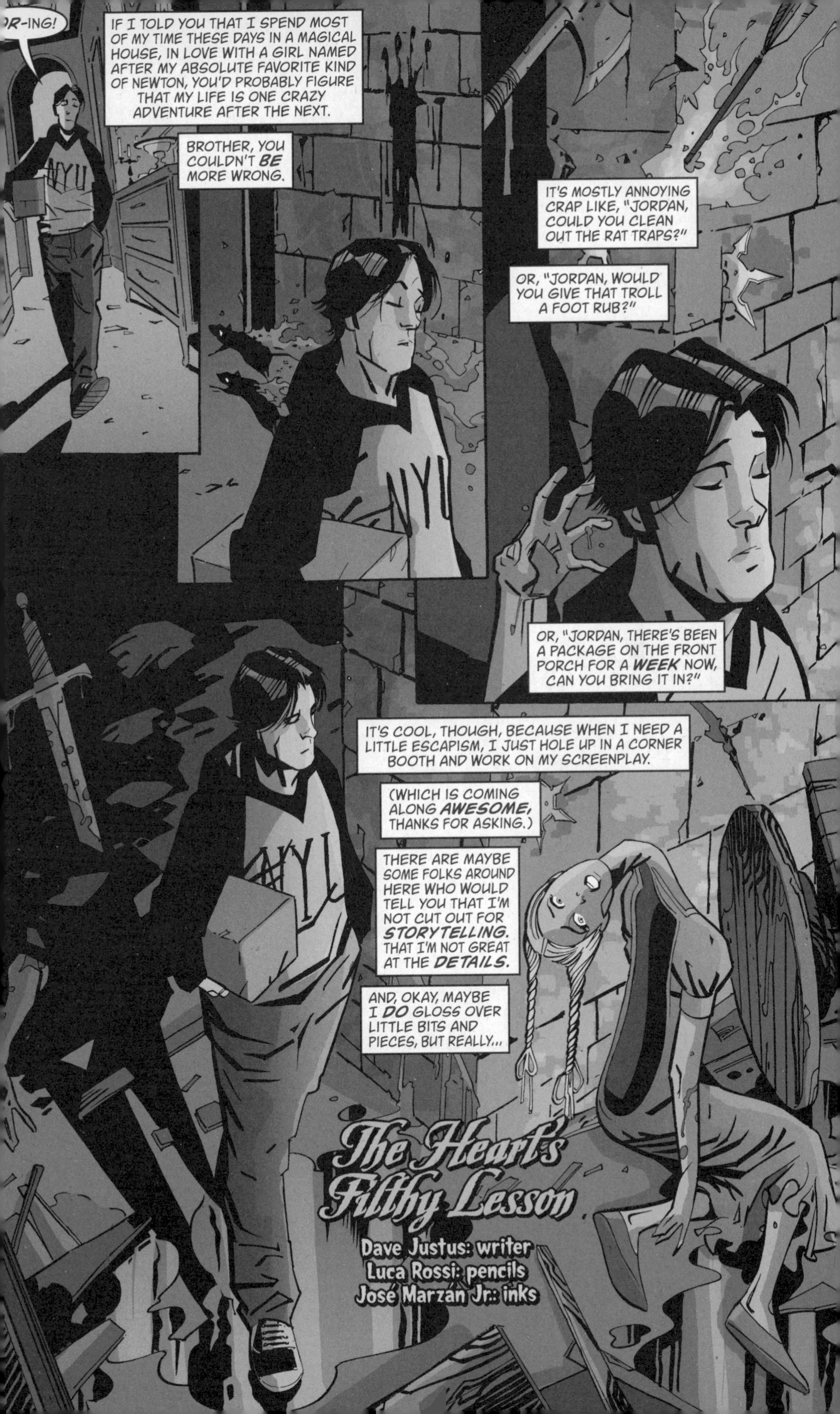

...R-ING!
IF I TOLD YOU THAT I SPEND MOST OF MY TIME THESE DAYS IN A MAGICAL HOUSE, IN LOVE WITH A GIRL NAMED AFTER MY ABSOLUTE FAVORITE KIND OF NEWTON, YOU'D PROBABLY FIGURE THAT MY LIFE IS ONE CRAZY ADVENTURE AFTER THE NEXT.
BROTHER, YOU COULDN'T BE MORE WRONG.
IT'S MOSTLY ANNOYING CRAP LIKE, "JORDAN, COULD YOU CLEAN OUT THE RAT TRAPS?"
OR, "JORDAN, WOULD YOU GIVE THAT TROLL A FOOT RUB?"
OR, "JORDAN, THERE'S BEEN A PACKAGE ON THE FRONT PORCH FOR A WEEK NOW, CAN YOU BRING IT IN?"
IT'S COOL, THOUGH, BECAUSE WHEN I NEED A LITTLE ESCAPISM, I JUST HOLE UP IN A CORNER BOOTH AND WORK ON MY SCREENPLAY.
(WHICH IS COMING ALONG AWESOME, THANKS FOR ASKING.)
THERE ARE MAYBE SOME FOLKS AROUND HERE WHO WOULD TELL YOU THAT I'M NOT CUT OUT FOR STORYTELLING. THAT I'M NOT GREAT AT THE DETAILS.
AND, OKAY, MAYBE I DO GLOSS OVER LITTLE BITS AND PIECES, BUT REALLY...
The Heart's Filthy Lesson
Dave Justus: writer
Luca Rossi: pencils
José Marzán Jr.: inks

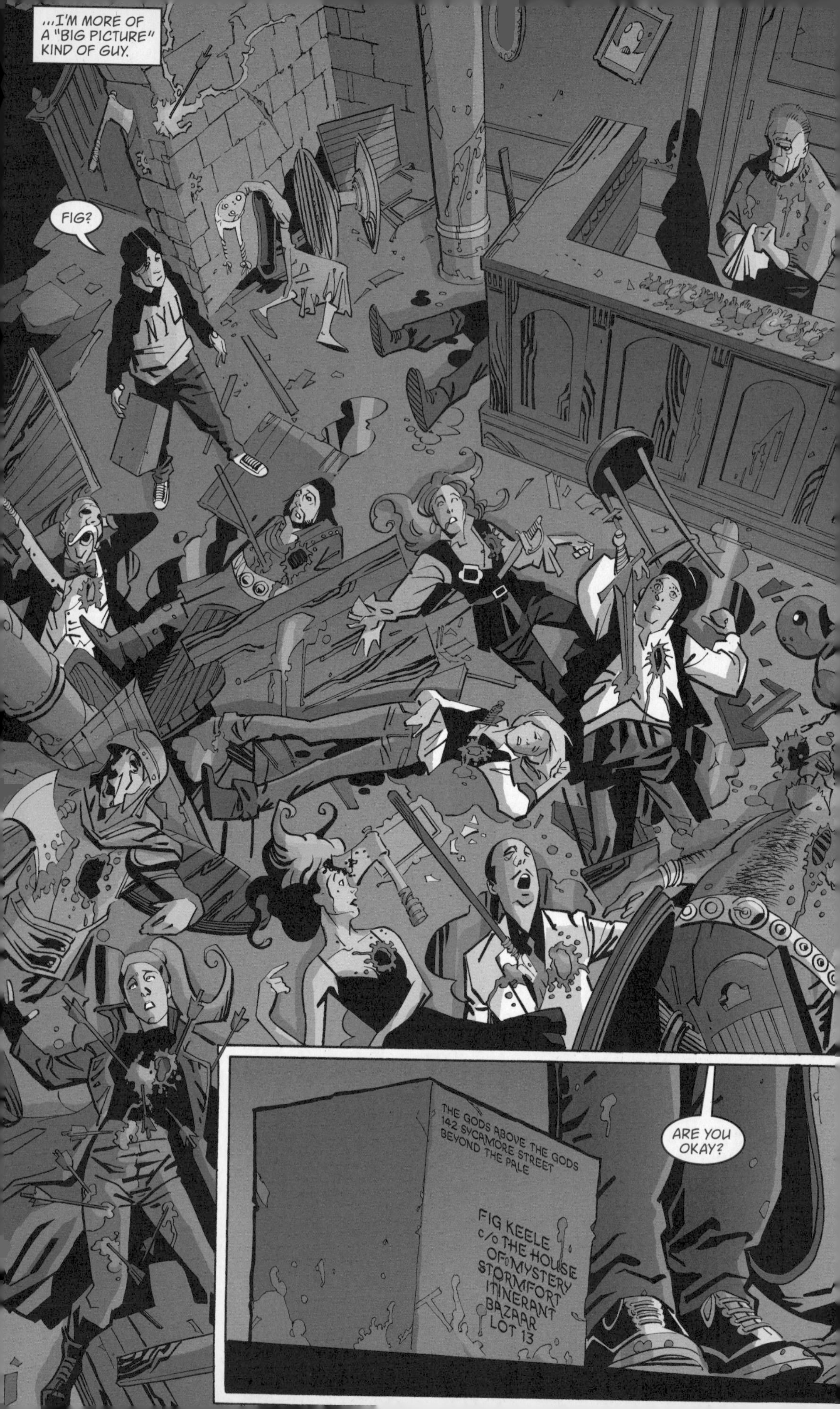
...I'M MORE OF A "BIG PICTURE" KIND OF GUY.
FIG?
ARE YOU OKAY?
THE GODS ABOVE THE GODS
142 SYCAMORE STREET
BEYOND THE PALE
FIG KEELE
c/o THE HOUSE OF MYSTERY
STORMFORT ITINERANT BAZAAR
LOT 13

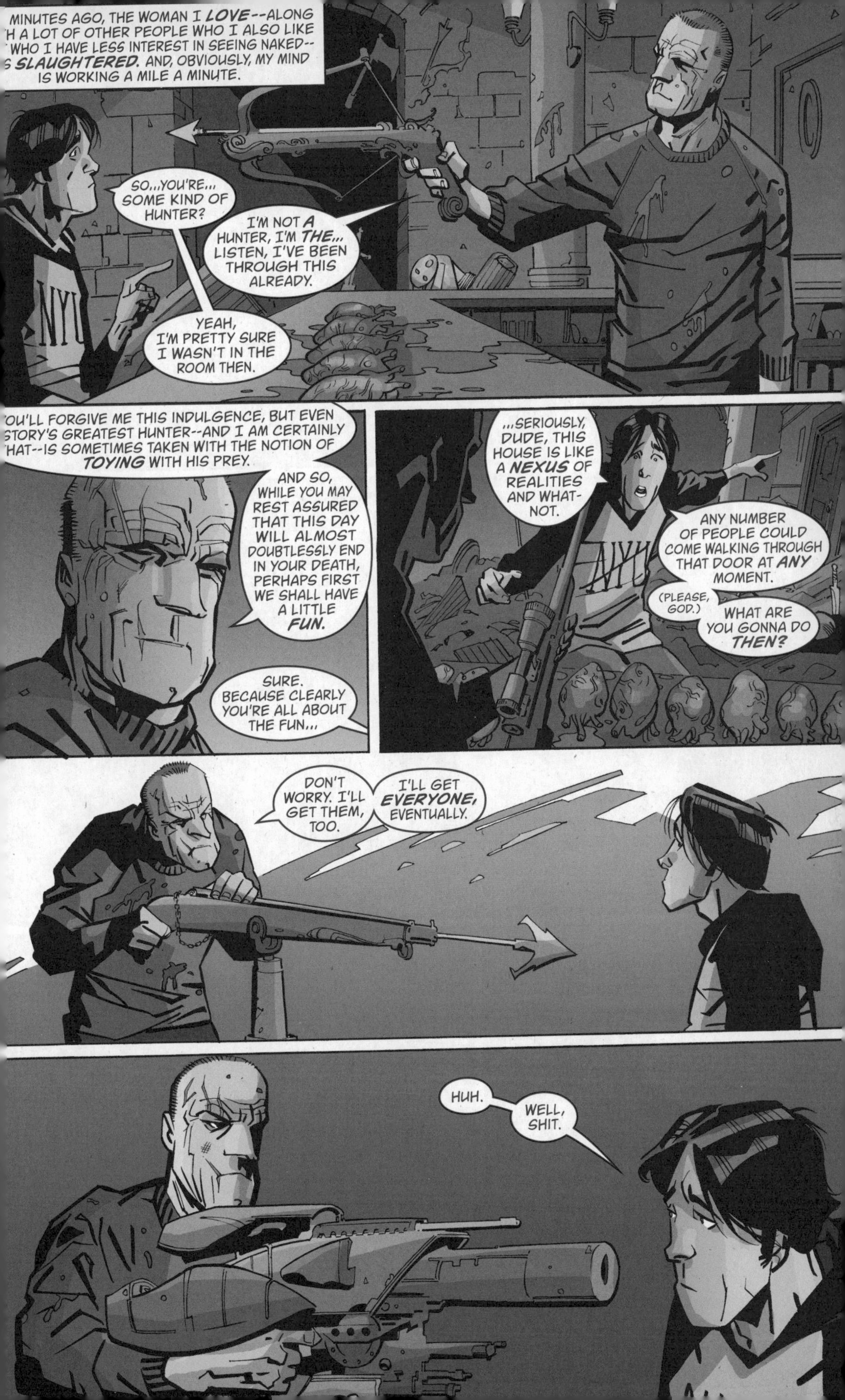
MINUTES AGO, THE WOMAN I LOVE--ALONG
H A LOT OF OTHER PEOPLE WHO I ALSO LIKE
WHO I HAVE LESS INTEREST IN SEEING NAKED--
S SLAUGHTERED. AND, OBVIOUSLY, MY MIND IS WORKING A MILE A MINUTE.
SO...YOU'RE... SOME KIND OF HUNTER?
I'M NOT A HUNTER, I'M THE... LISTEN, I'VE BEEN THROUGH THIS ALREADY.
YEAH, I'M PRETTY SURE I WASN'T IN THE ROOM THEN.
OU'LL FORGIVE ME THIS INDULGENCE, BUT EVEN STORY'S GREATEST HUNTER--AND I AM CERTAINLY HAT--IS SOMETIMES TAKEN WITH THE NOTION OF TOYING WITH HIS PREY.
AND SO, WHILE YOU MAY REST ASSURED THAT THIS DAY WILL ALMOST DOUBTLESSLY END IN YOUR DEATH, PERHAPS FIRST WE SHALL HAVE A LITTLE FUN.
SURE. BECAUSE CLEARLY YOU'RE ALL ABOUT THE FUN...
...SERIOUSLY, DUDE, THIS HOUSE IS LIKE A NEXUS OF REALITIES AND WHAT-NOT.
ANY NUMBER OF PEOPLE COULD COME WALKING THROUGH THAT DOOR AT ANY MOMENT.
(PLEASE, GOD.)
WHAT ARE YOU GONNA DO THEN?
DON'T WORRY. I'LL GET THEM, TOO.
I'LL GET EVERYONE, EVENTUALLY.
HUH.
WELL, SHIT.

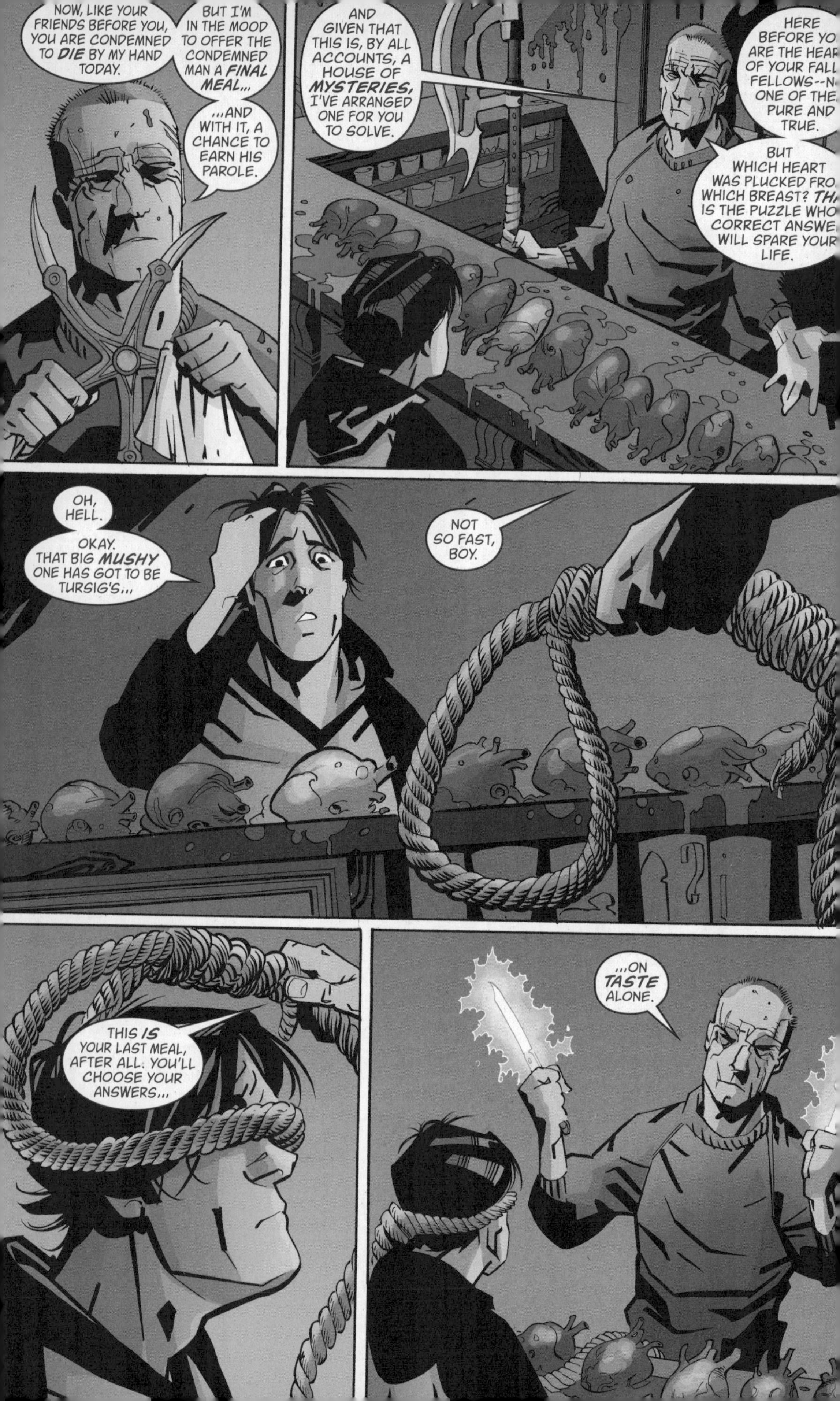
NOW, LIKE YOUR FRIENDS BEFORE YOU, YOU ARE CONDEMNED TO DIE BY MY HAND TODAY.
BUT I'M IN THE MOOD TO OFFER THE CONDEMNED MAN A FINAL MEAL...
...AND WITH IT, A CHANCE TO EARN HIS PAROLE.
AND GIVEN THAT THIS IS, BY ALL ACCOUNTS, A HOUSE OF MYSTERIES, I'VE ARRANGED ONE FOR YOU TO SOLVE.
HERE BEFORE YO ARE THE HEAR OF YOUR FALL FELLOWS--N ONE OF THE PURE AND TRUE.
BUT WHICH HEART WAS PLUCKED FRO WHICH BREAST? TH IS THE PUZZLE WHO CORRECT ANSWE WILL SPARE YOUR LIFE.
OH, HELL.
OKAY. THAT BIG MUSHY ONE HAS GOT TO BE TURSIG'S...
NOT SO FAST, BOY.
THIS IS YOUR LAST MEAL, AFTER ALL. YOU'LL CHOOSE YOUR ANSWERS...
...ON TASTE ALONE.

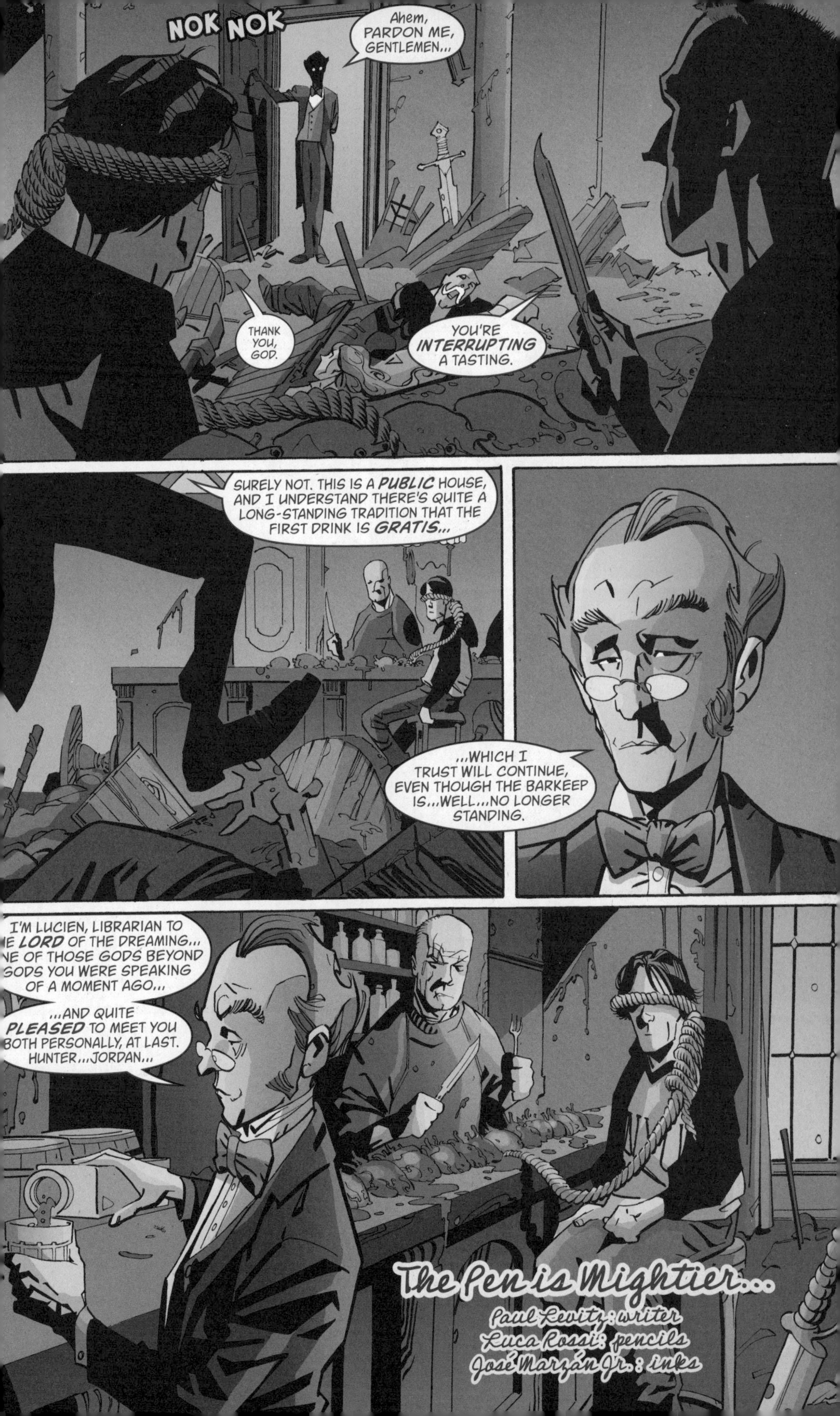

NOK NOK
Ahem, PARDON ME, GENTLEMEN...
THANK YOU, GOD.
YOU'RE INTERRUPTING A TASTING.
SURELY NOT. THIS IS A PUBLIC HOUSE, AND I UNDERSTAND THERE'S QUITE A LONG-STANDING TRADITION THAT THE FIRST DRINK IS GRATIS...
...WHICH I TRUST WILL CONTINUE, EVEN THOUGH THE BARKEEP IS...WELL...NO LONGER STANDING.
I'M LUCIEN, LIBRARIAN TO E LORD OF THE DREAMING... NE OF THOSE GODS BEYOND GODS YOU WERE SPEAKING OF A MOMENT AGO...
...AND QUITE PLEASED TO MEET YOU BOTH PERSONALLY, AT LAST. HUNTER...JORDAN...
The Pen is Mightier...
Paul Levitz: writer
Luca Rossi: pencils
José Marzán Jr.: inks

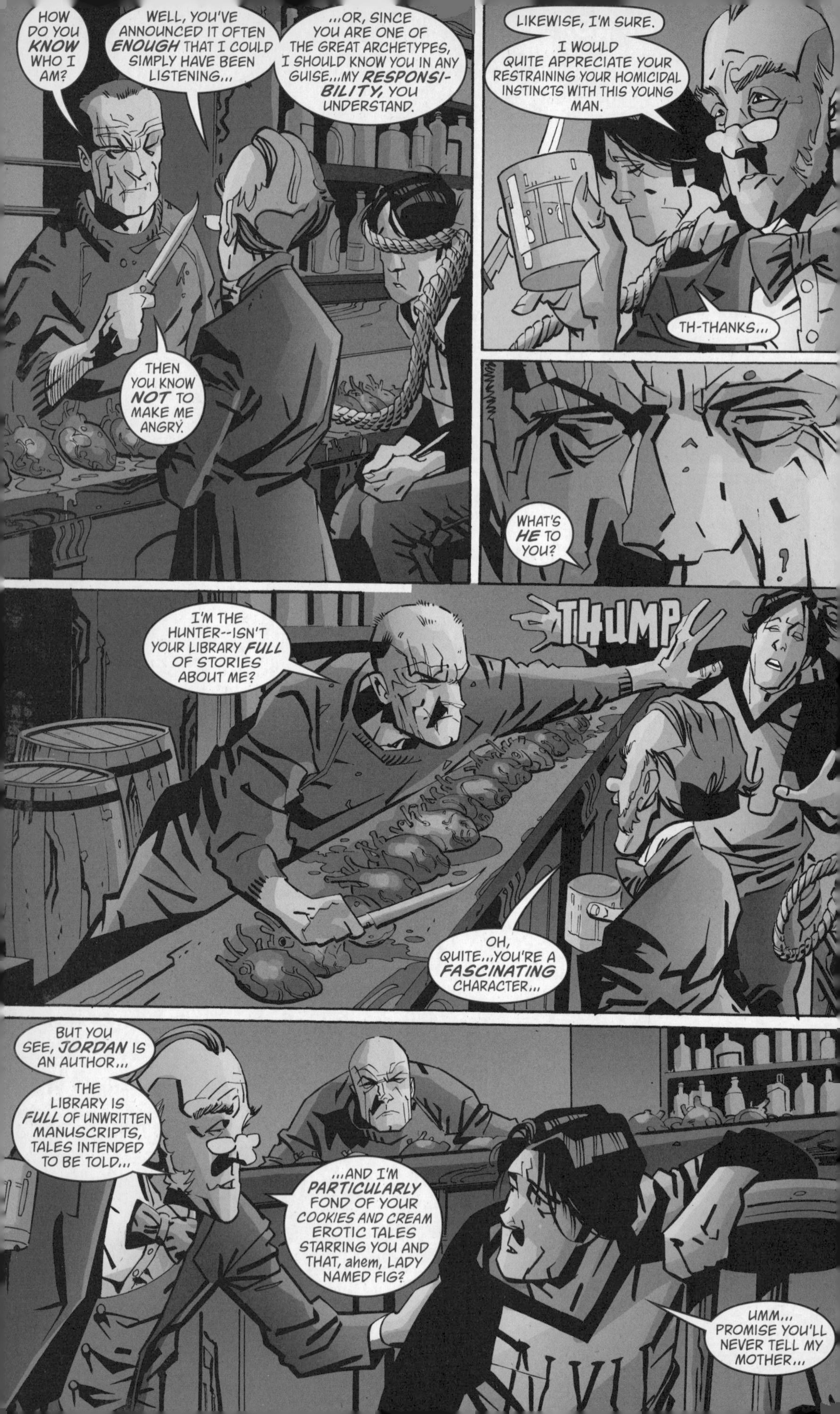

HOW DO YOU **KNOW** WHO I AM?
WELL, YOU'VE ANNOUNCED IT OFTEN **ENOUGH** THAT I COULD SIMPLY HAVE BEEN LISTENING...
...OR, SINCE YOU ARE ONE OF THE GREAT ARCHETYPES, I SHOULD KNOW YOU IN ANY GUISE...MY **RESPONSIBILITY,** YOU UNDERSTAND.
THEN YOU KNOW **NOT** TO MAKE ME ANGRY.
LIKEWISE, I'M SURE.
I WOULD QUITE APPRECIATE YOUR RESTRAINING YOUR HOMICIDAL INSTINCTS WITH THIS YOUNG MAN.
TH-THANKS...
WHAT'S **HE** TO YOU?
I'M THE HUNTER--ISN'T YOUR LIBRARY **FULL** OF STORIES ABOUT ME?
THUMP
OH, QUITE...YOU'RE A **FASCINATING** CHARACTER...
BUT YOU SEE, **JORDAN** IS AN AUTHOR...
THE LIBRARY IS **FULL** OF UNWRITTEN MANUSCRIPTS, TALES INTENDED TO BE TOLD...
...AND I'M **PARTICULARLY** FOND OF YOUR COOKIES AND CREAM EROTIC TALES STARRING YOU AND THAT, ahem, LADY NAMED FIG?
UMM... PROMISE YOU'LL NEVER TELL MY MOTHER...

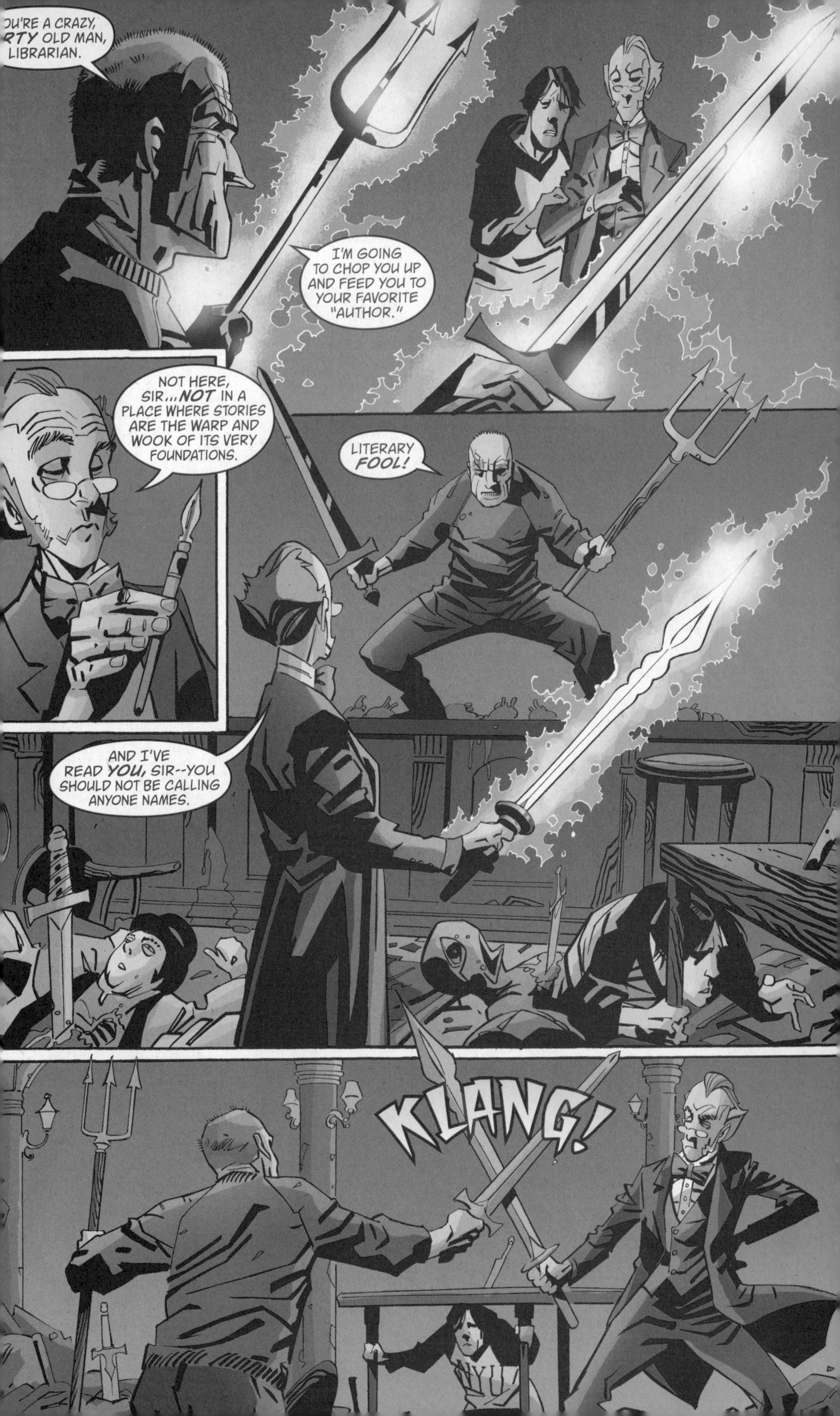
OU'RE A CRAZY, RTY OLD MAN, LIBRARIAN.
I'M GOING TO CHOP YOU UP AND FEED YOU TO YOUR FAVORITE "AUTHOR."
NOT HERE, SIR...NOT IN A PLACE WHERE STORIES ARE THE WARP AND WOOK OF ITS VERY FOUNDATIONS.
LITERARY FOOL!
AND I'VE READ YOU, SIR--YOU SHOULD NOT BE CALLING ANYONE NAMES.
KLANG!
NYU

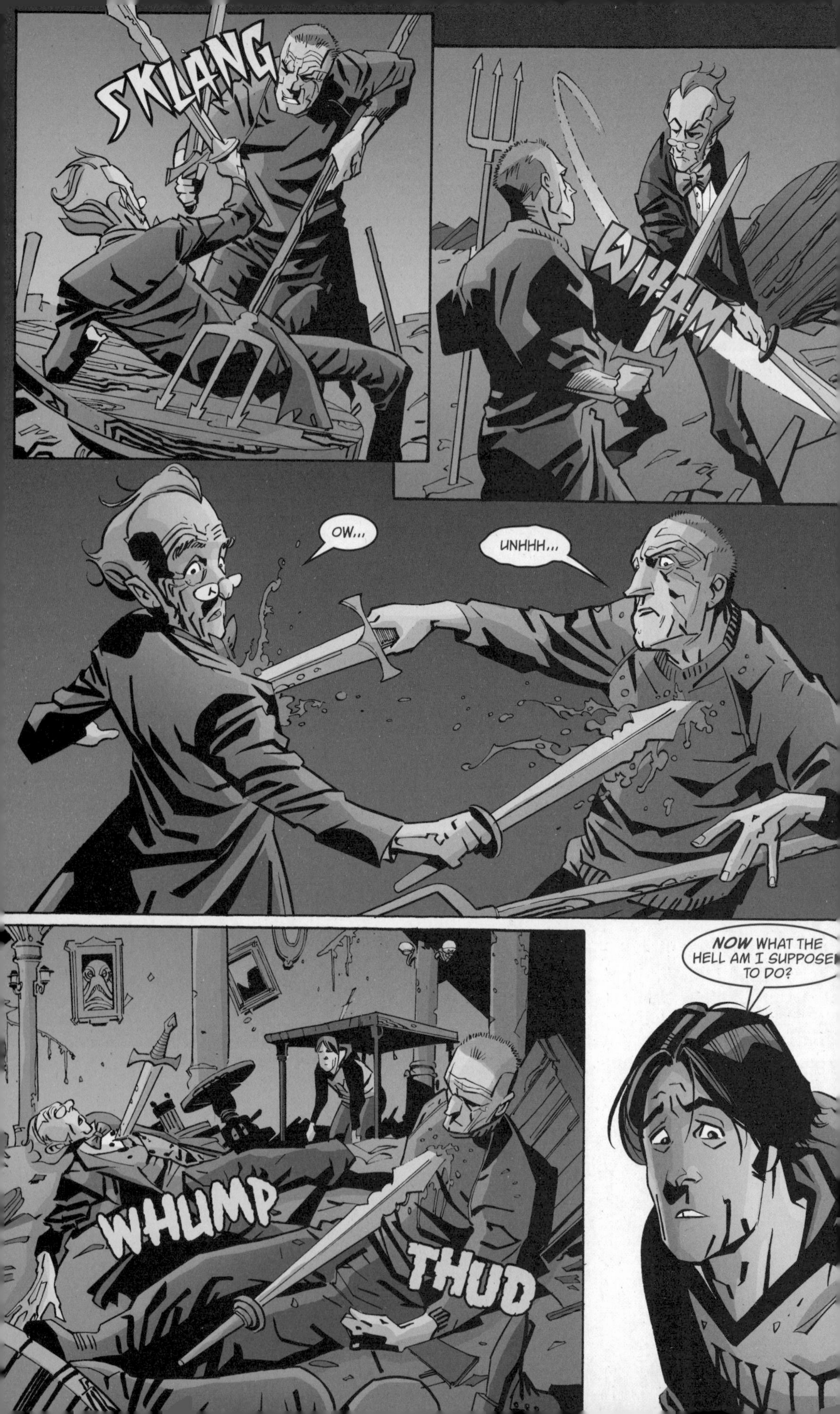
SKLANG
WHAM
OW...
UNHHH...
WHUMP
THUD
NOW WHAT THE HELL AM I SUPPOSE TO DO?

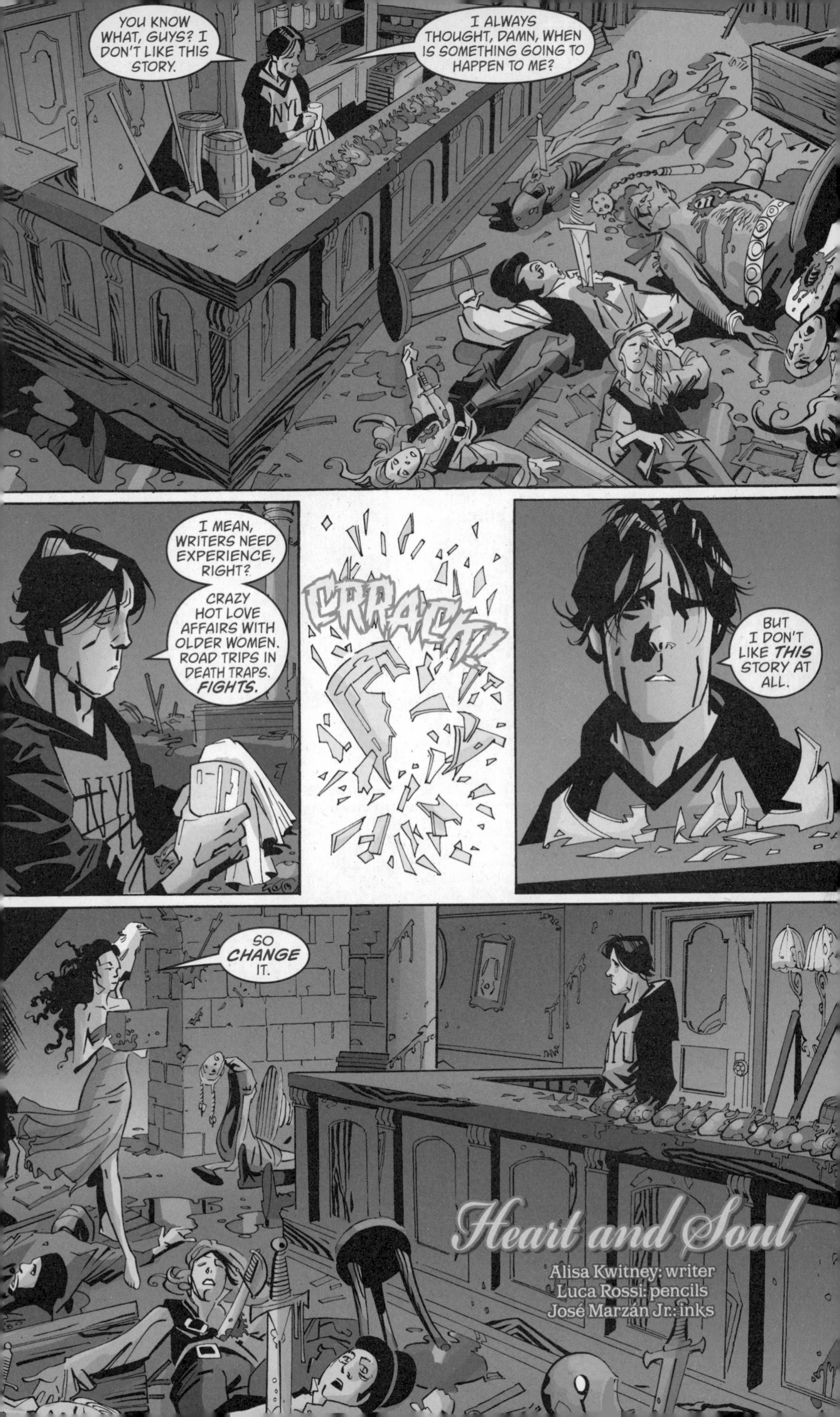
YOU KNOW WHAT, GUYS? I DON'T LIKE THIS STORY.
I ALWAYS THOUGHT, DAMN, WHEN IS SOMETHING GOING TO HAPPEN TO ME?
I MEAN, WRITERS NEED EXPERIENCE, RIGHT?
CRAZY HOT LOVE AFFAIRS WITH OLDER WOMEN. ROAD TRIPS IN DEATH TRAPS. ***FIGHTS.***
CRRACK!!
BUT I DON'T LIKE ***THIS*** STORY AT ALL.
SO ***CHANGE*** IT.
Heart and Soul
Alisa Kwitney: writer
Luca Rossi: pencils
José Marzán Jr.: inks

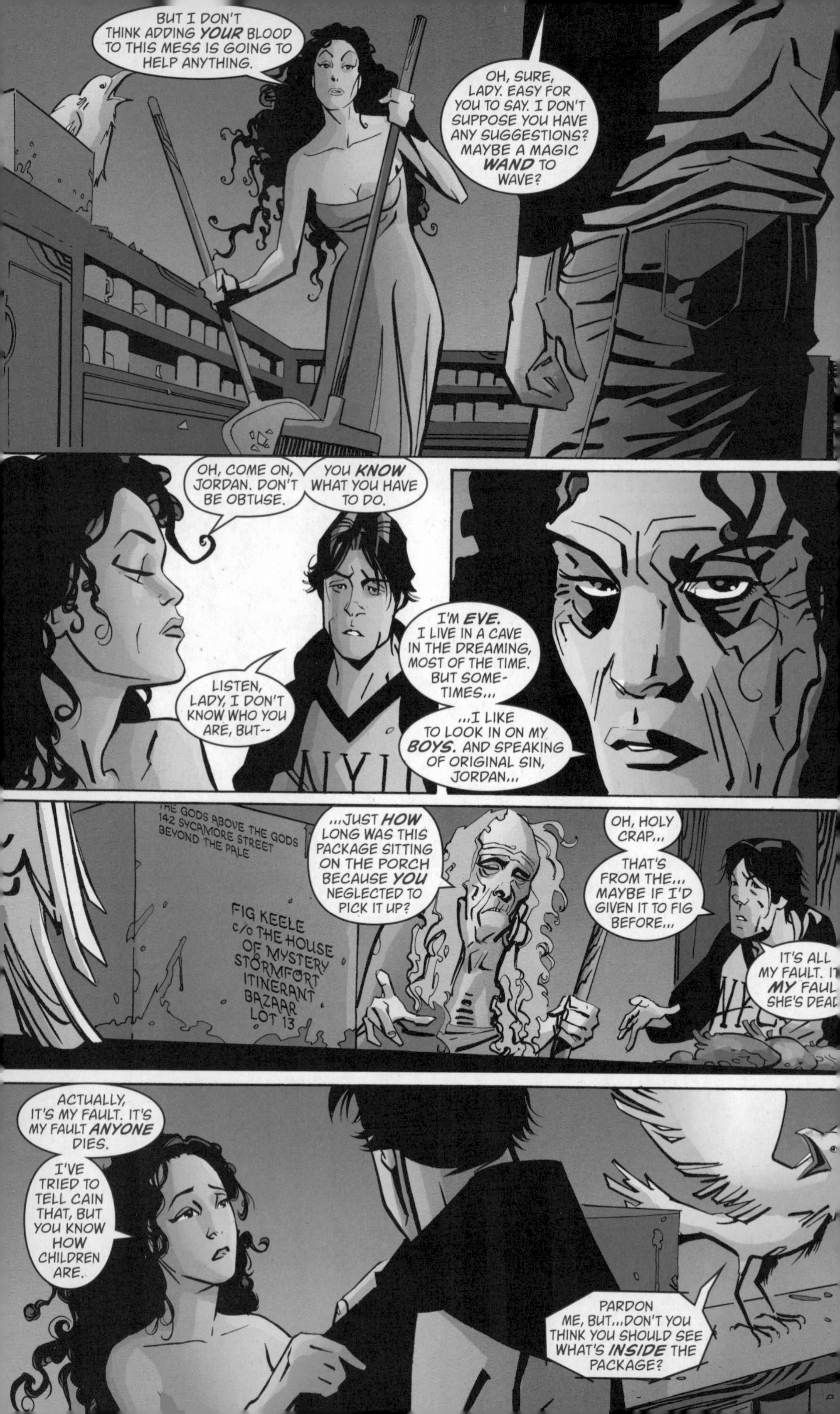
BUT I DON'T THINK ADDING YOUR BLOOD TO THIS MESS IS GOING TO HELP ANYTHING.
OH, SURE, LADY. EASY FOR YOU TO SAY. I DON'T SUPPOSE YOU HAVE ANY SUGGESTIONS? MAYBE A MAGIC WAND TO WAVE?
OH, COME ON, JORDAN. DON'T BE OBTUSE.
YOU KNOW WHAT YOU HAVE TO DO.
LISTEN, LADY, I DON'T KNOW WHO YOU ARE, BUT--
I'M EVE. I LIVE IN A CAVE IN THE DREAMING, MOST OF THE TIME. BUT SOME-TIMES...
...I LIKE TO LOOK IN ON MY BOYS. AND SPEAKING OF ORIGINAL SIN, JORDAN...
THE GODS ABOVE THE GODS
142 SYCAMORE STREET
BEYOND THE PALE
FIG KEELE
c/o THE HOUSE OF MYSTERY
STORMFORT ITINERANT BAZAAR
LOT 13
...JUST HOW LONG WAS THIS PACKAGE SITTING ON THE PORCH BECAUSE YOU NEGLECTED TO PICK IT UP?
OH, HOLY CRAP...
THAT'S FROM THE... MAYBE IF I'D GIVEN IT TO FIG BEFORE...
IT'S ALL MY FAULT. IT
MY FAUL
SHE'S DEAD
ACTUALLY, IT'S MY FAULT. IT'S MY FAULT ANYONE DIES.
I'VE TRIED TO TELL CAIN THAT, BUT YOU KNOW HOW CHILDREN ARE.
PARDON ME, BUT...DON'T YOU THINK YOU SHOULD SEE WHAT'S INSIDE THE PACKAGE?

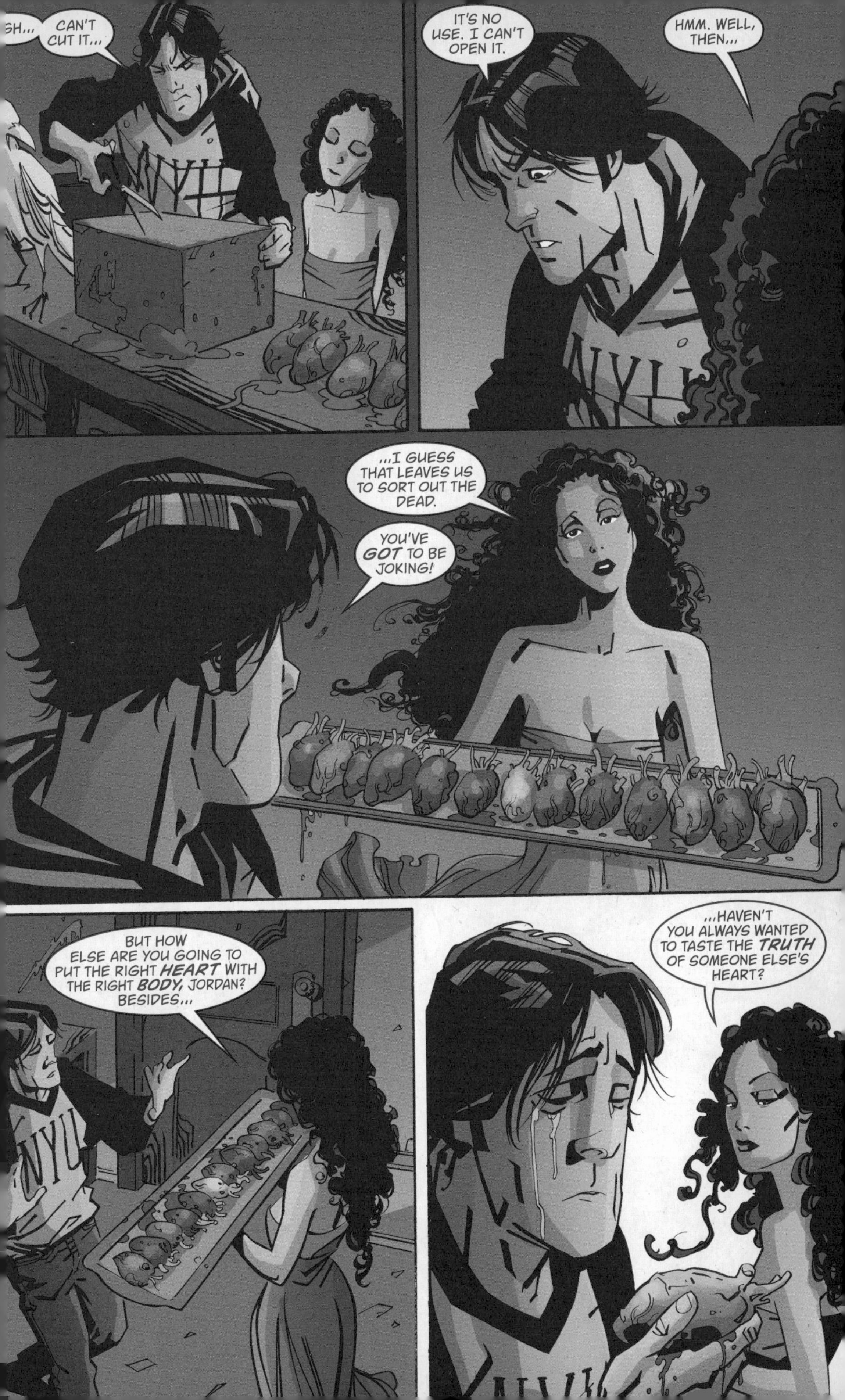
GH... CAN'T CUT IT...
IT'S NO USE. I CAN'T OPEN IT.
HMM. WELL, THEN...
...I GUESS THAT LEAVES US TO SORT OUT THE DEAD.
YOU'VE GOT TO BE JOKING!
BUT HOW ELSE ARE YOU GOING TO PUT THE RIGHT HEART WITH THE RIGHT BODY, JORDAN? BESIDES...
...HAVEN'T YOU ALWAYS WANTED TO TASTE THE TRUTH OF SOMEONE ELSE'S HEART?

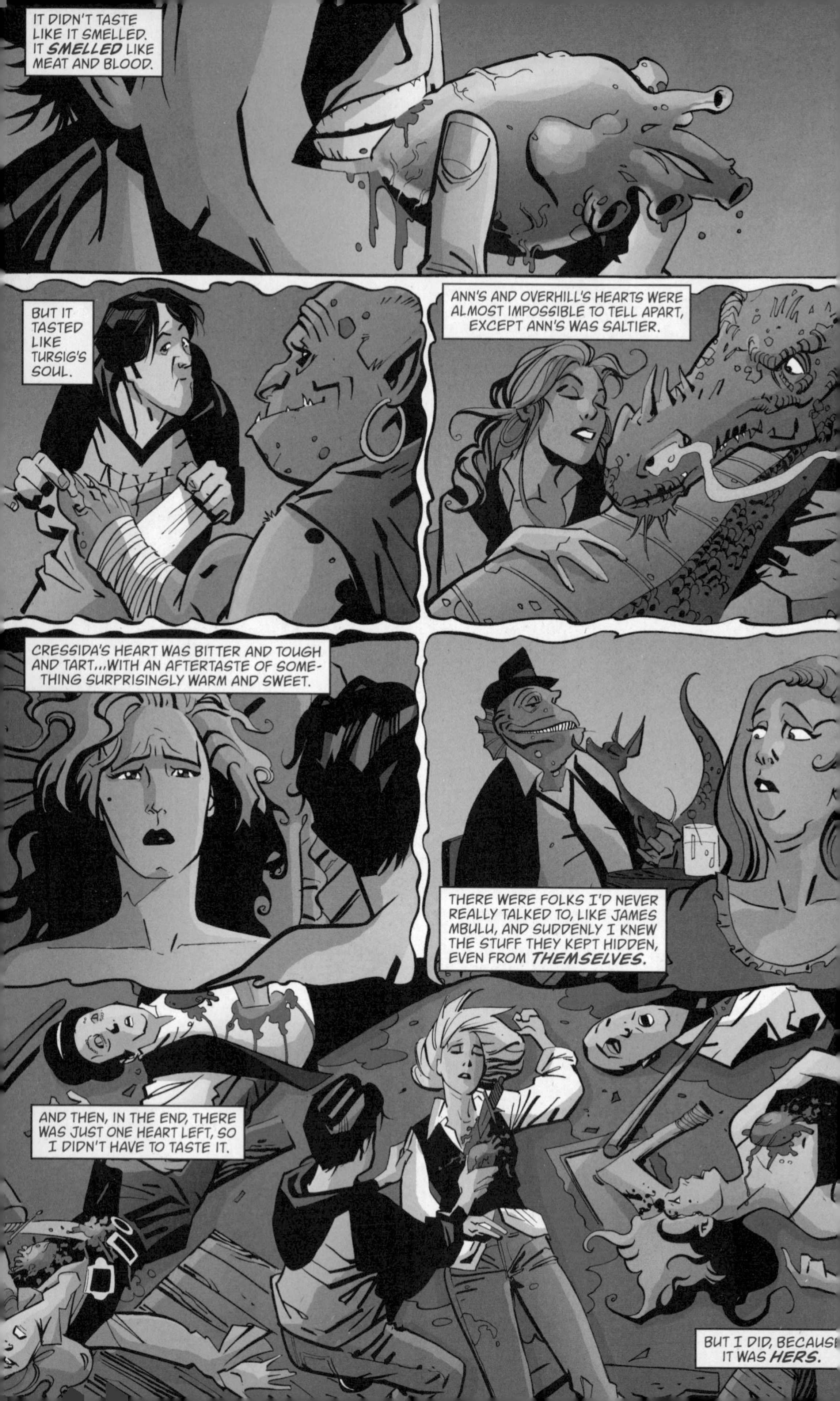
IT DIDN'T TASTE LIKE IT SMELLED. IT *SMELLED* LIKE MEAT AND BLOOD.
BUT IT TASTED LIKE TURSIG'S SOUL.
ANN'S AND OVERHILL'S HEARTS WERE ALMOST IMPOSSIBLE TO TELL APART, EXCEPT ANN'S WAS SALTIER.
CRESSIDA'S HEART WAS BITTER AND TOUGH AND TART...WITH AN AFTERTASTE OF SOME-THING SURPRISINGLY WARM AND SWEET.
THERE WERE FOLKS I'D NEVER REALLY TALKED TO, LIKE JAMES MBULU, AND SUDDENLY I KNEW THE STUFF THEY KEPT HIDDEN, EVEN FROM *THEMSELVES.*
AND THEN, IN THE END, THERE WAS JUST ONE HEART LEFT, SO I DIDN'T HAVE TO TASTE IT.
BUT I DID, BECAUSE IT WAS *HERS.*

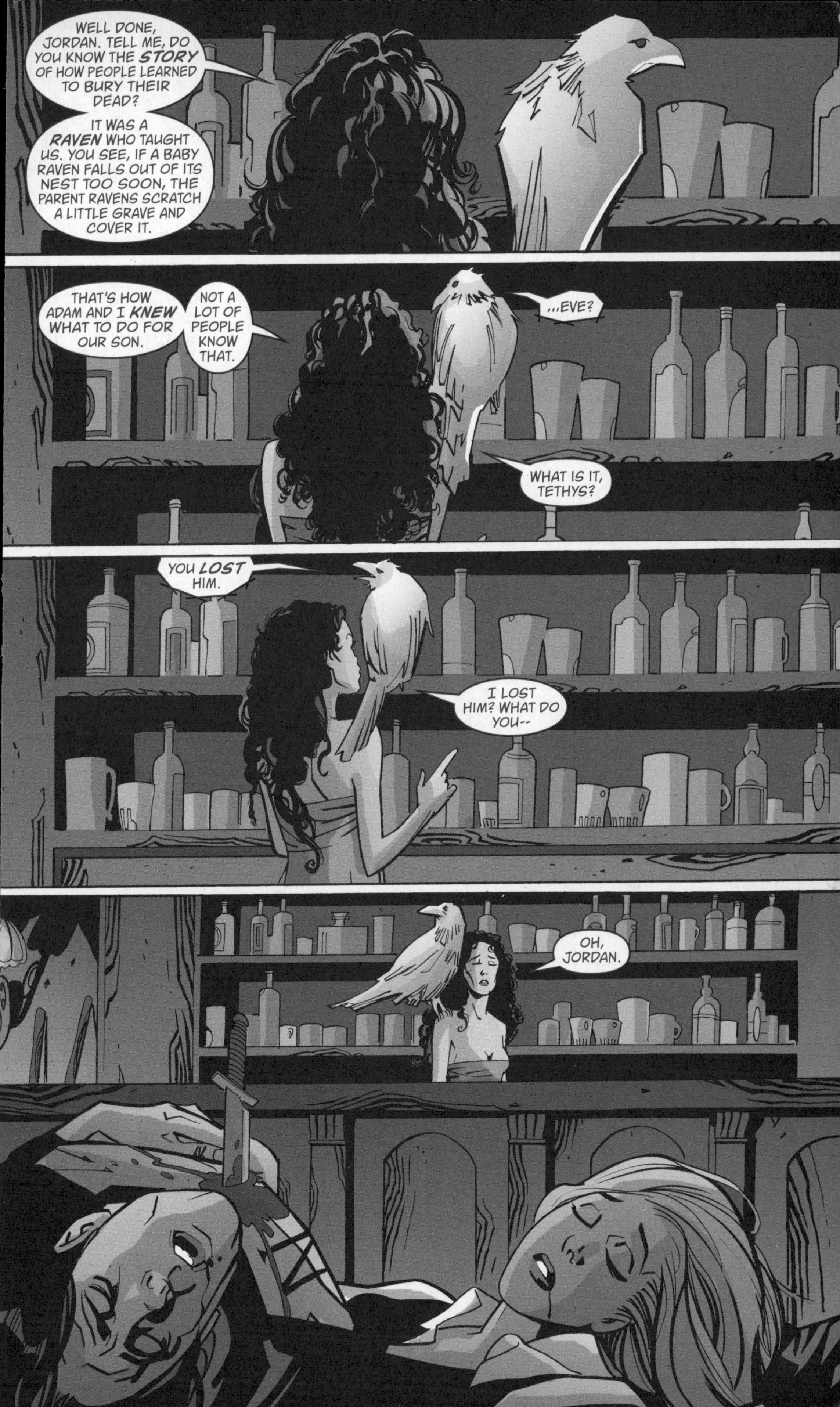
WELL DONE, JORDAN. TELL ME, DO YOU KNOW THE STORY OF HOW PEOPLE LEARNED TO BURY THEIR DEAD?
IT WAS A RAVEN WHO TAUGHT US. YOU SEE, IF A BABY RAVEN FALLS OUT OF ITS NEST TOO SOON, THE PARENT RAVENS SCRATCH A LITTLE GRAVE AND COVER IT.
THAT'S HOW ADAM AND I KNEW WHAT TO DO FOR OUR SON.
NOT A LOT OF PEOPLE KNOW THAT.
...EVE?
WHAT IS IT, TETHYS?
YOU LOST HIM.
I LOST HIM? WHAT DO YOU--
OH, JORDAN.

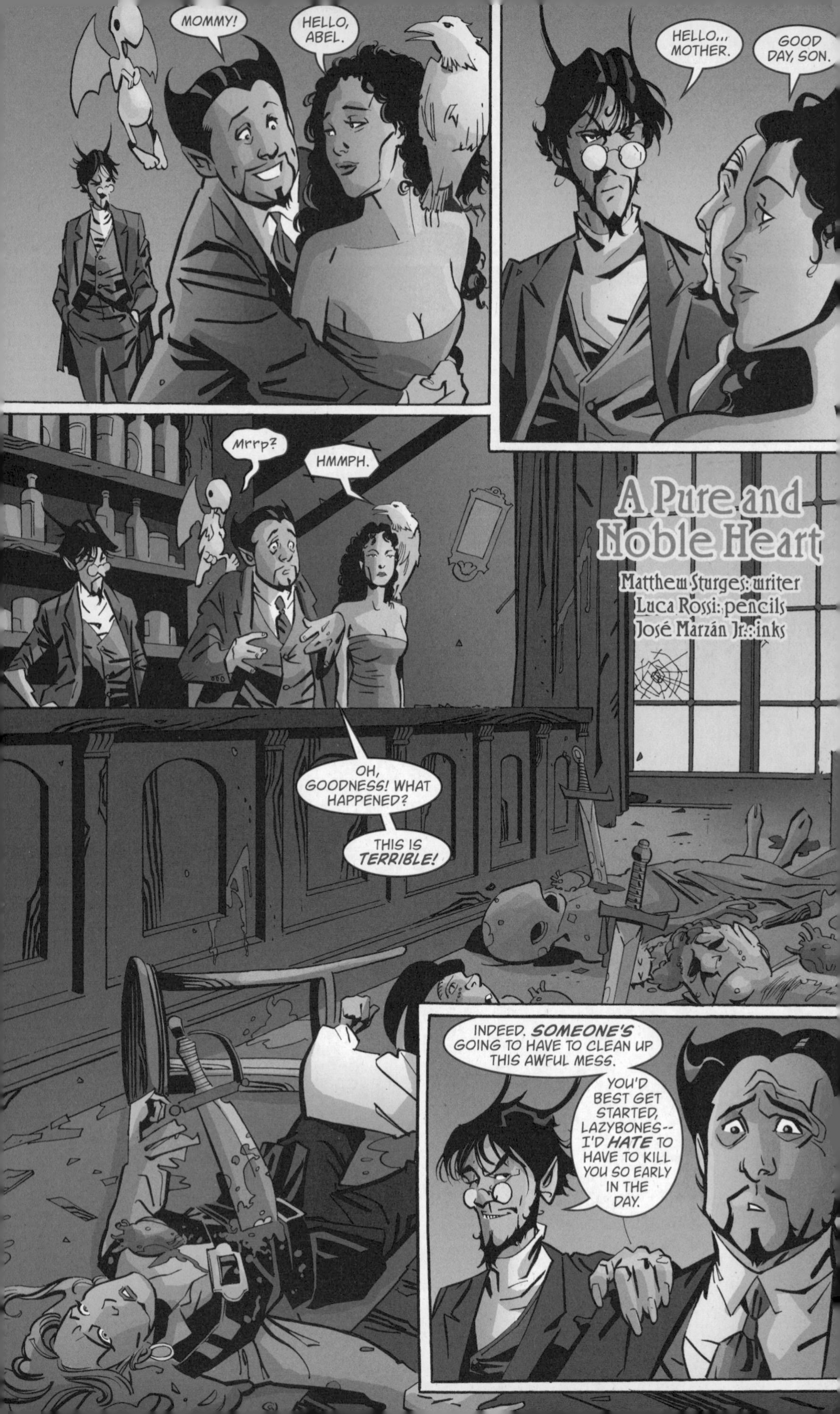

MOMMY!
HELLO, ABEL.
HELLO... MOTHER.
GOOD DAY, SON.
Mrrp?
HMMPH.
A Pure and Noble Heart
Matthew Sturges: writer
Luca Rossi: pencils
José Marzán Jr.: inks
OH, GOODNESS! WHAT HAPPENED?
THIS IS TERRIBLE!
INDEED. SOMEONE'S GOING TO HAVE TO CLEAN UP THIS AWFUL MESS.
YOU'D BEST GET STARTED, LAZYBONES-- I'D HATE TO HAVE TO KILL YOU SO EARLY IN THE DAY.

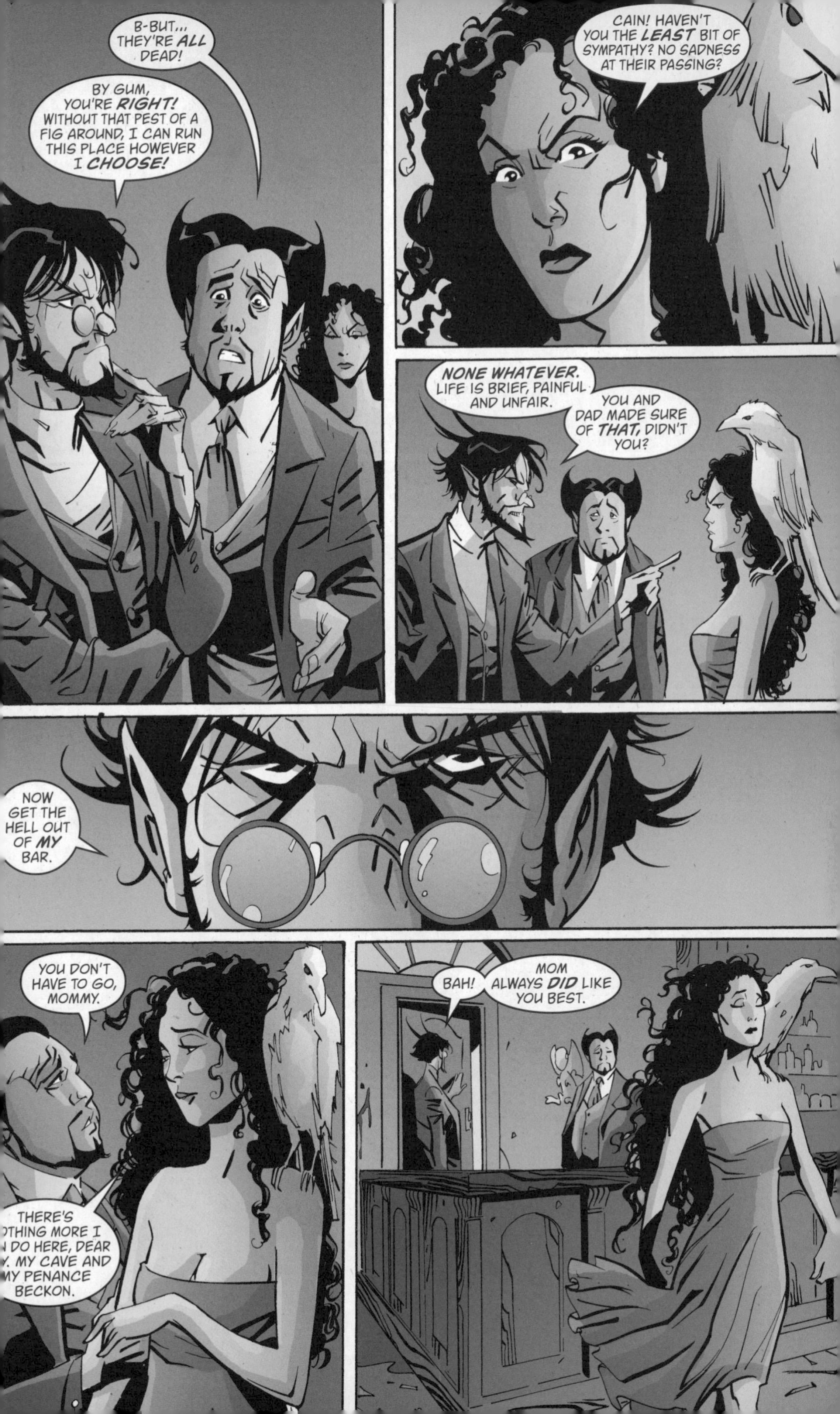
B-BUT... THEY'RE ALL DEAD!
BY GUM, YOU'RE RIGHT! WITHOUT THAT PEST OF A FIG AROUND, I CAN RUN THIS PLACE HOWEVER I CHOOSE!
CAIN! HAVEN'T YOU THE LEAST BIT OF SYMPATHY? NO SADNESS AT THEIR PASSING?
NONE WHATEVER. LIFE IS BRIEF, PAINFUL AND UNFAIR.
YOU AND DAD MADE SURE OF THAT, DIDN'T YOU?
NOW GET THE HELL OUT OF MY BAR.
YOU DON'T HAVE TO GO, MOMMY.
THERE'S
DTHING MORE I
I DO HERE, DEAR
Y. MY CAVE AND
MY PENANCE
BECKON.
BAH!
MOM ALWAYS DID LIKE YOU BEST.

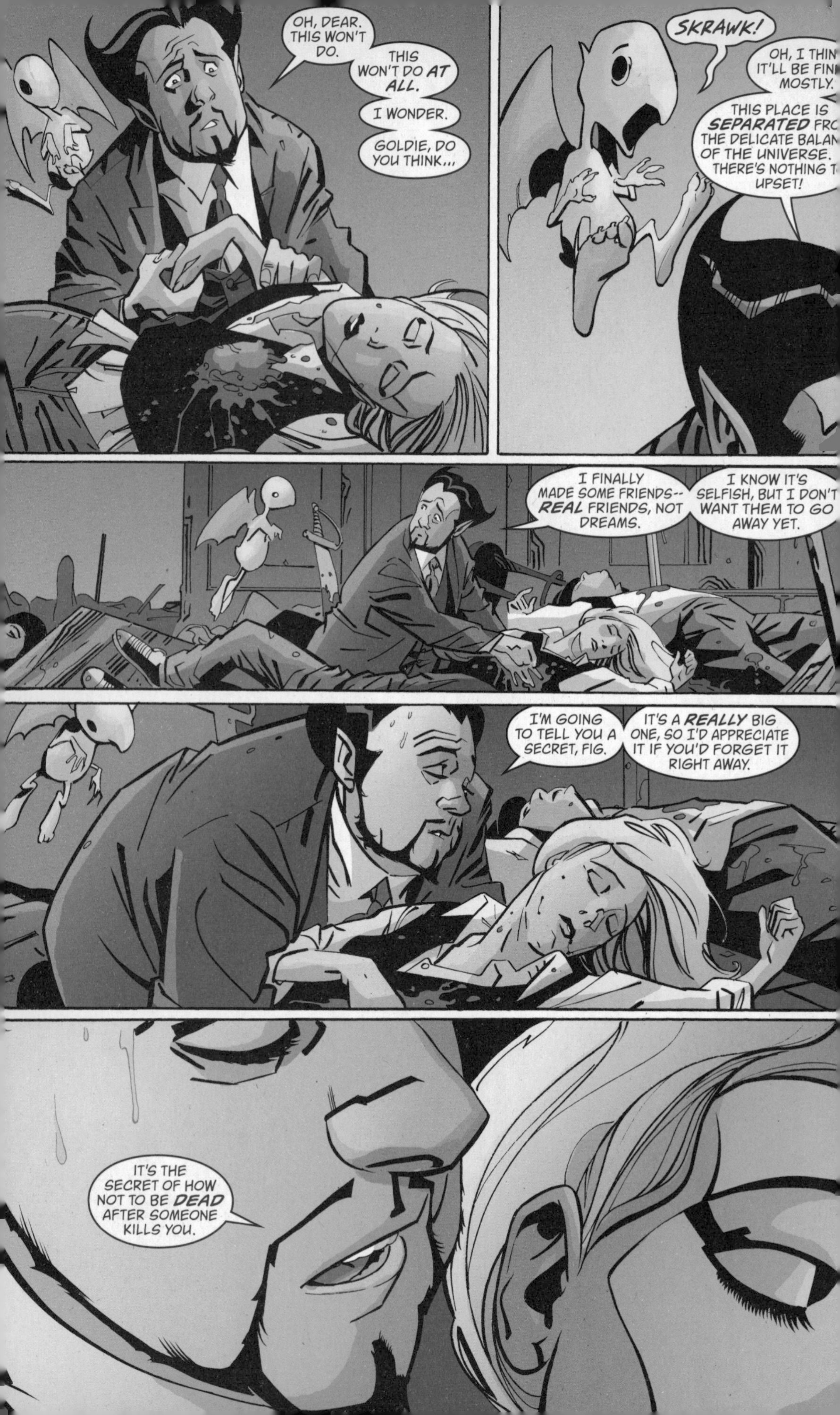
OH, DEAR. THIS WON'T DO.
THIS WON'T DO AT ALL.
I WONDER.
GOLDIE, DO YOU THINK...
SKRAWK!
OH, I THIN IT'LL BE FIN MOSTLY.
THIS PLACE IS SEPARATED FRO THE DELICATE BALAN OF THE UNIVERSE. THERE'S NOTHING T UPSET!
I FINALLY MADE SOME FRIENDS-- REAL FRIENDS, NOT DREAMS.
I KNOW IT'S SELFISH, BUT I DON'T WANT THEM TO GO AWAY YET.
I'M GOING TO TELL YOU A SECRET, FIG.
IT'S A REALLY BIG ONE, SO I'D APPRECIATE IT IF YOU'D FORGET IT RIGHT AWAY.
IT'S THE SECRET OF HOW NOT TO BE DEAD AFTER SOMEONE KILLS YOU.

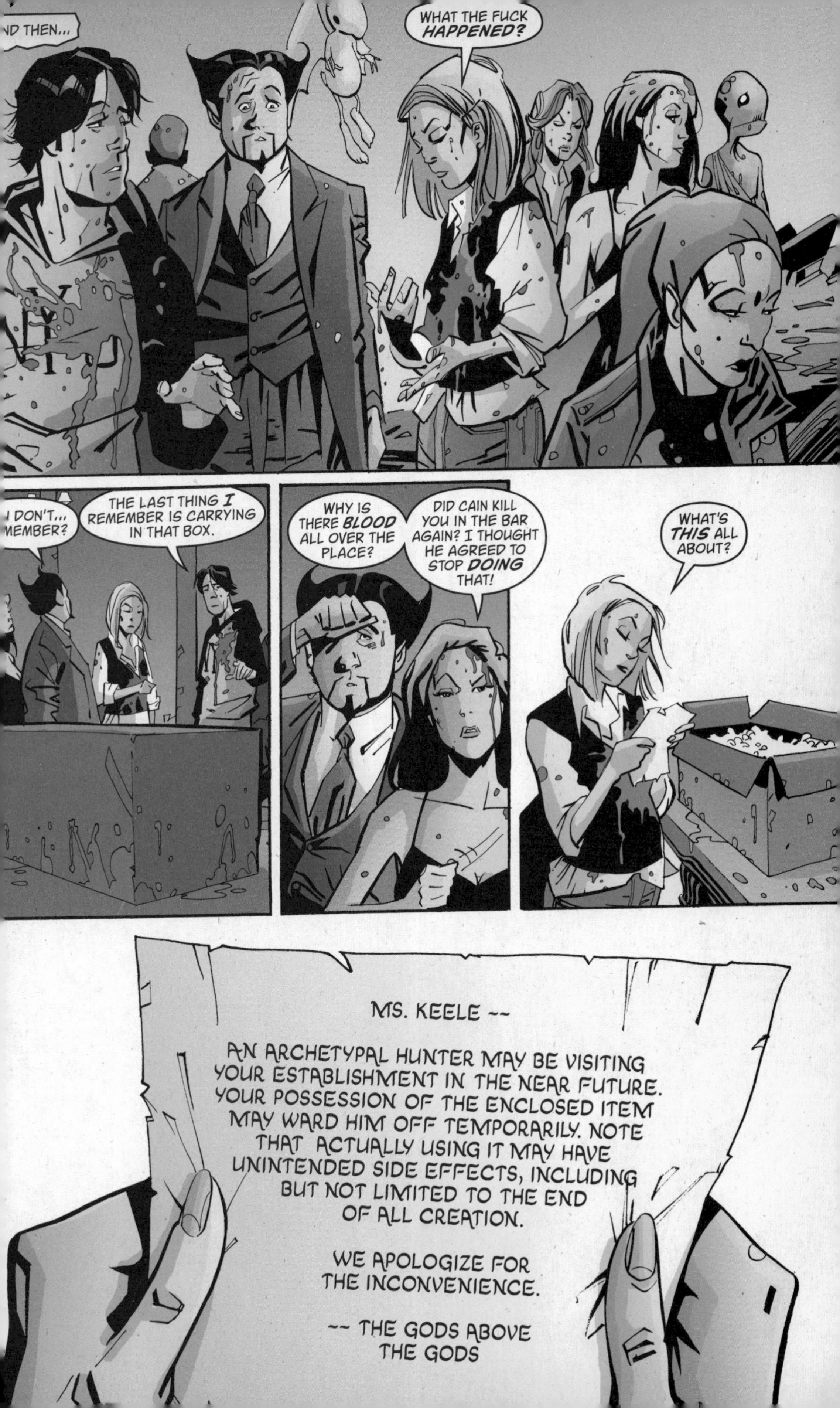

ND THEN...
WHAT THE FUCK HAPPENED?
I DON'T... MEMBER?
THE LAST THING I REMEMBER IS CARRYING IN THAT BOX.
WHY IS THERE BLOOD ALL OVER THE PLACE?
DID CAIN KILL YOU IN THE BAR AGAIN? I THOUGHT HE AGREED TO STOP DOING THAT!
WHAT'S THIS ALL ABOUT?
MS. KEELE --
AN ARCHETYPAL HUNTER MAY BE VISITING YOUR ESTABLISHMENT IN THE NEAR FUTURE. YOUR POSSESSION OF THE ENCLOSED ITEM MAY WARD HIM OFF TEMPORARILY. NOTE THAT ACTUALLY USING IT MAY HAVE UNINTENDED SIDE EFFECTS, INCLUDING BUT NOT LIMITED TO THE END OF ALL CREATION.
WE APOLOGIZE FOR THE INCONVENIENCE.
-- THE GODS ABOVE THE GODS

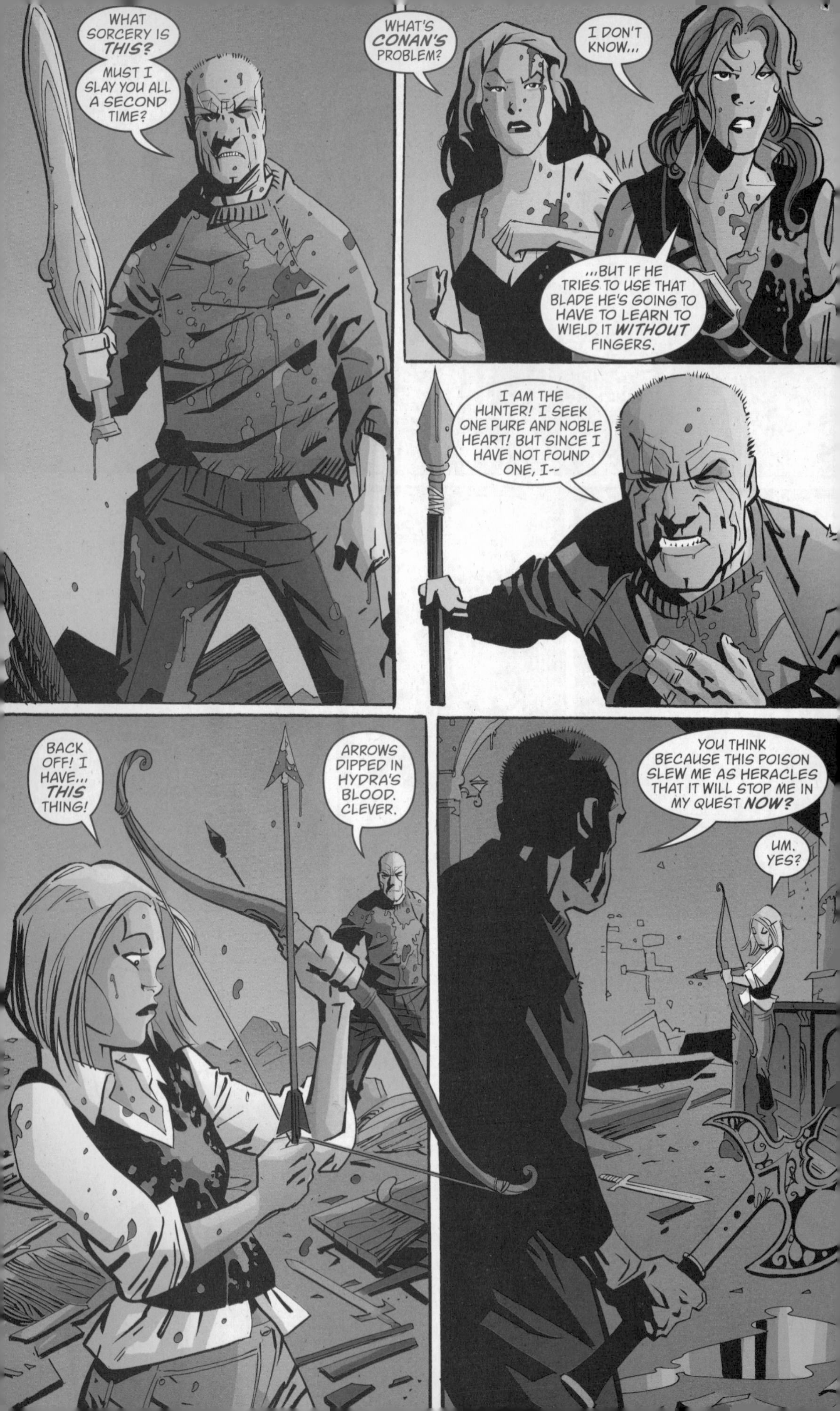
WHAT SORCERY IS THIS?
MUST I SLAY YOU ALL A SECOND TIME?
WHAT'S CONAN'S PROBLEM?
I DON'T KNOW...
...BUT IF HE TRIES TO USE THAT BLADE HE'S GOING TO HAVE TO LEARN TO WIELD IT WITHOUT FINGERS.
I AM THE HUNTER! I SEEK ONE PURE AND NOBLE HEART! BUT SINCE I HAVE NOT FOUND ONE, I--
BACK OFF! I HAVE... THIS THING!
ARROWS DIPPED IN HYDRA'S BLOOD. CLEVER.
YOU THINK BECAUSE THIS POISON SLEW ME AS HERACLES THAT IT WILL STOP ME IN MY QUEST NOW?
UM. YES?

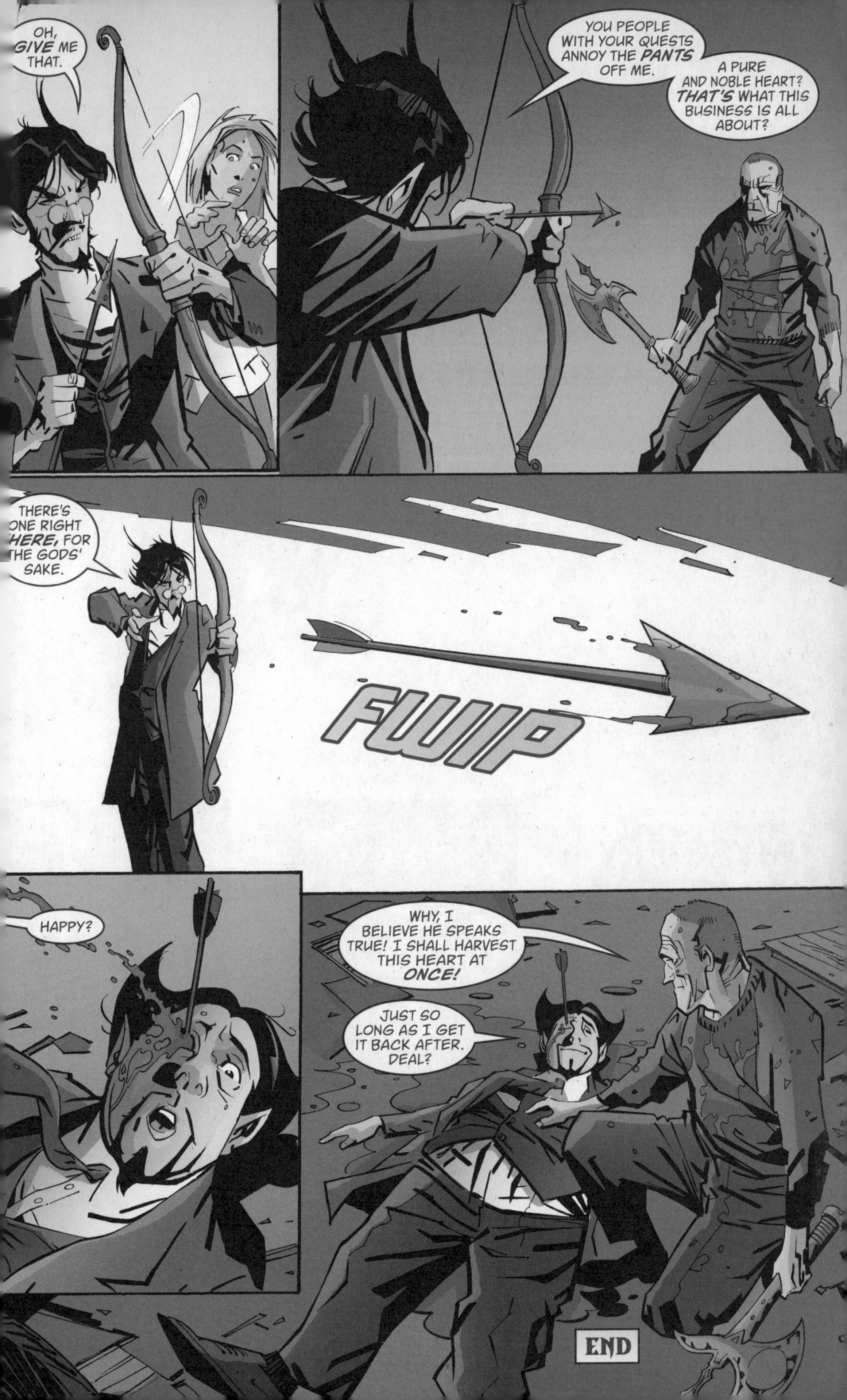
OH, GIVE ME THAT.
YOU PEOPLE WITH YOUR QUESTS ANNOY THE PANTS OFF ME.
A PURE AND NOBLE HEART? THAT'S WHAT THIS BUSINESS IS ALL ABOUT?
THERE'S ONE RIGHT HERE, FOR THE GODS' SAKE.
FWIP
HAPPY?
WHY, I BELIEVE HE SPEAKS TRUE! I SHALL HARVEST THIS HEART AT ONCE!
JUST SO LONG AS I GET IT BACK AFTER. DEAL?
END